Our National Parks and the Search for Sustainability

## DATE DUE

| | |
|---|---|
| OCT 2 3 2002 | |
| MAR 2 3 2009 | |
| NOV 1 1 2010 | |
| NOV 2 6 2014 | |
| WITHDRAWN | |
| | |
| | |
| | |
| | |
| | |
| | |
| | |

# Our National Parks

 UNIVERSITY OF

and the

# Search for
# Sustainability

## Bob R. O'Brien

*Drawings by Gary O'Brien*

T E X A S    P R E S S    *A U S T I N*

Requests for permission to reproduce material from this work should be sent to
Permissions, University of Texas Press, Box 7819, Austin, TX 78713-7819.

⊗ The paper used in this publication meets the minimum requirements of
American National Standard for Information Sciences—Permanence of Paper
for Printed Library Materials, ANSI Z39.48-1984.

Library of Congress Cataloging-in-Publication Data

O'Brien, Bob R.
    Our national parks and the search for sustainability /
Bob R. O'Brien. — 1st ed.
        p.      cm.
    Includes bibliographical references (p.    ) and index.
    ISBN 0-292-76049-3
    ISBN 0-292-76050-7 (pbk.)
        1. National parks and reserves—United States.    2. National parks and
    reserves—Multiple use—United States—Case studies.    3. Nature conser-
    vation—United States.    I. Title
    SB482.A4 O37    1999
    333.78'315'0973—ddc21                                                98-9011

FOR GARY, LAURA, AND MOM

# Contents

# Illustrations

# Preface

IT was, without question, the most spectacular spot for eating a picnic lunch that I had ever seen. The 8.2-mile climb to the summit of Half Dome with the accompaniment of booming waterfalls was certainly impressive, but this topped my greatest expectations of what Yosemite National Park had to offer. Just a few feet from the summit of Half Dome is one of nature's most stupendous vertical walls. At the very top of this wall was a little wisp of a rock that somehow had escaped the erosion that stripped away the rest of the dome and was left overhanging the face. That surprise was many years ago, but in retrospect it was the kind of experience— sitting on this ledge, dangling my feet in space, eating a mountain lunch and savoring the view—that I had come to expect from the national parks.

The year was 1947, and I was on a long-awaited tour of the national parks of the West from my home in Texas: the Grand Canyon, Mount Rainier, the Teton Range, Yellowstone, and the giant cliffs and waterfalls of Yosemite Valley. It was the culmination of a dream which went back as far as I could remember, when I first read books of mountains and parks and longed desperately to see them. I was not disappointed.

If that trip was sheer joy, a similar trip twenty years later was sheer agony. I was a little more sophisticated about the parks, I suppose. I had written a dissertation on Yellowstone National Park, been a ranger at Mount Rainier National Park, and been to many of the parks several times. But I was still thrilled by John Muir's "incomparable valley" and would return again and again to the picnic spot dangling in space nearly 5,000 feet above the valley floor. On this trip, though, I was shaken badly by what had happened to Yosemite Valley in the intervening years.

Yosemite Valley in July of 1967 would have had to be seen to be believed. There was never an empty campsite in the valley; you had to create a space for yourself in a sea of cars, tents, and humanity. If you couldn't find a spot in the campground you could still carry sleeping bags out into the meadow or sleep in your car in a parking lot. The Merced River flooded the campgrounds that summer, but some of the campsites which were flooded were used just as if nothing had happened. Spaces were too precious to vacate just because they happened to be under water. The camp next to ours had fifty people in it, with rugs hung between the trees, incense burning, and a stereo set going full volume. "Yosemite City" got a lot of bad publicity that summer, as it should have, peaking with riots three summers later on the Fourth of July weekend of 1970. These riots finally provided the impetus to change the "parks are for people" logic which had guided the park service from the beginning. A third Yosemite was beginning to emerge.

Since 1967 I have been to Yosemite many times, including a dozen class trips of up to a week in length, and it is easy to see the direction the National Park Service (NPS) is attempting to take. The 89 percent of the park which is undeveloped is probably in its best shape since the Yosemite area was first visited by Europeans in 1851. The rest of the park, and especially Yosemite Valley, is in the throes of the NPS's "search for sustainablity": to allow as many people as possible to visit a landscape which is kept in as natural a state as possible, and to keep it that way forever.

The perception of the national park mandate until after World War II was to save the basic amenities of the park—the walls and waterfalls of Yosemite Valley, the giant sequoias, the meadows and forests of the backcountry—from being despoiled. At that time, we were still worrying about the total loss of resources, from dams, chainsaws, and concrete. Tourists, and the tourist infrastructure of roads and hotels, were not considered an intrusion. The more tourists you had the better. The result was the Yosemite Valley of 1967, which was more crowded, and much noisier, than most city neighborhoods. Bad as the situation might have been, however, it was obvious that things could have been much worse. Without protection from grazing, lumbering, and homesteading when Yosemite became a park over a hundred years ago, the area would certainly have had a short life. Sheep can devastate an area quickly and thoroughly, and they were already doing so a century ago. John Muir himself worked in a lumber mill in Yosemite Valley. Imagine the area without protection: a lumber company in the sequoia groves, a dam across the head of Yosemite

Valley, summer homes in Tuolumne Meadow; there could be worse things than overcrowding the valley floor.

My first trip to the park after the NPS had started reacting to the overcrowding was an eye-opener. There were just as many people in the valley in the early 1970's as in 1967 and seemingly as many "hippies" as ever. It was, however, a totally different environment. A shuttle bus system was in place, and two of the largest parking lots in the valley had been closed. At the Happy Isles parking lot in the upper valley, which was once a sea of steel, glass, and exhaust fumes, the asphalt had been removed, and the experience of cycling through the forest was exhilarating. At Yosemite Village the asphalt was still there, but instead of cars in the blocked-off parking lot there were benches and people wandering around and enjoying the view.

Inaugurating the shuttle bus system, closing roads and parking lots, and drastically cutting overnight use by controlling camping were the first steps toward relieving pressure on Yosemite Valley. Subsequent steps, such as barring all automobiles from the valley, removing nonessential government and employee housing, and reducing accommodations and services, have proved much more difficult. Restoring Yosemite Valley is going to be more difficult still. A start has been made, such as rehabilitating the banks of a small part of the Merced River through the valley and trying to prevent the disappearance of the black oak through replanting, but this is *only* a start.

So what will my grandchildren see, twenty years from now, when they look down at the valley from the top of Half Dome? If nothing is done and visitation continues to increase as it always has, they'll be able to feel the chaos even from 5,000 feet above the valley. But I tend to be optimistic. I'd like to think that much of what will be discussed in this book about preserving and enhancing the parks *will* take place. Let us make that assumption and take a short look at the Yosemite Valley of the year 2019.

In 2019, Yosemite Valley is a good example of what has helped make tourism the world's leading industry for two decades. Congress and the president have finally fully awakened to the importance of the national parks to the nation and to the world, and have started to do what is necessary to make them even better. They realized that while wilderness in the United States had become more and more a rarity in a rapidly developing world, the natural landscape of the national parks, the "wilderness beyond the shoulder of the road," had become even more important. Ecotourism, on a scale few had thought possible, had arrived. People were willing to compromise their creature comforts a little in order to see some of the most beautiful scenery in the world.

The compromises, twenty years from now, are modest but crucial. It is unlikely that a large percentage of the campgrounds, hotels, stores, and food outlets will be removed from the valley. The miracle in restoring Yosemite to its original splendor would come from the shuttle bus system, in operation since the 1970's, being extended to serve the entire valley. Some cars could still use the roads to travel nonstop to campgrounds and hotels where their owners had reservations, but the parking lots and much of the traffic would be gone. The next logical step, which will probably be even further in the future, would be a quiet, unobtrusive train which would replace all motorized transportation to the park. By then the number of campgrounds and hotels would be much reduced, and restoration projects would have caused a dramatic improvement in the appearance of the valley. Instead of the present "Yosemite City" it would be the Yosemite wilderness, with people.

This brief look at Yosemite—past, present, and future—introduces the theme of this book: how the NPS is attempting to make the nation's most attractive landscapes available to the public and still retain them in their natural state. This conflicting mandate is made all the more difficult by the different ways Americans look at their landscape: from those who would preserve far more than the few percent presently protected in national parks and wilderness areas to those at the other extreme who would tap most of the geysers in Yellowstone to generate electricity. While this conflict is never likely to be fully resolved, the natural landscape must be preserved from further deterioration. The search for sustainability must end at a level of environmental quality much better than what we see today.

I have chosen several topics to illustrate the methods used by the NPS to pursue the elusive goal of sustainability. The subjects, from administration to wildlife, are not what everyone interested in the national parks would choose. The core interest in the parks is, and should be, the natural landscape. I have chosen, however, to focus most of my attention on the *use* of the parks, which I feel is the crucial factor in achieving a sustainable future for the parks. I have also tried to take an *evolutionary* view of what the national parks can and should be. Although bold plans must be pursued, the "best" should not be the enemy of the "better."

The size and diversity of the National Park System present an almost endless list of examples to use in this book. Time and space are limited, however, and my discussions will focus on the big Western national parks, especially Yosemite, Yellowstone, and the Grand Canyon. I know these parks well, and I also feel many of the critical issues in the National Park System tend to concentrate there.

The greatest fringe benefit of doing a book on the national parks is working with the personnel of the National Park Service. Despite their extreme time constraints, from the superintendent who might be the most sought-after public speaker in a region to the ranger who answers questions nonstop all day, I always return from meetings with them enthusiastic and hopeful. The list that follows is only a fraction of those who have helped me in my long association with the national parks: Norman Bishop, Michael Finley, Marshall Gingery, Jean Muencraft, Linda Olson, Noel Poe, John Reed, and Henry Snyder. They provided me with all the information I requested; what I did with that information is my responsibility entirely.

I also want to mention my colleagues in the Geography Department at San Diego State University, for providing an excellent environment of intellectual integrity and support in which to work. I can truthfully list every member of the department, and the staff, as contributing to this book. The students of my national parks course have, through the years, also furnished many of the insights found here, plus giving me an excuse to go to Yosemite twice a year. Tom Herman has mastered all the intricacies of electronic mapmaking to furnish the maps seen in the text. Douglas Strong contributed immeasurably through his critical reading of the manuscript and his support. Others, who have probably heard more about the national parks than they wanted, but constantly offered encouragement, include Jim Blick, Patti Dodgen, Marilu Harms, Diana Richardson, Barbara Fredrich, and the Sessions, Pages, and Nosells.

I doubt seriously if this book would have been written without the support and guidance of Shannon Davies, my sponsoring editor at the University of Texas Press. A subject as big, diverse, and dynamic as national park management has allowed unlimited latitude for hesitancy and doubt in my ability to finish this book. Whether I reach my goal of a fair and hopeful view of the future of the national parks is entirely up to me, of course, but Shannon increased the odds considerably. The same could be said about the entire staff at the University of Texas Press, but I would like to single out Mandy Woods, manuscript editor, Carolyn Cates Wylie, managing editor, Paul Spragens, copy editor, Heidi Haeuser, designer, and Nancy Bryan, marketing.

Finally, I want to acknowledge my family—my children, Gary O'Brien and Laura McCarthy, and my parents, Randolph and Bernice. While my father was alive we went to the mountains every summer, which usually included the national parks. I continued that tradition with my family, and the travel bug bit my children in astounding ways. My mom, now ninety-one, accompanies me to the parks almost every year. Laura, a former English major and current geography professor, helped with much of the early writing. Gary, a Grand Canyon river guide, geology graduate student, and accomplished artist, answered many of my questions concerning the Grand Canyon and provided the drawings which introduce the case studies. Mainly, though, my family have offered me their total support, something I will always remember.

Our National Parks and the Search for Sustainability

# 1 Introduction

WHEN we complain about lack of political concern with the environment we should think back 125 years, to the time when the first national park was established, and be thankful for what we have. Then, there were no environmental legislation, no environmental organizations, and almost no ecological concern. There were of course far fewer people in the United States, only about 40 million in 1872,[1] but they were capable of immense destruction with no environmental laws or ethics to stop them. Most of the big game animals in America, such as bison, elk, and antelope, were in danger of becoming extinct, and landscapes from forests to grasslands were losing their productivity.[2] The entire natural landscape had little value for most people, and without the environmental consciousness that came with the national parks movement, the nation would be far bleaker than it is today.

I consider the establishment of Yellowstone National Park one of the real miracles of American history. In the midst of one of the most rapacious eras in our history, we quietly set aside an area the size of one of the original states to be preserved in perpetuity. The establishment of national parks has probably been the most copied of American institutions, emulated by over a hundred nations today.

President Grant signed the Yellowstone National Park Act on March 1, 1872. The key words in this act of only six hundred words were: "[Yellowstone Park] . . . is hereby reserved and withdrawn from settlement, occupancy, or sale under the laws of the United States, and dedicated and set apart as a public park or pleasuring-ground for the benefit and enjoyment of the people . . . [and] such regulations shall provide for the preservation from injury or spoliation of all timber, mineral deposits, natural curiosities, or wonders within said park, and their retention in their natural condition."[3]

Here we have an act that breaks new ground in two major fields: it gave to the *people* of the United States—not individuals, not states—a large parcel of land to enjoy as a park, and it called for the preservation of that landscape in its natural state, in perpetuity. We have then the forerunner of thousands of areas throughout the world preserved as parks, wilderness areas, game refuges, and other areas for the enjoyment of the people. We also have, in reality, one of the first attempts at a sustainable use of a landscape.

Sustainability is the key word for environmentalists today, or for that matter anyone who cares about the future of this planet. At one time it may have been possible to live off the capital of the land, to leave the world a little less able to support those who came afterwards; now we *have* to find a sustainable lifestyle to have any hope at all for the future. Yet, with so many people of the world living in grinding poverty, sustainability becomes an almost impossible dream. The rainforest and its priceless contribution to world biodiversity and climatic stability count for less than the few years' survival it can promise to those who slash and burn. On a different level, even in the United States and Canada it is hard to preserve the small amount of ancient forest left when jobs in lumbering are at stake. Here, and through much of the world where remnants of the natural landscape exist, ecotourism offers almost the only hope of saving those landscapes.

Ecotourism is a form of tourism that offers economic support to attractive tourist destinations that would otherwise be exploited for timber, minerals, agriculture, or water resources.[4] Classic ecotourism locations—Costa Rica, Nepal, Africa—are relatively poor areas where the influx of foreign travel dollars offers the alternative to cutting the rainforest, farming steep hillsides, or killing elephants. The same principles, however, can be applied to raft trips through the Grand Canyon, which helped keep dams out of the canyon, or making a tourist destination out of a historic village where a shopping center is planned.

The basic idea of national parks, from the beginning, was to preserve the parks for the people's enjoyment. It became obvious, however, that if a person's enjoyment consisted of breaking off pieces of one of Yellowstone's geyser cones for souvenirs or catching hundreds of trout in an afternoon, this brand of ecotourism was not going to work. The use must be sustainable. Protecting the parks meant preserving the park from commercial exploitation, *and* preserving it from the tourists. The first goal was the most important in the early years of the national parks, while the second has been the most important in recent years.

The national parks have been highly successful in achieving their earliest goals: to preserve the parks from commercial exploitation and to make easily accessible the most scenic portions of the United States. The preservation question is the subject of this book, but let's look at the geographic question: are the most scenic portions of the United States in the National Park System? One has only to flip through any travel brochure or picture book of the United States to answer in the affirmative, but listing superlatives also hints at the attractiveness of the national parks. Here are a few: tallest mountain in North America and one of tallest in the world from base to top (Mount McKinley in Denali National Park); most active volcanic area in United States (Hawaii Volcanoes National Park); most recent volcano in the conterminous United States (Mount Saint Helens Volcanic National Monument, run by the U.S. Forest Service); largest canyon in the world (Grand Canyon); tallest waterfalls in the United States (Yosemite); deepest lake in the United States (Crater Lake); tallest, largest, and oldest trees in the world (Redwood, Sequoia, and Great Basin National Parks); highest temperature in the United States (Death Valley); and greatest annual snowfall in the world (Mount Rainier).

Focusing on the unique and spectacular might cause us to ignore what ultimately will be the most important factor in park management: preserving habitat and ecosystems. The value of park areas has climbed sharply in the last few decades as the acreage of natural areas in the United States has been reduced. Rocky Mountain National Park was probably not the most beautiful section of the Colorado Rocky Mountains that could have been preserved in a park, but as the years go by it is becoming increasingly unique as ski resorts and backcountry vehicles scar the rest of the Colorado backcountry. It is becoming evident that we should have paid more attention to the "ordinary" landscapes such as prairie, coastal lagoons, marshlands, and hardwood forests, which might be ecologically more important than spectacular landscapes like mountains.

Other benefits seemed even more obscure when the national parks were first established. Wildlife, for example, was not particularly abundant in Yellowstone National Park compared to areas outside the park in the 1870's. Animals, like humans, prefer rich, warm lowlands to high, cold plateaus. The animals will live, however, where they need to live to survive, and in the days when game laws were virtually nonexistent they found safety inside park boundaries. Because it was protected, Yellowstone National Park became the home of the last wild buffalo herd in the United States, some of the last elk, and some of the last trumpeter swans. National parks gave breathing room to many species in the days before game laws had a chance to protect wildlife.

Watershed protection is an added bonus in having national parks. Many rivers, such as the Snake, Yellowstone, and Missouri, flow out of our parks pure and naturally regulated by uncut vegetation and undisturbed soil that absorbs the often copious rainfall. How many dams and water treatment plants would be necessary to replace what we get for free in the parks? The sight of a free-flowing stream, undammed and unpolluted, is a sight rare enough to thrill many park visitors.

Wilderness travel has become a major form of outdoor recreation. More and more people are discovering the ultimate delight in the out-of-doors, where the landscape is unmarred by roads, buildings, and the crush of people. In the national parks, wilderness begins just beyond the shoulder of the road and can be enjoyed by visitors the minute they enter park boundaries. Outside the national parks, roads invariably mean development, whether cutover forests, mined hillsides, or dammed streams. To the park motorist, roads seem numerous, but by far the greatest acreage in most national parks is roadless. Of course, the best wilderness experience comes when you leave roads far behind, and set out on foot to discover land affected only by nature.

Most visitors want only to escape the urban environment, and even the most crowded areas of the parks can fill that need. Visitors are apt to feel they are back in the city in the area surrounding Old Faithful, where thousands of people mingle for food, lodging, and parking. Then they catch a glimpse of a buffalo in the distance and can look miles beyond into pristine wilderness.

The first attention given to outdoor recreation by the federal government centered on the national parks, although it was not intended as a primary purpose of the parks. Recreational travel by car, bicycle, or on foot; recreational living in tent, trailer, cabin, or resort; boating, swimming, fishing, nature study, cross-country skiing, and mountaineering can reach their qualitative peak in the national parks. The escalation of these pursuits has worried many who feel that they could take place just as easily outside the parks, but most of the pursuits mentioned above can, with care, continue to be enjoyed at their present level, and some, like hiking, can be much expanded.

In a situation that makes local chambers of commerce happy and fills environmentalists with foreboding, the National Park System has become one of the top tourist attractions in the world. It would be hard to think of a way to extract a greater monetary benefit from developing the resources of any park than the tourist dollars that flow into it now. Even cutting back development within the parks would not stem the flow of tourist income into the surrounding areas, because the more beautiful the parks become, the more people are going to want to see them.

Finally, the educational value of the national parks is immense. People come to the Grand Canyon primarily to see one of the great natural wonders in the world. Many of them will also just look awhile, take a picture, and leave. But most will wonder how the canyon was formed and stand in awe at the unimaginable duration represented by one of the greatest exposures of geologic time in the world. They might also wonder how the area is being preserved by the National Park Service (NPS) for future generations and what is being done about current problems such as the noise from overflights and overcrowding. The answers are available there from rangers, in visitor centers, and in an extensive literature on the canyon and the park, although lack of funds has reduced the educational potential of this and other national parks.

We must be proud of our wisdom in setting aside national parks. We all sometimes look at our past and think of ourselves as heartless exploiters of the country's natural wealth. Thanks to the national parks, however, and other forms of preservation that have followed, we have probably saved more of the country's outstanding scenic, historic, and scientific areas than we have lost. Furthermore, there is every expectation that the national parks might someday represent one of the largest areas of sustainable use in the world.

# 2  Nature of the System

THE National Park System is a complex grouping of 374 parks containing over 83 million acres in forty-nine states, four territories, and the District of Columbia. There are national parks, historical areas, monuments, battlefields, seashores, parkways, recreation areas, lakeshores, scenic rivers, scientific areas, and more.[1] At one point the NPS attempted to simplify the system by placing each park in the category of natural, historic, or recreational area. Few parks fit neatly into this system, and the NPS has rejected it, but I still feel the classification is useful.

## NATURAL AREAS

The first national parks—Yellowstone, Yosemite, and Sequoia—were big, beautiful natural areas. Such parks are still the backbone of the National Park System. National parks, national monuments, and preserves make up 93 percent of the acreage of the system. At the core of this stand the 54 national parks.

### National Parks

The 54 national parks are not spread evenly across the United States. Alaska and California have 16 between them, while the twenty-six states east of the Mississippi have only 7 altogether. Still, it is hard to come up with any really spectacular area in the United States that is not represented, at least in part, by one of the national parks. The following geographic description covers each of the national parks.

*Old Faithful in Yellowstone National Park is one of the prime examples of unique and spectacular features of the National Park System. There are 374 units in the system, with highly varied reasons for their establishment. (National Parks photo)*

Acadia National Park, Maine, contains the most rugged coastline, the highest mountain—Cadillac Mountain, 1,530 feet—and the highest sheer cliff along either the Atlantic Ocean or the Gulf of Mexico in the United States. Mammoth Cave National Park in Kentucky was the first of three "cavern national parks" set aside, and besides containing the world's longest cave system, it also has unique water features and important historical and scientific associations. Shenandoah National Park, Virginia, logged before becoming a park, is becoming increasingly a prime example of the northern Blue Ridge Mountains after over half a century of protection. Great Smoky Mountains National Park contains the most impressive part of the Blue Ridge Mountains, the largest section of uncut forests in the eastern United States, and the finest example of the rich vegetation of the Appalachian Mountains. Everglades National Park in Florida is a large, subtropical paradise for plants and birds, but is highly

*Bathhouse Row in Hot Springs National Park, where the distinction between a natural and a historic park is blurred.*

endangered because of water diversions. Biscayne National Park, near the Everglades just south of Miami, has amazingly remained natural, mainly because most of its features are underwater. It was upgraded in the 1980's from a national monument to a national park. Dry Tortugas National Park, beyond the tip of the Florida Keys, is one of the nation's newest national parks, also upgraded from a national monument. All but a tiny percentage of its acreage is underwater, like Biscayne. Virgin Islands National Park, one of several parks that have benefited from the generosity of John D. Rockefeller Jr., is as important for saving underwater areas as for preserving the mostly cutover tropical forest.

There have only been three parks downgraded from national parks: Platt National Park in Oklahoma, which became part of Chickasaw National Recreation Area, Mackinac National Park in Michigan, which became a state park after being the first national park established after Yellowstone, and Sullys Hill National Park in North Dakota, which became a game preserve. Hot Springs National Park in Arkansas, set aside as a federal spa-type reservation as early as 1832, will probably remain a national park, although it might make more sense as a national historical park. It encloses an area of only 5,549 acres, mostly surrounded by the wooded tourist town of Hot Springs, and most of the springs have been enclosed in bathhouses.

Badlands National Park preserves a large and beautiful prairie area in South Dakota, and Theodore Roosevelt National Park a similar area in North Dakota. Wind Cave National Park is part of an important complex of natural features in the Black Hills of South Dakota that also contains Mount Rushmore and Jewel Cave National Monuments. Isle Royale National Park, Michigan, is a good example of the north woods ecosystem, and is the largest island in the largest of the Great Lakes, Lake Superior. The park is also roadless, and has been the focus of important animal ecology studies—on wolves and moose—for decades. Another park with a similar ecosystem is Voyageurs National Park in northern Minnesota.

Big Bend National Park, Texas, located in a bend of the Rio Grande, contains impressive canyons and supports several plants and animals unique to the United States. Guadalupe Mountains National Park, Texas, an "ecological national park" with unique flora and fauna, also contains the highest mountain in Texas and, geologically, one of the world's largest limestone reefs. Carlsbad Caverns National Park in New Mexico, possibly the most spectacular caverns in the United States, also contains the equally impressive, newly discovered Lechuguilla Caverns. Lechuguilla may never be opened to the general public because of the unavoidable damage any movement through it causes. Rocky Mountain National Park north of Denver offers a good sample of the Colorado Rocky Mountains and, as the years go by, a more natural area than the rest of the state, with its intensive ski and tourist resorts.

Grand Teton and Yellowstone National Parks are part of the 28,000-square-mile Greater Yellowstone Ecosystem of Wyoming, Montana, and Idaho, one of the largest relatively intact temperate ecosystems in the world. Within the area the Teton Range includes some of the country's most beautiful mountains, while Yellowstone has over 10,000 thermal features. The area contains large herds of elk and bison, some of the last grizzly bears in the conterminous United States, and the recently reintroduced gray wolf. Glacier National Park, Montana, protects an impressive section of the sedimentary northern Rocky Mountains and also has grizzlies and wolves.

The Colorado Plateau, a physiographic province in southeastern Utah and adjoining sections of Arizona, Colorado, and New Mexico, has the greatest concentration of national parks of any area of similar size in the country. Flat-lying sedimentary formations on the plateau have been uplifted, incised by the Colorado River and its tributaries into great canyons, and eroded by wind and water into fantastic and colorful landforms. Grand Canyon National Park, Arizona, contains one of the best-known landforms in the world and is the most heavily visited natural park in the western United States.[2] Canyonlands National Park, Utah, has also been cut by the Colorado River and its main tributary, the Green River, but is better known for its erosional features adjacent to the main canyons. Neighboring Arches National Park has the world's greatest concentration of natural arches. Capitol Reef National Park, Utah, protects an enormous geologic feature: the Waterpocket Fold. Bryce Canyon National Park, Utah, is one of our most beautiful national parks, with extensive erosional features cut in pink sandstone. Zion National Park, also in Utah, has been cut by the Virgin River, a tributary of the Colorado, and is the only canyon national park where you can drive into the bottom of the canyon. Mesa Verde National Park, Colorado, has the distinction of having the world's largest concentration of cliff dwellings as well as being the only "archaeological" national park. Saguaro National Park, Arizona, south of the Colorado Plateau in the Sonoran Desert, preserves the giant saguaro cactus, and is the "newest" national park, although it was proclaimed a national monument in 1933.

Washington has three mountain-oriented national parks, although they are quite different. North Cascades National Park was established as recently as 1968. Its alpine peaks and glaciers are wild and remote, the factor that kept such an impressive area little known for so long. Olympic National Park's primary attraction, in addition to its heavily glaciated mountains, is the nation's premier mid-latitude coastal rainforest. Mount Rainier is the tallest volcano and the most heavily glaciated peak in the conterminous United States, with some of the finest flower fields anywhere. Crater Lake National Park, Oregon, is the only national park (there are several national lakeshores) based entirely on a lake. It is arguably the most beautiful lake in the world—2,000 feet deep, clear, and intensely blue.

Some of the oldest and most impressive national parks in the country are in California. Yosemite National Park contains a combination of soaring cliffs, tall waterfalls, and a spectacular valley that epitomizes the quality of the National Park System. Yosemite also contains large groves of the world's largest living things, the sequoias, and a section of the Sierra Nevada mountains. Sequoia National Park contains the highest mountain in the conterminous United States, Mount Whitney, as well as the largest and most accessible groves of sequoias. Kings Canyon National Park is largely wilderness, with an outstanding section of the high Sierras. Lassen Volcanic National Park contained the only active volcano in the country when it was first made a park, although now that Alaska and Hawaii are states and St. Helens has erupted, it has lost some of its original meaning. Redwood National Park took almost a century of effort before being established, while old-growth redwoods, valuable lumber trees as well as the world's tallest, almost disappeared. Death Valley, an outstanding desert area, only recently was upgraded from a national monument to a national park. It is now the largest unit of the National Park System outside of Alaska, replacing Yellowstone. Joshua Tree National Park, with its beautifully eroded rock formations so beloved of rock climbers, was made a national park at the same time as Death Valley. Channel Island National Park contains unique island environments and one of the country's largest marine preserves.

Hawaii has two national parks on separate islands, and they are both based on volcanism. Hawaii Volcanoes National Park is one of the most continuously active volcanic areas on earth, while Haleakala contains an enormous extinct crater and the rare silver sword plant. The National Park of American Samoa, our fiftieth national park, is a small park in the South Pacific with good examples of tropical rainforest and some of the healthiest coral reefs in the world.

Alaska contains 58 percent of the total acreage of the National Park System, including enormous areas of unspoiled wilderness. The Alaskan parks offer wildlife not normally encountered in the lower forty-eight: caribou, Dall sheep, grizzly bears, and wolves. Parks that stand above even the Alaskan norm for spectacular scenery include Denali National Park, with the tallest mountain in North America, Wrangell–St. Elias National Park, the largest park in the country (six times larger than Yellowstone), and Glacier Bay National Park, the favorite of cruise lines. Other national parks are Gates of the Arctic, Kobuk Valley, Katmai, Lake Clark, and Kenai Fjords.

## National Preserves

"National preserves" is a new category, first used at Big Cypress in Florida in 1977, which allows noncompatible uses such as sport hunting without jeopardizing traditional national park values. The major use of this category is in Alaska, where huge areas of parkland contain Native Americans, whose rights most people felt had been violated enough without adding hunting restraints. Of the 15 preserves, 10 are in Alaska. The Wrangell–St. Elias National Preserve in Alaska contains 4,852,773 acres, larger than any park in the conterminous United States, yet is a part of a national park twice as large. The same is true of Gates of the Arctic National Park and Preserve, and Noatak National Preserve, which, with Kobuk Valley National Park, is the largest contiguous national park protected area in the United States: 17,180,158 acres.

The national preserve category took on a new meaning in 1995 as the environmental landmark Desert Protection Act worked itself through Congress. The most controversial part of this wide-ranging bill was the proposed establishment of a Mojave National Park in what had once been public domain. One use after another was allowed as the proposal moved toward acceptance, including, finally, even hunting. By then, national park designation was impossible, and it became Mojave National Preserve.

## National Monuments

The national monuments, half of which are historic, do not fit easily in any category. This is because of the way they are established. National monuments are the only units in the National Park System that can be established by presidential proclamation rather than by act of Congress. The intent of the national monument enabling act, the National Antiquities Act, was to allow the president to act quickly in saving archaeological sites on public lands before they could be plundered. The act as written, however, applied to any area of "historic or scientific interest."[3] Such an area may not lose its value because of development as quickly as an archaeological site to thievery, but the principle is the same. National monuments are often "holding areas" for national parks, as half the national parks were once national monuments, including Acadia, Grand Canyon, Zion, and Olympic National Parks.

Conservation-minded presidents have used the Antiquities Act frequently to save potential park areas, while others have ignored it. Franklin and Theodore Roosevelt founded several national monuments, for example, and Jimmy Carter pressured the U.S. Congress to act on the Alaska Native Claims Settlement Act by setting aside 59 million acres of national monuments in Alaska, a total almost as large as the entire National Park System in the rest of the United States. The last national monument to be established was by President Clinton in September 1996: the Grand Staircase–Escalante National Monument, protecting 1.7 million acres between Bryce Canyon National Park and Glen Canyon National Recreation Area in Utah from a proposed coal mine.

## HISTORICAL AREAS

The one thing historic units in the National Park System have in common is their small size. Although there are about 180 historic parks, half of the National Park System, they make up less than 1 percent of the total acreage of the system.[4] Their value to the nation, of course, is far greater than their small size indicates.

The reorganization of the executive branch of our government in 1933 brought 53 areas into the National Park System, mostly historic parks. One of them, the White House, predated Yellowstone as a park. The majority of such areas came from the War Department, mostly Civil War and revolutionary battlefields. The Civil War is still a common theme for historic parks, with 24 parks. The names—Shiloh, Antietam, Chickamauga, Vicksburg, and Gettysburg—are familiar to many Americans. The primary management problem in such parks is trying to keep landscapes characteristic of the Civil War period intact, in the face of intense tourism and commercial development. Other war-oriented parks number

*Scotts Bluff National Monument in Nebraska preserves an important landmark and stopover on the Oregon Trail. Approximately half of the units of the National Park System are historic.*

16, with only 2 from World War II. Some of the parks are a result of our changing attitudes about our actions in past wars. Manzanar, one of the newest national historic parks, commemorates the suffering of Japanese-Americans in World War II because of unjust internment. Custer Battle-field National Monument in Montana has become Little Bighorn Battlefield National Monument as we have rethought our part in certain conflicts with Native Americans.

National expansion is another important category for the historic parks, with 30 parks commemorating our westward movement. These include forts in the new territories, trading posts, sites along trails heading west, new settlements in Alaska and Hawaii, and forms of industry such as gold mining that formed the impetus for such movement. Jefferson National Expansion Memorial is notable primarily for its 630-foot stainless steel arch, but St. Louis was the starting point for much of the national expansion.

Historic parks commemorating former presidents and other famous Americans make up the largest category of historical parks: 44. For the presidents there is a certain selectivity: only a third of the presidents before Hoover are commemorated in historic parks (9 out of 29), although 4 parks each are devoted to Theodore Roosevelt and Lincoln. On the other hand, probably because of greater familiarity, six of the ten presidents since Hoover have been honored. Lifestyle might also be a factor. Theodore Roosevelt lived in a palatial mansion with beautiful grounds in Oyster Bay (Sagamore Hill National Historic Site, New York). He was also the obvious candidate, as our most conservation-minded president, for the name of a wooded island in the Potomac (Theodore Roosevelt Island). Finally, he is one of four presidents on Mount Rushmore, his birthplace and inauguration location are set aside as national historic sites, and because of his period as a cowhand in North Dakota, the Theodore Roosevelt National Park in North Dakota is named after him.

Famous Americans besides presidents are recognized in 23 historic parks. There is great variety in the choices. Some, like John Muir, Henry Wadsworth Longfellow, Thomas Edison, Robert E. Lee, Edgar Allan Poe, and the Wright brothers, are nationally recognized figures. Others are well known to people in their fields: Frederick Law Olmsted (landscape architecture), Clara Barton (American Red Cross), George Washington Carver (agronomy), and Eugene O'Neill (playwright). The rich are often remembered: John D. Rockefeller Jr. for his work in establishing several national parks, especially the Grand Teton National Park, and Cornelius Vanderbilt for the magnificent estate he left the nation.

The fastest-growing category of historic parks deals with American life. There are 3 concerned with railroads (Allegheny Portage Railroad, Pennsylvania, Golden Spike, Utah, and Steamtown, Pennsylvania), 2 dealing with early ironworks (Saugus, Massachusetts, and Hopewell Furnace, Pennsylvania), an armory (Springfield, Massachusetts), a park commemorating the Homestead Act, and a town where the Industrial Revolution started in this country (Lowell, Massachusetts).

Historic parks, which are small and may not involve changing land uses, can be noncontroversial and are likely to expand in number in the future. The further we get from events the more historic places become. Finally, it is well to remember that all the parks are historic to a degree, even the wildest Alaskan parks. Good examples from two of our most "natural" national parks include Cades Cove in Great Smoky Mountains National Park, an early 1900's rural farmstead, and all the places and events surrounding the establishment of the world's first national park in Yellowstone National Park.

## RECREATION AREAS

The first national recreation areas were established in the 1930's, partially for depression relief, and represented a departure from natural scenic parks, where the primary concern was *protecting* an area for use by the people. The first of these projects, in fact, involved building parkways and reservoirs for recreational use. They were included in the system because they involved federal projects with recreational benefits and there were no other agencies in the federal government with the authority or expertise to manage the new units. In building Hoover Dam, for example, an enormous reservoir was created with obvious recreational potential, so the NPS was called in to build the boat ramps, campgrounds, and picnic areas and to manage it afterwards.

### National Parkways

The earliest parkways, authorized in the 1920's, were limited-access roads in Washington, D.C., meant for recreational use and later incorporated into the National Capital Parks. The earliest parkway to stand as a separate unit in the National Park System, and the most famous, was the 470-mile-long Blue Ridge Parkway, which was started in 1933. It was built to furnish access to remote areas in the scenically beautiful Blue Ridge Mountains in North Carolina and Virginia. The areas were preserved by buying only the land immediately adjacent to the road and using scenic

easements and cooperation with states, national forests, and private landowners to control billboards, phone lines, and other developments.[5] Despite many national parkways being proposed, only a few exist because of
the great expense in managing and maintaining them. The parkways also
have high visitations. In 1995 Blue Ridge Parkway had 17,169,062 visitors, the highest in the National Park System, and there was a 7.7-million-
visitor average for the 4 parkways in the system.[6]

## Reservoirs

Including reservoirs in the National Park System has been controversial
from the beginning, as they depend on the flooding of natural areas. Glen
Canyon National Recreation Area is a good example. The canyon flooded
by the Glen Canyon Dam in 1963 was one of the most beautiful canyons
in existence.[7] To flood it seemed like the ultimate hypocrisy: destroying
the very thing that national parks were created to save and *then* to make
a park of it. The fight against Glen Canyon Dam was not as bitter as it
might have been because Glen Canyon was virtually unknown at the time
the dam was authorized. Afterwards, it became a symbol of the preservation movement almost as famous as Hetch Hetchy. Still, things change,
and people forget. The lake itself is beautiful, and Glen Canyon National
Recreation Area has become one of the most popular parks in the system.
A move to drain the lake, which loses an enormous amount of increasingly valuable water to evaporation and seepage, will likely be as strongly
opposed by recreationists as by power users.[8]

The era of big federal dams and reservoirs seems to be over; it has been
twenty years since the last national recreation area was established
around a reservoir, and none is being proposed. The greater possibility
is for them to be deauthorized, unless there are large amounts of park-
quality landscapes around the reservoir. If there are no preservation issues involved, state, local, or even private recreational units should be
able to do the job as well as the federal government.

## National Seashores

In 1934 the first national seashore, Cape Hatteras, North Carolina, was
authorized. It was to be thirty years before the second, Cape Cod National
Seashore, Massachusetts, was authorized, and then largely because we
elected a new, conservation-minded president who happened to be from
Massachusetts: John F. Kennedy. A study issued by the NPS in 1955, *Our
Vanishing Shoreline*, indicated that if something were not done to protect

our shorelines, especially in the East and South, most Americans would one day be cut off from the sea. In the decade of the 1960's, 8 of the 10 national seashores were established. Several were purposely set aside close to major population centers: Cape Cod near Boston, Fire Island near New York City, and Point Reyes near San Francisco, although the central purpose was still to preserve the natural landscape of beach areas.

## Rivers and Lakes

In the dam building era, the 1930's through the 1960's, it looked as if any free-flowing stream would be a museum piece. In the 1960's people were also beginning to discover one of the most rewarding forms of outdoor recreation—river running. The growing popularity of river-oriented tourism led to the NPS protecting 15 sections of river, starting with the Ozark National Scenic Riverways in 1964. The National Wild and Scenic Rivers Act, signed October 2, 1968, seemed as if it would obviate the need for other river parks in the National Park System, but others have followed. There is some confusion in the management of units of the Wild and Scenic Rivers System. Some, like Alatna Wild River in Gates of the Arctic National Park, Alaska, lie wholly within a national park. Others, like the Merced River, which forms the spectacular Nevada and Vernal Falls in Yosemite, flow through national park, national forest, and national resource lands. Most of the rivers of the Wild and Scenic Rivers System are on federal lands other than national parks.[9]

The Great Lakes are among the most unique and interesting lakes on earth, yet before 1966 only Isle Royale National Park, which few people visit, gave national recognition and protection to any part of the Great Lakes. There are now 4 national lakeshores, including Indiana Dunes in the heavily urbanized Chicago-Gary area. Some people shook their heads about a park within sight of steel mills, but recent studies have shown the biodiversity of Indiana Dunes National Lakeshore to be the highest in the National Park System. It seemed in the 1960's that other lakeshores, such as portions of the Great Salt Lake or Lake Tahoe, would follow, but it has been over twenty years since the last national lakeshore was established.

## Urban Parks

The newest, and among the most heavily used, units of the National Park System are national recreation areas lying within and just adjacent to large cities. There are only 4 of them: Golden Gate (San Francisco), Gateway (New York City), Santa Monica Mountains (Los Angeles), and Cuyahoga Valley, which connects Cleveland and Akron, Ohio. The idea behind the establishment of such parks is that since many Americans cannot afford to visit the parks, which are mostly located in the least populated parts of the country, parks should be brought to cities, especially those where attractive landscapes still exist. The initial impetus for the idea came in the 1960's in the Kennedy-Johnson administration, when inner-city riots received a lot of attention and an NPS program—Summer in the Parks—in Washington, D.C., seemed to be working.[10] As President Johnson put it, "a park, however splendid, has little appeal to a family that cannot reach it."[11] The first urban parks were established in 1972, when parks with similar names but at opposite ends of the country—Gateway National Recreation Area in New York City and Golden Gate National Recreation Area in San Francisco—were brought into the system. They both benefited from attractive waterfront sites that could be transferred from other federal ownership, especially the military, at small cost. The idea was good and it has worked. Many inner-city children in San Francisco and New York City have seen the wonders of nature for the first time in these parks. Unfortunately, such parks are also very expensive, for obvious reasons, and it is a wonder that they survived the cost-cutting of recent years.

*Golden Gate National Recreation Area (GGNRA)*
San Francisco is one of the nation's most beautiful cities, and with the founding of GGNRA in the city and Point Reyes National Seashore to the north, there are over 50 miles of beaches, hills, and open space stretching through San Francisco and to the north managed by the NPS.[12] The provider of all this largess was the military, which owned large sections of land in San Francisco and just north of the city at the Marin Headlands. Total acreage of the park is 73,185. The best-known and most controversial of these areas is the 1,480-acre Presidio, one of the oldest and most beautiful military bases in the country. The Presidio contains a wealth of natural features, including the only free-flowing stream in San Francisco, and citizens lobbied to have it included in GGNRA if or when the post ever was deactivated.[13]

Deactivation came sooner than many people expected, and by 1994 the NPS was in charge of the base, with hundreds of buildings to care for and responsibility for removal of toxic substances and possible retrofitting of buildings to meet earthquake standards.[14] The Army spent $40 million a year taking care of the Presidio when it was in charge, which would make it the most expensive unit in the National Park System.[15] This would represent a real change from the 1995 budget, when GGNRA, although expensive overall at $9,481,000, was one of the cheapest parks in the system on a "per visit" basis at only 57 cents per visitor (compared to $486 per visit for Gates of the Arctic National Park).[16] This expense, and the fact that it is worth $4 billion as urban real estate, have put it near the top of "park closure lists."[17] A bill establishing a "Presidio Trust" that could perhaps save the Presidio as a unit in the National Park System, was recently passed as part of the Omnibus Parks Bill.[18] The trust would be an independent government corporation that would oversee the leasing and maintenance of hundreds of buildings in the Presidio.

## NEW NATIONAL PARKS

The question of whether the National Park System is complete, whether all the Yosemites, Yellowstones, and Denalis are safely within the system, will never be answered. Nor should it. Potential historic parks will grow in importance as time unfolds, as will "ecological parks," as we attempt to save as many diverse American landscapes as we can. "Park barrel" will continue, budgets will stand as obstacles to a larger park system, and many will feel the National Park System should be confined to a few "crown jewels." The establishment of the great parks in Alaska in 1980, however, and the recent establishment and expansion of desert parks in California, suggest that increased political support, and new parks, only await the inevitable swing in the body politic sometime in the future.

# 3  History

T HE first national parks were founded during a highly unfavorable time in American history. In the 1860's, America was at the peak of a period of environmental exploitation which was threatening to lay waste to half a continent.[1] From wildlife to grassland to timber to mineral deposits, we were destroying our natural heritage as fast as any nation in history. Voices of reason were heard, but with neither laws nor precedent to carry out the necessary reforms, an effective counter to the destruction did not exist.

Most of the western United States was public land during that period, obtained from the Louisiana Purchase and other land acquisitions, but none of it was earmarked for public retention. Law followed law, including the Homestead Act, to get the public domain into private hands as quickly as possible. An area larger than France and the United Kingdom combined was granted to railroad companies alone, for example, although the subsidy was probably unnecessary.[2] There were no parks or national forests or wildlife refuges. Private ownership was the dream, not public preservation.

Well before Yellowstone, there were people crying out for preservation of the natural landscape, or at least singing its praises. Ralph Waldo Emerson and Henry David Thoreau are obvious examples, but few of the early American explorers were unaffected by the magnificent landscapes they were seeing. Some even went a step further and speculated on the means of saving that which was disappearing so rapidly. George Catlin, one of the foremost artists of the American Indian, even called for a nation's park focusing on the Indians and their way of life as early as 1832.[3]

Hot Springs Reservation in Arkansas was set aside in 1832, but it did not become a national park until 1921.[4]

## THE FIRST NATIONAL PARKS

Yosemite and Yellowstone National Parks should both be credited with the start of the national parks movement, as they shared important attributes for that birth. They were highly scenic and did not, at the time of founding, have important economic resources. They also became parks shortly after their discovery.

### The Yosemite Park Act of 1864

Yosemite Valley was the first rural natural landscape in the country to be set aside as a park, an act that took place only thirteen years after the first exploratory party saw, and appreciated, the stupendous scenery of the valley.[5] Within that short period writers (Horace Greeley, Thomas Starr King), photographers (C. E. Watkins), and artists (Albert Bierstadt) introduced the wonders of Yosemite and the giant sequoias to the nation. The Yosemite Park Act of 1864, signed by President Lincoln, called for transferring Yosemite Valley and the Mariposa Grove of sequoias to the State of California. The success of the bill deeding Yosemite Valley to the state probably had as much to do with what was not there as what was. A century ago even the most extreme "wise use" adherent of the day would not have seen much future in the valley for farming, lumbering, or mineral extraction. Possibly the most important thing about the Yosemite grant was a law, upheld by the Supreme Court, which prevented homesteading in the valley and whose vindication established the constitutionality of national parks (and all public land).[6] The state did not take care of its holdings, however, allowing farming and salvage lumbering, and Yosemite Valley in 1905 became part of Yosemite National Park, which had been established in 1890.[7]

### Yellowstone National Park

The Yellowstone Plateau of 1872, encompassing most of the Yellowstone National Park of today, had been traversed by trappers and mountain men for at least half a century, yet was essentially untouched.[8] The native population consisted of only a few members of a poor Indian tribe living in the northern part of the plateau. The physical environment of the Yellowstone National Park area, predominantly a volcanic plateau averaging 8,000 feet in elevation, strongly discouraged human settlement. The area had long winters, with temperatures as low as −40 °F and up to 400 inches of snowfall at higher elevations.[9] Attempts at agricultural settlement were unsuccessful. The timber cover was three-fourths lodgepole pine, an inferior lumber tree. No minerals were found which could have been mined economically. Dams for water power and storage could be important in the area today but were not considered so until the 1920's. All of this was important at the time in the United States, because to go from an economic policy of every place having a price tag to the total exclusion of economic value was an enormous step. With very few exceptions, national parks, even today, are not established if there is any economic use for the land they would occupy.[10]

The first large exploratory expedition to Yellowstone, the Washburn Expedition in 1870, was generally credited with generating the national park idea. Trappers, miners, soldiers, and other expeditions had passed through the region for half a century, but the information they brought back of wonders encountered was neither accepted nor widely disseminated. This was not to happen with the Washburn Expedition. The difference in this expedition was that the group included several articulate and well-known individuals, including N. P. Langford, who was to become the world's first national park superintendent. The expedition members commanded a respect that gave credence to the claims they made of the wonders of Yellowstone.[11]

The origin of the national park idea, although this claim is challenged by several leading historians,[12] was said to have occurred on the expedition's last night in the park, when expedition members sat around a campfire and discussed how they could profit from staking claims in the park area.[13] As the conversation progressed, the explorers began to realize the effect this would have on the future of the park. The expedition's route had touched on most of the scenic points of the park, and in the total wilderness of that day, the effect of the scenic wonders on expedition members, who had not known what to expect, had been overwhelming. Their feeling, simply stated, was that visitors of the future should be able to repeat that experience in an area free of private claims, a pristine wilderness.

The next year an official government expedition, the 1871 Hayden Survey, was sent into the area to record its geology, flora, and fauna.[14] The expedition also contained Thomas Moran and W. D. Jackson. These individuals were to expose the world of Yellowstone through the media of photography and painting, with a quality that has scarcely been equaled since. Reproductions of Moran's paintings of the Grand Canyon are still sold in the park today, and Jackson's photographs are considered among the finest ever taken of the Yellowstone region. Minimal economic conflicts and maximum pressure from concerned and well-spoken individuals, including those representing the Northern Pacific Railroad,[15] led to Yellowstone's establishment as the world's first national park on March 1, 1872.

## MANAGEMENT PROBLEMS OF THE NEW PARKS

The period before the establishment of the National Park Service (NPS), and well before the post–World War II explosion in visitation, was spent in establishing new national parks, fighting off attempts at noncompatible use, and finding ways, including new laws, of meeting the protection mandate of the national parks. Yosemite and Yellowstone National Parks' first few years showed the problems the new parks could expect in the years ahead, especially those relating to lack of funds and a tendency to put accommodation of visitors ahead of preservation in park management. In Yosemite, nothing was done with early recommendations to site accommodations outside Yosemite Valley, and it soon filled with hotels, roads, fences, and even plowed fields. Protection was further handicapped with California's extreme reluctance to spend anything on the park: Galen Clark, the valley's first "guardian," was not paid for several years, although his salary was only $500 a year.[16]

Yellowstone fared even worse in some respects, although its visitation was much less (about 500 yearly through 1896 compared to 4,936 in Yosemite as early as 1870), and there was little pressure in the first few years for development.[17] Yellowstone's first superintendent, N. P. Langford, received no salary and only visited the park twice during his seven-year term of office. Visitors hunted, broke up geyser formations for souvenirs, and were careless with fires.[18] The solution to this state of affairs for Yellowstone, and Yosemite once it became a national park, was to put the parks under the care of the U.S. Army, which continued until the NPS was formed in 1916.[19]

Most environmentalists believe there are too many roads in the national parks, yet there would have been many more if the funding had been provided. They wouldn't find much to complain about in the dirt roads being built in the first half-century of national park history, traversed occasionally by the wagons and horses of the time. Even with the shortage of funds, the roads of Yellowstone were completed in approximately their present configuration as early as 1905.[20]

Sequoia, General Grant (later Kings Canyon), and Yosemite (minus Yosemite Valley) followed Yellowstone as national parks in 1890. They all benefited from the work of America's premier conservationist, John Muir, who worked hard in getting the California parks as well as Washington's Mount Rainier into the system. His impact was immeasurable in championing the preservation end of park management at a time when visitor use was preeminent. His part in founding and heading the Sierra Club, his fight against the Hetch Hetchy dam in Yosemite, and especially his skill as an environmental writer all contributed to furthering preservation in the national parks.[21]

Sixty-four areas had been established as parks prior to the August 25, 1916, National Parks Act, including 14 national parks, 5 national monuments which would become national parks, and other national monuments and historical sites which were administered by the War Department and Agriculture Department as well as the Department of the Interior.[22] There were also a number of national parks and monuments that were decommissioned, including the second national park, Mackinac Island.[23]

Possibly the worst setback in national park history was the building of a Hetch Hetchy dam in Yosemite National Park. The city of San Francisco wanted a site in the park on the Tuolumne River for a revenue-producing hydroelectric dam, despite the destruction of a highly scenic valley, the invasion of a national park, and the existence of alternate sites outside the park. Some might say that the dam stood as a horrible example to keep dams out of other parks; dams were proposed for Yellowstone, Grand Canyon, Kings Canyon, Dinosaur, Glacier, and others, and all were defeated. A dam proposed for Yellowstone National Park, for example, would have completely cut off the flow over Upper and Lower Yellowstone Falls by transferring the water by tunnel into the Snake River drainage for irrigation in Idaho.[24]

Just about everything has been proposed for the national parks, from farms to lumber mills, and it is unlikely that a tiny segment of the population will ever accept limitations on what they can do to any piece of land in the country. Looking at the behavior of some contemporary legislators from the western United States toward grazing and mining rights, it is easy to imagine how difficult it must have been for the early rangers to resist economic excursions by the locals into the parks. When we fault the early rangers for spending much of their energy courting the visitor or residents of lands bordering the park, rather than aggressively protecting the environment, we must realize how tenuous their position was in the early days. The nation had spent two centuries cutting forests, mining hillsides, plowing fields, and killing wildlife; *preserving* a landscape was new.

## THE NATIONAL PARK SERVICE

Even as the public was learning to care for its parks and the Army was doing a good job in its "temporary" situation of control, it was obvious that there had to be a greater sense of direction for the national parks if they were to survive. The agencies running the national parks and monuments—mainly the Department of the Interior but also the Departments of Agriculture and War—had as their primary goals the development of resources, not the protection of them. A new "national parks agency" needed to be established.

Two individuals, Stephen Mather and Horace Albright, are strongly linked to the founding of the National Park Service. Mather was described by park historian John Ise thus:

> Mather was a man of prodigious and explosive energy, a tireless worker, a born promoter, "a practical idealist of the live-wire type" with a generous devotion to his job which is reminiscent of some of America's greatest—Washington, Thomas Paine, and Gifford Pinchot. He had been a lover of the outdoors, a mountain climber, a member of the American Civic Association and of the Sierra Club since 1904, and had made a fortune in borax before [Franklin K.] Lane called him to Washington. Handsome, of winning personality, he commanded respect and admiration and was able to win many friends to the parks. . . . In his years in the Park Service he gave much of his fortune to the promotion of the parks, and gave of his energies so prodigally that his health broke several times and he died in 1930 at the age of sixty-three, after only twelve years as Director.[25]

Horace Albright had no fortune, but he had immense talents in public relations, especially with Congress, which he courted assiduously during his twenty-year association with the national parks. He was actually the NPS's first director, taking over the its operation the first year when Mather became ill. I came across Albright's name frequently in the research for my dissertation on Yellowstone in the 1960's, both as superintendent of the park from 1919 to 1929 and director of the NPS from 1929 to 1933. I had assumed that, after a third of a century, he had passed on years before. I hadn't considered that he was only twenty-six when he became acting director of the NPS. I visited him several times in his home near UCLA after I had moved to San Diego, and like most people who have known him, I was absolutely amazed at the clarity of his memory, and delighted by his stories of the early NPS.

Mather and Albright were to build the NPS as we know it from scratch, without any similar organization in the world to copy. Mather came to Washington in 1915 as Franklin K. Lane's assistant in charge of parks. While there, he and Albright lobbied incessantly for the establishment of a new national parks bureau, finally succeeding with its establishment on August 25, 1916. Opposition to the new bureau came mainly from the U.S. Forest Service, which saw, rightly as it would prove, that it would lose land and influence in the future to the NPS. Support for the new parks department came from those who stood to gain the most from it, namely the tourist and travel industries, the railroads, and conservation groups. There were also legislators who could see the value of the new parks department from the beginning.

The Mather-Albright era covered the period 1916 to 1933, which included Mather's term as NPS director, 1917–1928, and Albright's terms as superintendent of Yellowstone, 1919–1929, and NPS director, 1929–1933. In short, these gentlemen created the service much as we see it today. Neither had political ambitions, but both felt fervently about what they were doing. Their program could be divided into three parts: (1) solidifying the newly created federal agency by vigorously courting friends of the parks, the U.S. Congress, influential people, and the general public; (2) expanding the National Park System by working for the inclusion of appropriate areas; and (3) protecting park resources by showing the public the wonders of their parks and enlisting them in the fight to preserve the parks.

We look at the strength of the NPS today—with a $1.6 billion budget, thousands of employees, and a reputation as one of the most beloved and respected government agencies—and have a hard time imagining how fragile it was in the beginning. When its doors opened for the first time in 1916 its handful of employees fitted comfortably into a couple of offices, it controlled only 16 parks, and its entire budget was $19,500, which included Mather and Albright's salaries, plus those of the entire staff.[26] Furthermore, the NPS had a very powerful enemy in the Forest Service, which felt it could do the same job better and cheaper.

The selling job of Mather-Albright was helped immensely by what they were selling—such incredible portions of the earth's surface as Yosemite and Yellowstone—and by their allies: conservation groups like the

Sierra Club, progressive groups like the General Federation of Women's Club, and special friends in Congress. Mather made the expansion of this support, especially among the rich and influential, nearly a full-time job. Individuals such as John D. Rockefeller, Gilbert Grosvenor, editor of the *National Geographic,* heads of railroads, members of Congress, and several presidents came under the persuasion of Mather or Albright. The building of a loyal and efficient group of rangers and employees was another accomplishment of the Mather-Albright era. Albright is said to have known the first names of every ranger in the service during its early years and to have instilled a sense of mission so strong that many felt they were doing "the Lord's work." [27]

Although promotion received more attention than preservation, that portion of park management was not neglected. Attacks on the parks were nearly continuous from the beginning, from mining, power, lumbering, irrigation, and livestock interests. Albright and Mather understood that if the areas threatened were not included in national parks, even if they were in a national forest, any battle to preserve them would likely be lost before it began.

Before World War II many new parks were added to the system, including such giants as the Grand Canyon and Denali. Just as important, however, were the parks *not* added to the system. The establishing of national parks for economic or political reasons continues to be a problem today; imagine what it would have been like in the beginning. The classic example of a proposal for a worthless national park was "Mescalero Park" in New Mexico, proposed by Secretary of the Interior Albert Fall of "Teapot Dome" infamy, for an area adjoining Fall's ranch.[28] The park would be made up of small isolated tracts of little scenic value, would be open to mining and grazing, and—height of irony—would have included land taken from the Indians without compensation. It is easy to envision a much lower-quality National Park System than we have today without Mather and Albright's fight against inferior parks.

The keynote of the Albright administration was the transfer of most park-type lands from other government bureaus into the National Park System.[29] Albright always considered historic areas as much a part of the country's heritage as the natural areas, and he helped arrange the transfer of such areas as military parks and battlefield sites from the War Department to the NPS. Much of this, according to Albright's recollections, came about because of a ride he shared with Franklin D. Roosevelt in 1933, when the logic behind such a reorganization was explained to the president.[30] Albright resigned his office shortly after this accomplishment, citing the difficulties of sending children to college on a director's salary ($9,000 per year), thus ending the Mather-Albright contributions to the NPS.

## DEPRESSION AND WAR YEARS

The 1930's Depression held great danger for the national parks as visitation dropped and concessioners were forced to cut their services sharply. However, thanks to the Civilian Conservation Corps (CCC), a public works program under President Roosevelt, the national parks enjoyed one of their best periods. By the time the Depression ended with the onset of World War II, some 3 million men had worked on park projects, spending a half-billion dollars in appropriations.[31] In virtually every park, when you see a beautifully laid out trail, or a striking bridge, or an architecturally interesting building, chances are good that it was built by the CCC.

This period of attention to the national parks was followed by one of great neglect. The parks almost closed down during World War II as gas rationing took effect. Visitors to Yellowstone dropped to 64,144 in 1943, compared to 581,761 in 1941 and 814,907 in 1946.[32] There were efforts to exploit the parks also, such as allowing grazing in Mount Rainier National Park, but little came of them. The most serious threat was the potential logging of Sitka spruce, necessary for the aircraft industry, in Olympic National Park, but better supplies were found in Canada and the shift to aluminum planes had begun.[33] What happened after the war, however, was the most harmful to the national parks. For various reasons appropriations stayed at near-wartime levels through the postwar era, in spite of an American public acting as if it were starving for what the parks had to offer. Visitation doubled within seven years of the end of the war.

The result of the constant increase of visitors to prewar facilities was predictable: utter chaos. Bernard DeVoto, a popular American historian, wrote an article in 1953 entitled "Let's Close the National Parks."[34] It was a national shame, he maintained, to let something all Americans claimed to love fall into such a disreputable state.

## MISSION 66

Much of what DeVoto was unhappy about, a badly deteriorating infrastructure of roads, ranger housing, and museums, was improved by "Mission 66." This ten-year, billion-dollar program was intended to bring the National Park System up to date on the fiftieth anniversary of the NPS, 1966.[35] Environmentalists were not that happy with Mission 66, however, as it dealt almost entirely with development which would attract even more people to the national parks. Still, coming during the Eisenhower privatization era, and following the severe neglect of the previous sixteen years, Mission 66's accomplishments were impressive, including homes for two thousand park families, and 150 new visitor centers. The accomplishments would have been better received if they had not run head-on into the new environmental movement.

## THE ENVIRONMENTAL MOVEMENT

The environmental community seemed strong, particularly in the fight for the Wilderness Bill in the late 1950's and early 1960's, but it usually involved a relatively small number of people. Earth Day, April 22, 1970, signaled a change, as well as rapid growth, in the environmental movement. Issues such as the Santa Barbara oil spill and dramatically worsening air pollution indicated that protecting the environment was going to involve more than national parks and wilderness areas. Fortunately for the parks, the much greater attention given the overall environment did not diminish attention given the national parks, whose visitation continued to increase.

A strong push for the national parks came with the election of John F. Kennedy in 1960. He chose as his Secretary of the Interior Stewart L. Udall, author of *The Quiet Crisis* and one of our strongest conservation secretaries ever.[36] Founding new national parks, which had been on hold since the 1930's, started again. New kinds of parks, like national seashores, national lakeshores, and urban parks, were established, starting with Cape Cod National Seashore, Massachusetts, in Kennedy's state, and Canyonlands National Park in Udall's area.

Indeed, the 1970's, including the climactic year of 1980, was the period of greatest growth in national park history. Much of this was due to the Alaskan Land Bill, which essentially doubled the National Park System. There was also unprecedented growth in every part of the system, so much so that national park supporters started to worry about "park barrel" bills that used the potential of local spending to push inferior parks through Congress. Environmentalists had little time to celebrate the 1970's growth in attention given to the national parks before a shocking

29

event (for the environmental community) took place: the election of Ronald Reagan as president and his appointment of James Watt as Secretary of the Interior. Events of the 1980's are recent enough to receive attention in all the chapters to follow. Suffice it to say that the NPS has built enough support through the years that the disaster everyone predicted, but whose anticipation ironically led to the greatest growth period for environmental organizations ever, never happened.

# Case Study:
# Yellowstone National Park

$B$EING the oldest national park in the world certainly makes Yellowstone stand out. But a claim could also be made that it is the most interesting. Years ago, when I was spending part of each summer climbing in Grand Teton National Park, I'd make an occasional trip to Yellowstone: "people, moose, and mosquitoes," I thought at the time. Then I wrote my dissertation on the park, making more than a hundred trips there, and changed my mind completely. I think it mainly has to do with Yellowstone's size, diversity, and great variety of features. No matter how many times I visit the park I know there is more to see and know. Not to put down Crater Lake, the Grand Canyon, and Yosemite, for example, but once you have seen the main features—the lake, the canyon, and the valley—you might *feel* as if you had seen it all. How could you ever feel that way after seeing just Old Faithful?

So what are the features of Yellowstone that have stimulated so much interest? The thermal areas are certainly unique; Old Faithful is one of the symbols of the National Park System, and the thermal areas originally caught the public's imagination and led to Yellowstone's being established as the world's first national park. The park, with over ten thousand thermal features, is, and has been in the geologic past, one of the world's most active thermal areas (its eruptive material through time has been estimated at 3,800 cubic kilometers, compared to Mount St. Helens's 1 cubic kilometer).[1] Its collection of geysers is unique in that they are essentially untouched, whereas most of the world's other great geyser basins, such as those in Iceland and New Zealand, have been tapped extensively for thermo-power. The first explorers into Yellowstone's geyser basins were tremendously impressed by the great geysers. Present-day visitors, more traveled and sophisticated, are still impressed. Thousands of people gather for each eruption of Old Faithful in the summer months, and walking away after the eruption, they seem pretty happy with what they've seen.

Lower Yellowstone Falls is neither the tallest nor the largest waterfall in the country, and the Grand Canyon of the Yellowstone is nowhere near the largest or even the most colorful canyon in the country—but put all these features together and you have one of the world's most dramatic scenic views. It isn't hard to imagine how impressed members of the Washburn Expedition must have been in 1870 when they came on the falls and canyon without knowing what was there. Yellowstone, the birthplace of great rivers and located on a plateau thousands of feet

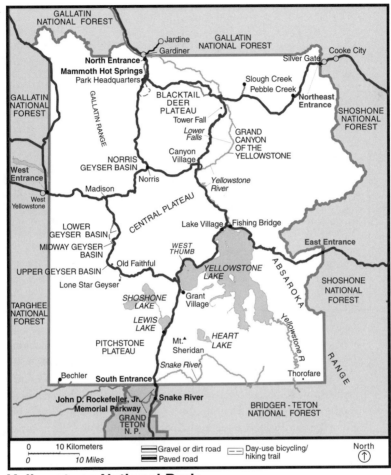

## Yellowstone National Park

*Lamar Valley in Yellowstone National Park seems almost ordinary by national park standards, but has become one of the hot spots in the National Park System for wildlife viewing. Bison, elk, antelope, black bear, grizzly bear, and gray wolves can all be seen here by the patient viewer.*

above the surrounding countryside, contains an abundance of waterfalls: Tower, Osprey, Upper Yellowstone, Lewis, and many others.

The thermal features and waterfalls are appreciated by present-day visitors, but wildlife seems to have replaced them as the main reason people visit the park.[2] Driving the 140-mile Grand Loop Road you'll almost certainly see elk and bison, possibly moose or antelope or coyotes, a great variety of bird life—some like the trumpeter swan among the most spectacular anywhere, small critters of great variety, and finally, if you're lucky: bear or wolves. Early one brisk morning in May 1997, I stood for two hours on a hill above Slough Creek in the park's northeast corner and saw an amazing parade of animals: eight wolves; five grizzly bears; assorted black bear, bison, elk, antelope, bighorn sheep; and a bald eagle. In few places in the world is the visitor's interest in an area so absorbed with wildlife.

Wilderness is also of much greater interest to the visitor than it was in the past, and will almost certainly be so in the future as wild country in the United States diminishes. In Yellowstone, wilderness isn't valued so much for actual or anticipated excursions into it, as in Sequoia or Kings Canyon National Parks, but for simply knowing it is there and being able to look at it from the window of a car. Most people are not used to driving through an area where all you can see on the distant horizon is wilderness. It provides an immersion in the natural scene that stamps Yellowstone as unique in the conterminous United States.

Water plays a big part in the Yellowstone experience—the falls already mentioned, Yellowstone and other lakes, and a number of special rivers. There is a place in the park, Two Ocean Pass, where fish can theoretically swim over the continental divide. Of the three major tributaries of the Missouri, the Madison and the Gallatin start in the park, and the Missouri's main tributary is the Yellowstone River. The Snake River, a major tributary of the Columbia, also starts in the park. Adding uniqueness to the rivers and lakes is their association with falls, wildlife, and thermal features.

Historical features here are among the most important of all the "natural" national parks. Because Yellowstone was the world's first national park, much of the history of the National Park System seems to rest on the Yellowstone Plateau. Finally, its size (eleventh in the National Park System but largest in the conterminous United States after newly expanded Death Valley National Park), its visitation (one of the highest in the system on a "visitor hours" basis),[3] the number and variety of its wildlife, and the diversity of its features have meant that many of the problems the National Park Service has had to try to solve have begun here. As examples, newsworthy items in just the last few years have included the great wildfires of 1988 and the wolf reintroduction of 1995.

## DEVELOPMENT

There is a large amount of development in Yellowstone compared to other large natural national parks, although the developed areas still only cover a tiny percentage of the park. Attempts to reduce development include changing the size, quality, and location of roads, hotels, stores, and campgrounds in the park.

## Roads

I'm unaware of any road system in the national parks which taps such a high percentage of the scenery of an area, and yet gives such an overall feeling of wilderness and wildlife, as the Grand Loop Road in Yellowstone National Park. There is also good access to the outside, with access roads north, south, east, west, and northeast, more recreational vehicles

*Visitors waiting for Old Faithful Geyser to erupt in Yellowstone National Park. Old Faithful Inn is in the distance.*

(RVs) than on any road I've ever seen, and tremendous problems with maintenance because of heavy use and severe weather. The road system has also had major problems accommodating the crowds using it, especially during the era of the roadside bears and "bear jams" prior to the early 1970's.

In retrospect it seems as if a single road across Yellowstone from West Yellowstone to Cody via Canyon with a side road to Old Faithful would have given a good sampling of the scenery in the park, including most of the outstanding sites, would have increased park wilderness, and would have decreased the cost of running the park significantly.[4] This will never happen, and neither will longer road systems be built, encircling Yellowstone Lake and giving access to the Lamar and Bechler Rivers, although these could easily have been accepted in the past.[5] The road system was completed in approximately its present configuration in 1905, and all that prevented a much longer system in the days before wilderness concerns was the cost.[6] Since then, most of the concern with the roads has been with a steadily growing use of the roads and steadily increasing needs for maintenance.

The problem of Yellowstone road crowding became intense in the decade or two after World War II when tourists flocked to the parks on roads up to half a century old, none of which had been built to handle the crowds which were now using them. The situation was exacerbated by the completely uncontrolled access on park roads and the profusion of wildlife. The wildlife, and especially bears, could be seen anywhere around the Grand Loop, often where there was no place to safely pull off the road. Having experienced "bear jams" in Yellowstone from my first trip to the park in 1947 until the last roadside bear disappeared in the 1970's, I thought it inevitable that park traffic would someday, somewhere, hopelessly jam. People would act as if they had never seen a bear (and the photographers as if no one had ever seen a picture of a bear) as they jumped from cars parked anywhere on the road and ran to see what was causing the excitement. Rangers had a hard time getting to the bears and scaring them away because of the congestion. The lack of an open lane for fire trucks or emergency vehicles was also serious, and the NPS knew it had to do something. Removing the roadside bear was crucial, but only as a first step toward improving park roads. Any animal, including bison and elk, would cause people to slam on the brakes and grab camera or binoculars, although none of them came close to the attraction of a bear and cubs. The obvious solution was to modernize the roads, but modernization raises a number of problems.

The logical way to handle more visitors to the park in a safer environment is to upgrade the roads—to widen them, straighten them, flatten them, and add shoulders. This would definitely improve the traffic flow, especially on highways which were originally built for another era. It's expensive, however, and opens the debate on the purpose of roads in the National Park System. A park-type road, as narrow as possible and laid out with respect to the topography, can be almost invisible from a short distance away. If the goal of park roads is just to allow the visitor to see the park, speed becomes a detriment. At 60 mph on a six-lane highway, drivers see mostly sky and pavement—only 17 percent of their vision encompasses the surrounding landscape.[7] In fact the NPS has resisted wide, fast roads, building only one four-lane highway in all the natural national parks in Yellowstone at the Old Faithful bypass (see page 42), yet it continues to upgrade its road system when the money is available.

Public transportation seems the obvious answer to the potential gridlock of Yellowstone roads in the future. Before the automobile was allowed in Yellowstone Park in 1915, the vast majority of visitors toured the park by public transportation.[8] Public transportation has several advantages over the private automobile: several times more visitors can be moved over the same road space than by private car, the visitor experience can be enhanced by better interpretation, park protection can be increased by better control of the visitor, and deterioration of the park road system can be slowed by lighter use. The use of public transportation, which plummeted to 1 percent of park visitors by the mid-1960's, had risen to only 3 percent by the early 1990's, despite much greater foreign visitor totals.[9] The major problem with public transportation is that Yellowstone is not a single-interest national park that would easily lend itself to rapid transit scheduling. Most visitors to Yellowstone see Old Faithful, the Grand Canyon of the Yellowstone, and Yellowstone Lake, and a few might see only these features during a trip to the park. However, there are a multitude of things in Yellowstone attracting visitors and causing them to stop. *Haynes Guide*, for example, lists twenty-eight points of interest in the 21 miles between Mammoth and Norris, but there are still the animals which might be seen and a wide variety of general landscape views obtainable in this section.[10] Yellowstone is also a park where action, rather than observing static scenery, usually dictates travel through the park. You wait for Old Faithful or other geysers even less predictable to erupt, you wait for the bear up on the hillside to come into view, and you know if you're patient enough you'll see the famous Yellowstone wolf run across a meadow. Having your time dictated by a bus schedule may not be the best way to see the park.

Cost, however, will probably be the final arbiter on a public transportation system in Yellowstone. It is already there, and 97 percent of the public chooses not to take it. The answer is either banning private cars altogether, a move politically impossible for the foreseeable future, or providing a system so attractive that people will abandon their beloved cars for it. Certain fragile areas of the park, like the Grand Canyon of the Yellowstone, Hayden Valley, or Dunraven Pass, could benefit from partial systems. Annualized costs for those predicted to use the system run from $6.80 per person for large shuttle buses to $75.78 per person for an elevated monorail, using a recent study of Hayden Valley as an example.[11] The future will probably bring such projects, but for now the existing road system needs massive upgrading.

While the grand plan for the future Yellowstone National Park road system is being formulated, the existing roads are falling apart. An evaluation of the 329 miles of the system in 1988 rated only 28.4 percent of the system in good or fairly good condition, with the remainder rated fair to very poor. Of the 1,228 motor vehicle accidents which occurred in the park 1982–1984, 25 were attributed to road defects.[12] The roads were simply not built to handle the huge volume of cars now found in the park, the heavy trucks supplying concessioners in the park, or the mix of traffic, from oversized RVs to bicycles, using the often narrow or shoulderless roads. A "permanent" solution to Yellowstone's deteriorating road system, bringing it all up to date, is currently being sought under a twenty-year, $300 million Federal Lands Highway Program.[13] Delays in road work in Yellowstone are perennial and will probably be so far into the future.

## Yellowstone "Towns"

With the exception of Mammoth and Old Faithful (open for snowmobiles), Yellowstone towns are closed from sometime in November until about the middle of April. They boom for only a few weeks, from the Fourth of July till Labor Day. They're pure recreational towns. You can go shopping in them, do your laundry, even go to the post office or bank, but their only "business" is to provide access to the park.

*Mammoth*
The area around Mammoth is my favorite part of the park. The park headquarters and research library are there, where I spent many busy but pleasant days researching my dissertation in the 1960's. It isn't quite so crowded and hectic as the southern area of the park, and the campground in the area is smaller, friendlier, and often populated, on its edge, with herds of elk. Mammoth was the site of old Fort Yellowstone, and the army buildings are still there and in use. It has an excellent museum and visitor center. Any direction from Mammoth, especially to the east toward Tower Junction over Blacktail Butte, and to the south up onto the Yellowstone Plateau, leads to quintessential Yellowstone country: grasslands, rolling hills, timber, plenty of edge environment, and, usually, plenty of animals. Mammoth is the only development in the park accessible by car which is open all year, with the national park headquarters, homes, and a school in addition to a hotel, a restaurant, cabins, a general store, a gas station, a campground, and a visitor center. Mammoth seems a sustainable village. There is constant fine tuning, but the lower popularity of the northern part of Yellowstone compared to the south and central has saved it from the worst effects of overcrowding.

*Mammoth Hot Springs: NPS headquarters at rear, visitor accommodations to the left, and the open landscape of Yellowstone National Park surrounding it all.*

### Canyon

The Grand Canyon of the Yellowstone and its falls can be observed from several lookouts on both sides of the canyon, and from trails to the top of the falls on one side and to near the bottom of the falls on the other side. Nearby Hayden Valley is an excellent wildlife area. It is a large, grassy valley, opening on the flat, beautiful Yellowstone River, with two or three small creeks cutting through it. I flew over the area once, and it looked like an American Serengeti, with large herds of bison and elk. The animals can usually be seen, and there are overlooks where, in season, you can see Canadian geese, trumpeter swans, white pelicans, and an occasional moose. In 1957 a number of structures were built in the Canyon area as part of the overall Mission 66 program to upgrade facilities and move them back away from scenic attractions, in this case the Grand Canyon of the Yellowstone. The area, located on the travel corridor between feeding areas on Mount Washburn and in the Hayden Valley, is important to the grizzly. Grizzlies were also attracted to the area by the bear feeding area with a grandstand at nearby Otter Creek, which was closed in 1941, and the Trout Creek open dump, which was closed in 1973. Shortly thereafter, grizzlies were causing trouble in the Canyon campground, leading to a "hard side trailer"–only policy. Recent proposals to shrink and upgrade the area would result in replacing 488 cabin rooms with rooms in compact buildings.[14]

*Yellowstone Lake*

Yellowstone Lake is the largest in the country at this altitude, and its association with thermal areas, wildlife, and wilderness makes it unique. Four developments are located on the lakeshore, and highways parallel it for miles, yet most of the shoreline is wilderness. The original choices for development were adjacent to the Yellowstone River outlet (Fishing Bridge), a beautiful shoreline location (Lake), and near the largest thermal area on the lake (West Thumb). Fishing Bridge was a terrible location for campgrounds and other developments because of conflict with grizzlies; Lake, nearby, was not a lot better; and the stores and cabins at West Thumb were practically in the hot springs. Grant Village was built in a supposedly uncritical area to replace Fishing Bridge and West Thumb, but has also had problems with critical grizzly habitat. West Thumb has been cleared of development, and Fishing Bridge is much smaller than in its heyday in the 1960's. Political pressures kept it from being further reduced, as will be discussed in the wildlife chapter.

*Old Faithful*

There are geyser basins scattered throughout the park, but the ones that receive the most attention are the Lower, Middle, and Upper Geyser Basins on the road between Old Faithful and Madison Junction, and the Norris Geyser Basin. These are the most tourist-active portions of the park, with the most short trails, walkways, interpretive signs, and turnouts. Eighty-four percent of Yellowstone visitors stop at Old Faithful, for example, more than visit any other part of the park.[15] In the 1960's a bypass road was built around Old Faithful, and the campground was closed. The area is still very crowded, however, and both pedestrian and road traffic are confusing. Some road reconstruction, and concentrating facilities as at Lake and Canyon, will gain some space and make the area a little more user-friendly.[16]

## THE YELLOWSTONE FIRES OF 1988

Despite all that has happened to Yellowstone National Park in its long history, the fires during the summer of 1988 drew the most attention. The $120 million fire fighting effort was one of the greatest in American history, yet did little to halt the spread of the fires that eventually consumed 1.4 million acres in the Greater Yellowstone Area.[17] Losses to wildlife were amazingly light—257 elk, 2 moose, 9 bison, and 4 deer— and much of the burned area was not as badly scorched as originally had

*This complex of parking lots and visitor services surrounding Old Faithful Geyser in Yellowstone National Park used to also contain a campground. The only four-lane highway in the 54 national parks is in the background.*

been thought.[18] Driving the loop road the summer after the fires, I was surprised to find much of the area unburned, and much of the burned area had only been burned in patches, with large untouched areas. Grass was growing under the dead trees, and the bison and elk grazed as if nothing had happened. Only the area between Mammoth and Norris seemed to have been really devastated.

The publicity given the fires was enormous.[19] People who had had trouble with the park service in nearby communities, and antigovernment people of all stripes, had a field day. Although the conditions were the most severely fire-prone on record, and a maximum effort was made to extinguish the fires, the NPS was accused of actually welcoming the fires to put "nature in balance." In fact, Yellowstone has had a policy since 1976 of letting burn wilderness fires which wouldn't affect buildings or spread to nonpark or private land, with scarcely a problem. It was accepted by most experts that the longer an area went without fires, the greater the future problem with fires, and usually, the less the biodiversity of an area. Controlled burns can mimic the natural situation, and reduce future fires, but Yellowstone contains far too much roadless country for most controlled burns to be feasible.[20] People have received an education from the fires, which prompted revision of the Yellowstone National Park fire management guidelines in 1992.[21]

## SAFETY

National parks, most of them anyway, are safer than the cities. The dangers people face in the city are familiar ones, however, and visitors to the parks have to cope with icy lakes, rushing streams, cliffs, hot springs, storms, wild animals, and a lot of other "natural phenomena," perhaps for the first time. Furthermore, Yellowstone is not Disneyland, where the animals are fake and the mountains plastic. I think many people are shocked when a bison charges or a deer kicks or a raccoon bites. Shouldn't the NPS take care of all that? Unfortunately, there are a lot of people who want just that—parks that are as safe as Disneyland, which would require the removal of every grizzly, mountain lion, and wolf from the national parks and erecting high wire fences around all the thermal features. So far attempts at such a scenario have failed, but who knows what litigation lies ahead for the park? Lawsuits have been filed by people whose children crawl under fences and get burned by hot springs, who go down ice-covered paths to fall to their deaths in the Grand Canyon of the Yellowstone, or who are killed by grizzlies while sleeping in an area closed to camping because of grizzly danger. These are all actual cases which the NPS won, and all of them could have had far-reaching effects on the future operation of the national parks. Actually only seven people have been killed by wildlife in Yellowstone, two by bison and five by bear, and another nineteen by deaths from hot springs; most of the hundreds of deaths in the park are from natural causes and automobile accidents.[22]

## PRESERVATION OF THERMAL AREAS

It is hard to believe that a bill with the avowed purpose of keeping the thermal areas of Yellowstone from going the way of those of New Zealand and Iceland would have had trouble getting through Congress, but the Old Faithful Protection Act failed in the 103d Congress. The bill passed the House of Representatives easily but was killed by the threat of a filibuster by two senators from Wyoming and Idaho worried about private property rights.[23] Essentially the bill would ban geothermal development on federal land within 15 miles of the park and would limit development on private land which might harm Yellowstone's thermal features. Ironically, while this was happening (1994), the $10 billion biotechnology industry was making a major breakthrough by discover-

*Thermal features, dangerous animals, rushing streams, and cliffs may all be threats to the Yellowstone visitor. A spot where a hot spring intersects the Gardner River near Mammoth is one of the few spots in the park where bathing adjacent to a thermal feature is reasonably safe.*

ing a molecule, living in the Mushroom Spring of the Great Fountain Group in the park, which allows scientists to duplicate DNA.[24] A journalist reporting on the discovery said, "It's as if Yellowstone's 10,000 hot springs and geysers hold a microscopic American rainforest full of biological mysteries."[25] Industrial strength collecting of enzymes is not allowed in Yellowstone, although at least one company has offered to pay royalties for the smaller-scale collecting which is allowed, and the possibility of biological riches in the future is great. Preservation is still what the parks are all about. Environmentalists have been saying for years that throwing away (allowing to become extinct) even the tiniest part of nature before we know its importance might lead to disastrous effects in the future.

## SUMMARY

The first national park continues to be the bellwether for problems facing the National Park System. Sometimes, it seems that solving Yellowstone's problems would solve many of the problems facing the entire system. The following examples of current crises in Yellowstone, which are discussed elsewhere in the book, are by no means exhaustive. The most serious problem a national park has recently faced, and supposedly solved, was a proposal for a massive mine just outside the park (Chapter 4). Three of America's most interesting animals—the grizzly bear, bison, and gray wolf—are meeting challenges in Yellowstone which could decide their future in this country (Chapter 7). The future health of forests in the United States, not just in the national parks, will be affected by lessons learned from the great Yellowstone fire of 1988. One of the largest controversies concerning recreational use of our national parks is whether limits should be placed on the use of snowmobiles in Yellowstone (Chapter 9). The future of one of the few completely natural aquatic ecosystems in the country could be determined by attempts to slow the growth of introduced lake trout in Yellowstone waters (Chapter 7). The vast maintenance backlog of national park facilities, and our desire to face the problem by starting to pay for it, are reflected in our starting to meet the incredible job of upgrading Yellowstone roads. Finally, the great strain on the national parks caused by rising visitation will someday have to be met by visitor limitation, ironically started in Yosemite by the current superintendent of Yellowstone, Mike Finley.

The future of the park looks very problematical when the litany of problems is laid out. But arrayed against these problems is just what Yellowstone is—the country's oldest national park, its best-known national park, and probably its most beloved national park. If any park is truly national, belonging to all the people in this country, Yellowstone would have to be it. A hundred and twenty-five years of overcoming such problems in the past can certainly be extended into the new century.

# 4 Preserving the Parks from Commercial Use

THE most important reason for establishing a national park is to protect it from commercial exploitation. Concern over park wilderness, wildlife, and the quality of visitor experience is meaningless if the landscape is devastated. It is a tribute to the earliest managers of our national parks that we can be concerned today with the finer points of park management. For much of park history, there was neither public understanding nor precedent and tradition to support park preservation. There were, however, laws protecting the parks from the very beginning.

The act establishing Yellowstone National Park prefigured the definitive statement set forth in the National Park Act of 1916: "The service thus established shall promote and regulate the use of Federal areas known as national parks . . . in such manner and by such means as will leave them unimpaired for the enjoyment of future generations."[1] Numerous policy statements have followed, but they all point to a consistent, overriding policy for the parks: there shall be no commercial use of the parks, and the parks shall remain as natural as possible. Getting an act through Congress and into law is one thing, and following the spirit of the act and preventing loopholes is quite another. There have been threats to the parks, both real and potential, throughout park history, and every law can be rescinded outright or in part.

The parks would have been under still greater pressure for development of their natural resources if they had not been of low economic potential. Scenic beauty and economic vitality are often mutually exclusive. Flat country generally contains the richest soils, the best building sites, the easiest terrain for transportation facilities, and the greatest water, timber, and mineral resources. Conversely, what we generally consider "scenic" areas are often too high, cold, rugged, dry, wet, or remote for viable economic activity. The Alaskan parks are good illustrations of this. In the debate over adding Alaskan parks to the National Park System, the major argument was not about lost economic activities, but about individual and states' rights. Most of the areas that were being examined for potential parks had been opened to homesteading for a century, yet virtually no one lived in them, not even natives. Most of the parks were too high or too far north for any timber resources, and the potential areas for petroleum resources were in flat country, which was set aside in wildlife refuges, not parks.

The vast majority of parks in the lower forty-eight follow the same pattern—too high (Rainier), too dry (Death Valley), too wet (Everglades), or too rugged (Grand Canyon). The only economic potentials in most of the parks are timber and water resources. Maps show that major farming areas of the country, or oil fields, or factories, or population, or virtually any form of economic activity except tourism is noticeably separated from natural parkland.

It is fortunate that America has managed to have its cake and eat it, too, by converting some of its resource "wastelands" into important economic areas by making them national parks. Tourism is the first, second, or third most important industry in all the Western states, and the national parks are leading attractions in most of them.[2] Scenery has become a rich commodity, and the very fact that the parks lacked high commercial potential has allowed them to be retained in their natural and most valuable state.

Even if it is generally recognized that tourism is the highest economic use of an area, however, this will mean little to those seeking commercial exploitation of the parks. A park earning money from tourism is not earning anything for the lumberer. An area might take in ten times more money through tourism than it would through a lumber operation over the long run, but normal economic competition does not usually decide the outcome. If the lumberer, or miner, or rancher has more effective representatives in Congress than the general public, potential park areas will not become parks. The following discussion will focus on different economic commodities and their impact on the National Park System.

## AGRICULTURE: CROP FARMING

One of the most basic forms of American industry, crop farming, has had little effect on the national parks. National park lands tend to have extreme temperatures, poor soils, and short growing seasons, and to be too dry or too wet for producing crops. Some farming operations have occurred in the parks in the past—there were homesteaders in Great Smoky Mountains and Shenandoah National Parks—but all were marginal and the farmers were glad someone wanted to buy their land. The total number of farmers that could be supported in the parks is so small, compared to the parks' value for tourism, that the political pressures which farmers could exert to get into the parks are nonexistent.

Where farmlands might become more of an issue is next to national parks, especially where wildlife is concerned. Had Yellowstone National Park been planned with the benefit of present-day hindsight, it would have included much more low-lying land next to the park for winter feeding by the elk and bison. There is a conflict currently between sugar growers and the park service north of Everglades National Park on how much water might flow through farmlands to nourish the vegetation in the park.

## AGRICULTURE: GRAZING

Cattle grazing, the most extensive form of land use in the country, has had much more effect on the parks than crop farming. Grazing is more suited for the national parks because it can take place in areas that are too rough or where the climate is too unfavorable for farming. In poorer sections of the world, like Peru or Nepal, or in areas where agriculture is heavily subsidized like Switzerland, the practice of transhumance—the seasonal movement of animals to and from high locations—allows the most rugged or the most isolated areas to be used. Even in the United States we find cattle and sheep grazed in the deserts of Nevada or the high alpine areas of Colorado. Many of the national parks were being used for grazing when they were first established, and as in Yosemite, the damage being done by overgrazing was one of the reasons for establishing the parks.

Some grazing still takes place in the national parks. Jackson Hole in Grand Teton National Park, when seen in great Western movies like *Shane*, seems the epitome of the American West. Appearances are deceptive. Jackson Hole is no rich agricultural preserve. The basin is high, the soils thin, and the growing season short. Years before it became a park, dude ranching and tourism appeared, representing the maximum potential of the area, not ranching. Still, cattle ranchers were present when John D. Rockefeller Jr. started buying land in the 1930's to allow the addition of Jackson Hole to the parkland, and they strongly opposed the expansion. The grazing interests leaned heavily on the American cowboy mystique and its claimed virtues of self-reliance and freedom, while the taking of land for the park was considered socialistic or worse. Ironically, ranching south of the park, where the ranching is better, is disappearing because of the subdividing of the land into homes, and residents are trying to maintain some of the Western ambience by new forms of zoning.

Today, the legacy of the bitter battle to establish Grand Teton National Park, where the NPS allowed for some noncompatible uses of the park to appease those who opposed it, means that ranching still exists within park boundaries. In one section of the park next to the highway, where ranching is currently ongoing, the visitor can get an "Old West" photo with cattle and a picturesque split rail fence. Of course, many feel the bison, which originally grazed these lands but have been displaced by cattle, would be even more picturesque and a lot more in keeping with national park goals.

A potential prairie national park has been held up for years because of grazing. The tall-grass prairie, originally found in Illinois, Iowa, and the eastern halves of the Great Plains states of the Dakotas, Nebraska, Kansas, and Oklahoma, was once home to one of the world's great herds of wildlife, some 50 million bison, along with elk, deer, antelope, puma, coyotes, wolves, and a profuse bird life. The tall-grass prairie also signaled the location of some of the best soils in the world in combination with weather ideal for the growing of corn or wheat. Later, when settlement pushed farther west and the steel plow was introduced, the Indians were mostly "removed," and the conversion of the prairie to crops began. Today, less than 1 percent of the original prairie remains, and there seems to be wide agreement, even among those in favor of downsizing the National Park System, that a prairie national park belongs in the system.[3]

It would be possible, certainly, to return parts of the tall-grass prairie land to its original ecological condition, but the political and economic consequences of doing so would be enormous. Buying large areas of rich farmland, in, say, Illinois or Nebraska, and letting it revert to tall-grass prairie, have never even been suggested. However, there are areas large enough for a viable park that for various reasons have never been plowed. One is in Kansas in a region called the Flint Hills, where limestone just below the surface has prevented plowing and led mostly to ranching. In the 1960's an area near Manhattan, Kansas, was proposed as a Prairie National Park, but was frustrated by opposition from ranchers and lack of support by Kansas legislators. A Tallgrass Prairie National Preserve was finally founded in 1996 on land bought by the National Park Trust, a 10,894-acre ranch in the Flint Hills, and turned over to the NPS.[4]

## LUMBERING

Pressure for lumbering is present in some of the parks, especially those of the Pacific Northwest such as Olympic National Park, where there is high-quality timber. However, when most of the western national parks were established there were vast amounts of commercial timberland in other, easier to reach areas. As the old-growth timber in the United States reaches a vanishing point, that remaining in the national parks will become more valuable. The land in Redwood National Park, however, has always been valuable; the redwood tree is one of the most sought-after lumber trees in the world.

The struggle to achieve a viable Redwood National Park offers a powerful bas-relief of the conflict between park and utilitarian values. The issues are simple. Redwood National Park breaks the rule that only economically poor land ends up in national parks. These are also some of the most noble forests in the world: the most lovely, the most majestic, the most serene. Giant trees tower up to the height of thirty-story buildings, allowing an isolated ray of light to highlight a fern, a young sapling, or a fallen giant in the first cycle of a new forest. Crystalline streams flow across the spongy earth, barely audible in the vast quiet. Surely no one could mar such overwhelming beauty. Yet this land has been marred with a vengeance.

The original uncut redwood forest, once stretching from Oregon to San Francisco, has been reduced to small isolated areas, many of them in state parks.[5] Some of the parks, unfortunately, are exposed to the vagaries of wind and water erosion through isolation by logging, and none of them offers the spacious wilderness associated with our great national parks. Despite efforts going back to the time of John Muir, establishing a national park on these valuable lands was unattainable. The Save-the-Redwoods League, founded in 1919, took the alternate route of buying smaller areas with private funds to be run by the state. As long as the privately owned areas surrounding the parks were uncut, it looked as if the redwood forest was being adequately preserved. As the years passed, however, and the "parks" were reduced to the small islands in a logged-over landscape, it was obvious that a much larger effort needed to be made.

The effort came during the Kennedy-Johnson administration when a Redwood National Park became a "showpiece" environmental goal. The *National Geographic* helped by publishing a special issue on the proposed park, announcing the discovery of the tallest tree in the world along Redwood Creek.[6] A Redwood National Park was established in 1968 encompassing 58,000 acres but including two existing state parks and much cutover land. Unfortunately, a portion of the watershed of Redwood Creek, which contained the world's tallest trees, was left in private hands. A proviso to the park bill added that efforts would promptly be initiated to acquire the remainder of the watershed.[7] The result has been one of almost total frustration for those who love the redwoods. While the government was busy trying to obtain money and legislation to buy the watershed of Redwood Creek, lumber operations were shifted there to make sure there was nothing to save. The big trees were felled, using the clear-cut method of forestry that absolutely devastates the forest. The debate between clear-cutting and selective logging has been long and virulent. Clear-cutting is more profitable, and the trees do come back. On the other hand, the redwood forest, if logging continues on schedule, is far less beautiful, and many question the sustainability of the logging industry because of soil erosion from the unprotected landscape.[8]

Rain falling in a redwood forest proves nature's dominant role as a conserver of life. The rain is absorbed into the forest floor completely; you can feel the moisture being drawn into the earth to succor the giants and the myriad life that belongs there. Remove the trees and the raindrops impact the earth, form into rivulets, coalesce into floods that rage down Redwood Creek, undercut the stream banks, and threaten to topple the giants. Incredibly, the world-record trees themselves have been threatened by the logging operations. "The eternal redwoods" becomes a macabre joke. The threat of this loss, after an increasingly acrimonious debate between loggers and environmentalists, finally resulted in the addition of 48,000 acres to the park in 1978 and the saving of the Redwood Creek watershed. Ironically, some of the money that would have been used to buy more land for the park was needed to restore the damage caused by logging in the area. There were 250 miles of abandoned logging roads and 2,000–3,000 miles of tractor trails that crisscrossed the recently logged-over lands.[9]

Interest in the saving of American forests has shifted from isolated areas to the country as a whole. Seeing rich forest-covered areas change into cutover lands, especially in the Pacific Northwest and southeast Alaska, has led people to question the whole concept of commercial forests on public lands. The spotted owl and the National Endangered Species Act have given the forests some reprieve, and the remaining ancient forests in the United States, a small number, may receive better treatment than those that have been logged.[10]

*A clear-cut forest near Mount Rainier National Park is in marked contrast to the ancient forest just inside the park.*

## MINING

The national parks are not great storehouses of mineral wealth, although this has not prevented mining from being a factor in preserving national parks. Our reluctance to set aside areas with actual or potential mineral resources is well illustrated by the mining companies' intense opposition to the National Wilderness Act, which was being debated in the early 1960's. The law establishing the National Wilderness Preservation System required a complete mineral exploration survey of all potential national forest wilderness areas before bringing them into the system, despite the existence of only a few small operating mines in such areas after a full century of exploration.[11] Still, even inferior deposits can yield benefits through open pit or strip mining, and there is no way of knowing what mineral might become important in the future.

Mining is related to the parks in three ways: through parks brought into the system with some mining potential (Death Valley National Park), potential parks with some mining in the area (Mojave National Preserve), and mining next to the parks (Yellowstone National Park). Mining in Death Valley, with its twenty-mule teams hauling borax, was so picturesque that the bill establishing the national monument met little resistance in recognizing existing mining claims and allowing mining to continue. The mule teams became a part of history even before the turn of the century, but limited mining activities have continued, the latest by ecologically destructive open pit operations. Enough people were concerned when operations started in view of Zabriskie Point, Death Valley's most impressive vantage point, that Congress passed a law to curb mining there and in other units of the system.[12]

The most critical law concerning preservation of public lands is the Mining Law of 1872, ironically adopted the same year as Yellowstone's founding.[13] This allows individuals to claim ownership of any public land, except national parks or wilderness, if they think valuable minerals are there. To purchase the land for extremely low amounts, the land does not have to be mined but merely "improved for mining," which could involve minimal work on the property. Many of the "inholdings" in national parks were originally mining claims, and, as most parks adjoin public land, there will always be the potential for other "New World Mines" like the one recently plaguing Yellowstone National Park.

## WATER RESOURCES DEVELOPMENT

The major threat to the national parks has been the development of water resource projects. The climate and terrain of the national parks might have made them poor areas for most economic pursuits, but they have made them excellent for dams and reservoirs. Many of the parks, especially in the western United States, are areas of high precipitation surrounded by relatively dry areas. These areas, such as Yellowstone and Yosemite, have high elevations and intercept rainfall, creating large streams that flow down into country where water is an extremely valuable commodity. Many of these parks also contain dam sites with good hydroelectric potential.

Dating from the turn of the century, there have been a number of controversies concerning water resource development in the national parks. In 1913 Hetch Hetchy was authorized and later built in Yosemite, and various irrigation and power projects in Yellowstone were hotly debated in the 1920's and '30's.[14] Projects in Glacier, Rocky Mountain, and Kings Canyon National Parks have also been proposed. The classic confrontation concerning dams and parks, however, took place in Dinosaur National Monument's Echo Park and in the Grand Canyon.

### Echo Park Dam

The battle over the Bureau of Reclamation's proposed dam in Echo Park on the Colorado-Utah border in the 1950's changed the face of conservation in this country. Before that, people who considered themselves conservationists (the word "environmentalist" was not used for another twenty years) were very small in number, and ineffective politically. They lost the battle of Hetch Hetchy, and the dams in Yellowstone might have been built except for officials of the NPS, especially Horace Albright. The Sierra Club had only a few thousand members. The battle against Echo Park Dam was led by the Sierra Club, however, and was won by showing hundreds of people the canyons of Dinosaur National Monument on river trips down the Yampa and Green Rivers, and by causing thousands of people to write letters to their representatives in Congress.[15] The club also produced high-quality books and articles, attracted gifted authors like Bernard DeVoto, who wrote for the widely disseminated *Saturday Evening Post,* and produced excellent propaganda films. The staff of the House Committee on Interior and Insular Affairs counted letters commenting on the building of the Echo Park Dam and found only 53 in favor out of 4,731 received.[16] The dam was defeated.

## CONCLUSIONS

I cannot believe, seriously, that we will ever go back to constructing dams, cutting trees, or grazing cattle in the national parks. Such uses will continue to be advocated, as the Wise Use Association is doing now, but the odds today are overwhelmingly against them.[17] When the newly formed National Parks Association helped defeat attempts at building dams in Yellowstone National Park in the early 1920's, it had a membership of only a few hundred and fought the dam virtually by itself. When the Sierra Club helped keep dams out of Dinosaur National Monument, it had only 6,000 members and several conservation organizations on its side. Supporting the Echo Park Dam were all the senators, all the representatives, and all the governors of the states involved—Colorado, New Mexico, Wyoming, and Utah—all the newspapers in the area, and all the federal agencies involved in the project. The NPS, acceding to the pro-dam position of the Secretary of the Interior, kept quiet. The dam was not built and it will not be built. Today the National Parks Association has more than 450,000 members, the Sierra Club almost 600,000, and the number of conservation organizations increases almost daily.

The National Park Act, the idea of national parks, and the great popularity of the national parks are powerful weapons against those who would change them. People will try. The more strength they gain, however, as when James Watt was Secretary of the Interior, the more counter-reaction you get from the general public. The parks have definitely had better times than they are experiencing in the mid-1990's, but as they have done in the 125 years since the first park was established, they will, I believe, pass through this period unscathed.

# 5   External Threats

$A$T one time national parks were considered islands of nature in a sea of development. The goal of environmental groups up until about the late 1960's was to save a sample of the country's beautiful wild places in national parks and wilderness areas where one could escape from the trials and tribulations of the outside world: "In wildness is the preservation of the world."[1] In the late 1960's when the Sierra Club opposed Disney's proposal to build a huge ski resort in Mineral King, adjacent to Sequoia National Park, many disagreed with the action.[2] The area chosen for the resort was not in a wilderness, it was not in a national park, so why did the Sierra Club even care? Most of the membership of the club, however, was beginning to understand John Muir's statement: "When we try to pick out anything by itself, we find it hitched to everything in the universe."[3] Even the protected areas in national parks were not free from outside influence. This was especially true with wildlife.

## WILDLIFE

Yellowstone was the first park where it became obvious that the land included in the boundaries of the park was not going to be sufficient to protect all of the park's resources. As protection in the new park grew, the herds of elk, once threatened, grew also. This growth accelerated with the NPS's elimination of predators in the first half of this century. Yellowstone National Park mainly protected the higher country. In winter, the elk would follow the Yellowstone River in the north and the Snake River in the south toward lower range. The smaller southern herd started encountering settlements in Jackson Hole to the south, while the northern herd, which soon numbered in the tens of thousands, was encountering hunters. There was an infamous "firing line" along the northern boundary of the park near Gardner, where thousands of elk were killed.[4] Eventually, the elk learned not to cross the border, which led to starvation and overgrazing within park boundaries. The NPS tried to cure this by supplemental feeding and the slaughter of surplus animals, poor solutions which were eventually discontinued.[5]

Virtually every national park has some problems with its boundaries and wildlife. The extent of these problems will depend on how wisely the boundaries were drawn in relation to migration patterns of wildlife, and on the wildness of the country next to the park. Unfortunately, few boundaries were ideally drawn, even when those in charge knew all there was to know about the animals, because boundaries usually involve political compromises. Yosemite National Park, for example, lost fully a third of its area in 1905, including areas of lower elevation important to its wildlife, because of political pressure to release lands of value to loggers and miners.[6]

Finally, public lands adjacent to the parks are seldom administered to protect park values. The Forest Service and the Bureau of Land Management, for example, allow economic exploitation of most kinds. Compounding the problem, the Forest Service subsidizes the building of roads for timber cutting on its lands, decreasing their value for wildlife.[7]

## AIR POLLUTION

Air pollution, which is obviously no respecter of boundaries, has been one of the most dramatic of the external threats to the parks. Visibility nationwide has been sharply reduced, and people are becoming accustomed to it. When there is a view to be seen, however, such as at the Grand Canyon, and when you can barely see across the canyon on some hazy days, people recognize that something is very wrong. For people who have been coming to the Grand Canyon for several years it is especially bad, as the Colorado Plateau used to have some of the clearest skies and longest views in the United States.[8] Much of the pollution drifted from as far away as Los Angeles, again underlining the weakness of park boundaries in protecting park resources.

When the Clean Air Act was first passed in 1970, its most important provision was the establishment of emission areas, where those within the areas were able to set their own standards, within reason, and their own methods of meeting those standards.[9] The dirty areas would have to have the most rigid standards; clean areas had leeway. Unfortunately for the national parks, particularly dirty industries, such as coal burning power generation plants, tend to move out of the cities into clean areas, like the Colorado Plateau. The power can easily be sent back to the consumers with power lines.

The Clean Air Act of 1977 attempted to rectify this situation by designating certain areas, including most national parks and wilderness areas, as "Class I areas."[10] The act sets "as a national goal, the prevention of any future, and the remedying of any existing, impairment of visibility in mandatory Class I federal areas where impairment results from man-made air pollution."[11] Unfortunately, except in the Grand Canyon, discussed below, no federal action has been taken in response to the Class I provision of the Clean Air Act.[12]

Visibility from the Blue Ridge Mountains was the main reason for the building of Skyline Drive in Shenandoah National Park. The views were magnificent; often the visitor could see a hundred miles. This is no longer possible. Overall visibility has dropped 80 percent in the summer months since 1948, according to a ten-year study at the University of California at Davis. The visibility at Shenandoah National Park can be worse than Los Angeles's.[13] Acid rain and dying trees are the results of the air pollutants. With many more coal burning power plants being built, the problem can only worsen.[14] Few national parks in the conterminous United States are free of this threat, from the Great Smoky Mountains to Big Bend to Mount Rainier.

Some air pollution threats in the national parks can best be fought within park boundaries, as in Yosemite National Park, where the narrow Yosemite Valley and temperature inversions can turn auto exhausts and wood fires into full-scale air pollution. Most national parks want to serve as good examples to the "outside world," and many have at least tried to reduce auto traffic and other sources of air pollution. Most battles against air pollution, and especially the threat of global warming, must ultimately be fought and won outside the parks, however, if the dire conditions just discussed are to improve.

Education is perhaps the most important role that parks can play concerning air pollution and especially global warming. While the causes, effects, and even the existence of global warming are being debated, visitors can look around them in the national parks and see that this is a problem

*Bryce Canyon is one national park which doesn't seem to have suffered from overuse or development pressures. In the Paria Valley in the distance, however, a huge coal mine that would have lowered the quality of the park was proposed.*

which must be solved. The sequoias, for example, are located within narrow parameters of rainfall and climate and could cease to exist. Rising sea levels could do away with the Everglades, Dry Tortugas, and other parks. Change is part of nature, but when our actions determine its extent, the necessity for learning and soul searching increases.

## WATER POLLUTION

Most inland national parks are spared damage from water pollution because they are in headwater areas, above most pollution sources. An exception is our most famous headwater park, Yellowstone, discussed below. The impact on downstream parks is much greater, as illustrated by Everglades National Park, whose entire existence is determined by water flowing through the park. Finally, the ocean or seashore parks, like Kenai Fjords in Alaska, are threatened by oil spills.

Yellowstone is a good example of how threats to the national parks can come from unlikely sources. Yellowstone is on a high plateau, located in a lightly populated part of the country, and mostly surrounded by federal land, including some of the largest wilderness areas in the conterminous United States. Sandwiched between Yellowstone Park on one side and the Absaroka-Beartooth Wilderness on the other, however, are the small tourist town of Cooke City and the proposed New World Mine nearby. This mine would take an estimated $600 million in gold and silver from the public lands there. The potential for an environmental catastrophe is enormous, as 4 tons of sulfide rock will have to be removed for every ounce of gold obtained, creating toxic waste material which will have to be stored in perpetuity to prevent acidic heavy metal effluent from spilling into streams on the mountain. One of these streams flows into Yellowstone National Park. The roads and the operation itself would further impact an enormous natural area. A Canadian firm called Crown Butte planned to develop the mine, and under the terms of the 1872 Mining Law, nothing would be paid for the value gained or the damage done. Furthermore, the company's liability is limited in case of environmental damage.[15]

President Clinton visited the site of the New World Mine in August 1995 and placed a two-year moratorium on mining claims around the site.[16] An international investigative team from the United Nations World Heritage Committee also visited the mine site and declared Yellowstone National Park a "world heritage site in danger" because of the mine.[17] Finally, in August of 1996, President Clinton announced a settlement with Crown Butte which would compensate shareholders in the company for their investment, and stop all exploration and mining activity in the area.[18]

Everglades National Park has the negative distinction of being our most endangered national park. The rich semitropical landscape of the Everglades is a result of the slow, shallow runoff of water southward from Lake Ocheechobee in southern Florida through the park, and into the Gulf of Mexico. The ecosystem was totally disrupted when federally funded canals intercepted most of the flow and shunted it off to the Atlantic, some for water supply but most to make the marshlike landscape suitable for farming. Sugar was a major crop, and high amounts of polluted water also flowed into the Everglades. The results have been devastating. The Everglades were once home to some of the largest masses of wading birds found anywhere, but only a fraction of their number remains. All the life in the park, from shrimp to panthers, have suffered similarly.[19] Many plans to save the Everglades have been made, but their costs would be enormous.[20] Recent attempts to include special funds in the U.S. budget and to levy a cent a pound tax on the sugar industry to help pay for the clean-up have failed. Environmental groups suggest diverting some of the enormous subsidies received by sugar owners in Florida into the clean-up.

The well-publicized *Exxon Valdez* oil spill in 1989 illustrates the damage one ship, piloted by one individual, can do. The spill coated more than a thousand miles of coastline and killed between 300,000 and 645,000 birds, up to 5,500 sea otters, 30 seals, 23 whales, and unknown numbers of fish.[21] Included in that shoreline was Kenai Fjords National Park. All our coastal national parks, including Channel Islands, Acadia, five parks in Alaska, and the national seashores, face the same threat. The *Exxon Valdez* tragedy could have been prevented by double-hull tankers, more effective radar monitoring in Prince William Sound, and a number of other oil tanker regulations that have been the subject of recent environmental legislation.

## NOISE POLLUTION

The largest impact of noise pollution in the national parks comes from aerial sight-seeing, especially over the Grand Canyon. The skies are almost a last frontier for park protection, as the parks have very little control over what goes on there. Special laws have been made for the Grand Canyon, but the problem of aircraft noise is spreading to many other parks. I remember waiting, with a thousand other visitors, for Old Faithful to erupt two summers ago. Obviously a passenger in a plane above us was also waiting, as its persistent whine was with us the whole period. I noticed several people looking up in annoyance—aren't we in a wilderness park? We can expect similar situations in Yosemite, Hawaiian Volcanoes, and many other parks in the years ahead.

In Canyonlands and Arches the problem is with helicopters, the noisiest of all aircraft. Although their number is still small compared to the Grand Canyon, the fact that they can hover just above the ground, and even land (illegally), gives them unprecedented nuisance value.[22] Stories of landings to allow a passenger to relieve himself or to approach climbers on sheer cliffs for photographs have led to the founding of a group called Citizens for a Heli-Free Moab.[23]

## THE ECOSYSTEM APPROACH

We have seen how smog, polluted water, and noise can cross park boundaries. Ideally, we should live in an unpolluted world where air and water are just as clean outside the national parks as within them. As a realistic alternative we need buffer zones, where at least a transition area exists from the spoiled to the protected landscape. Wilderness areas within many of the parks serve as buffer zones, but much more is needed.

Park officials and planners are working with the people who manage surrounding areas, especially if public land is involved, to try to establish buffer zones around the parks. Grand Canyon officials work with the Kaibab National Forest north and south of the park, the Navajo and Havasupai Indian Reservations east and west of the park, and the city of Flagstaff and the tourist community of Tusayan to the south. Saguaro National Park is closely associated with Tucson, whose suburbs are growing right up to park boundaries. Officials of Antietam National Battlefield and Gettysburg National Military Park fight to keep some ambience of historical interest and respect for those who died there in the face of private developments which threaten to engulf these small parks.

## Greater Yellowstone Ecosystem

The ideal situation blending parks and surroundings would be to set up a planning area for the region surrounding a park, including all the private and public agencies and individuals that would have an influence on the park. The Greater Yellowstone Ecosystem is a good example of such an area, a 28,000-square-mile contiguous region made up of Yellowstone and Grand Teton National Parks and the six surrounding national forests, three wildlife refuges, wilderness areas, public domain, and state and private land. It is one of the largest relatively natural temperate-zone ecosystems in the world.[24] The term "Greater Yellowstone Ecosystem" seems first to have been used by Frank Craighead in the book *Track of the Grizzly*, published in 1979, referring to the range of the Yellowstone grizzly population, about twice the size of the park. By 1984 more than 170 articles and books dealing with the ecosystem had appeared, and by 1989 both the U.S. Congress and the president had acknowledged the Greater Yellowstone Ecoystem's existence, in hearings and speeches.[25]

Recognition of the Greater Yellowstone Ecosystem is one thing; actually accomplishing something within the region by working together is quite another. All the federal, state, and local agencies mentioned above have different mandates. The national parks and national forest wilderness areas are managed for preservation and recreation; the rest of the national forests are managed for multiple use, including grazing, logging, and mineral exploration; private lands operate under restrictions in some areas, almost none in others, and so on. Cooperation is essential, however. Wildlife doesn't recognize boundaries and neither does wildfire. The thermal area underlying Yellowstone certainly isn't limited to park boundaries. River systems interconnect all the areas.

The first major example of cooperation within the Greater Yellowstone Ecosystem came with the joint preparation of *Vision for the Future*, by a committee from the NPS and U.S. Forest Service, which would present a framework for coordinating activities within the ecosystem.[26] It presented three fundamental philosophies: (1) conserve the sense of naturalness and maintain ecosystem integrity, (2) encourage opportunities that are biologically sustainable, and (3) use coordination and education to protect ecosystem values.[27] Unfortunately, the *Vision* document became more of a political target than a plan for cooperation. "Naturalness," "ecosystem integrity," and "sustainability" might be beloved buzzwords for environmentalists but not for the local ranchers, miners, and lumberers; it wasn't long before Senator Alan Simpson of Wyoming and White House Chief of Staff John Sununu under George Bush were attacking the document.[28] The result was the reworking of the document to be "politically sensitive," its reduction in size from sixty to ten pages, and the transfer and later resignation of the chief architect of the original document, Lorraine Mintzmyer.[29]

This episode did not lessen the importance of ecosystem planning to the Greater Yellowstone Ecosystem. Population in the twenty counties of the Greater Yellowstone Ecosystem is growing 33 percent faster than the average for Montana, Idaho, and Wyoming, with nearly all of the new jobs being created there more dependent on the quality of the ecosystem than on traditional mining, lumbering, and ranching.[30]

## SUMMARY

The days of the past, when we could escape our workaday world for the pristine environment of our national parks, are being rapidly replaced by a world where preserving the national parks will depend more on what happens outside the parks than within them. Certainly cooperation with public agencies and private groups and individuals adjacent to the parks is something every park superintendent knows must be at the top of any list of park improvements. The environmental quality of the Grand Canyon depends as much on the operation of a dam upstream from the park, power plants as far away as Los Angeles, and planes that fly over the park, as on what is done in the park itself, as the case study which follows shows. Ultimately, however, the educational value of the parks, as models of what the world outside the parks can be if we take care of it, might be the most valuable contribution they can make.

# Case Study:
# Grand Canyon National Park

EXTERNAL forces have a tremendous impact on Grand Canyon National Park, from air pollutants which drift in from as far away as Los Angeles and ruin the formerly crystalline views, to air tours that destroy what was once a quiet, peaceful environment, to a dam upstream which has changed the character of the Colorado River, which flows through the canyon. There is only one Grand Canyon, however, and losses which might be considered the price of success elsewhere are not acceptable here. It's possible that the Grand Canyon, at one time insulated from the travails of the outside world by being in a national park, might someday be a force in increasing the environmental quality for areas far distant from the canyon.

The Grand Canyon, the world's largest canyon, is one of the earth's most dramatic physical features. Although an argument could be made for everything from the Himalayas to Niagara Falls, if a vote for the number-one physical attraction in the world were made among travel experts, I believe the Grand Canyon would come out on top. This is amazing in a way because the canyon is far from being the deepest in the world, or even the United States; Hell's Canyon on the border between Oregon and Idaho and Kings Canyon in California are slightly deeper.[1] Hell's Canyon is not an important tourist destination, however, and one of the claimants for the deepest canyon in the world, the Kala Gandaki Gorge in Nepal, is not even known to most travelers.

The Grand Canyon has a number of features that make it stand out above all the rest. First, there is the visibility. You can drive for an hour, from the north or south, through pretty but not outstanding flat country, and then suddenly the earth just disappears. Twelve miles wide, a mile deep, and 277 miles long, the Grand Canyon is truly an inverted mountain range, and one that saves its splendor until the instant you arrive at the rim. The view is unencumbered by vegetation—naked rock is everywhere to be seen. And what rock! The colors range from pure white to blood red, and every shade in between. The shapes of the rocks are harmonious, with formations of a certain color standing as great cliffs, while others form gently sloping platforms. Volcanic flows are all that break the regularity.

The sustainability of the natural beauty of the Grand Canyon depends on giving it long-term protection as a national park, saving it from incompatible uses within the park, reducing external threats, and preventing overuse by visitors. The first of these, making it a park, was

*The basic reason for establishing national parks is to preserve America's spectacular landscapes. By any criteria, the Grand Canyon is one of the world's most impressive natural features.*

relatively easy. Mining was virtually the only potential use of the area before it became a park, and the difficulties of working in the canyon and the lack of bonanzas in gold and silver kept mining from being much more than a nuisance to the new park. Mining claims were used in one case to try to control the tourist trade on the South Rim of the canyon,[2] and successful mines removing uranium and guano in the past are now gone.[3] A far worse threat to the canyon as we know it today was the possibility of a railroad through the canyon. A company was formed to build one, but the president of the company drowned on an engineering survey of the canyon in 1889 and no other builders were interested.[4] Forests on the rim had not been exploited when they became part of a forest reserve in 1893.

In 1903 a very fortuitous thing happened—Theodore Roosevelt visited the canyon, two years after he became president. He fell in love with the canyon, visited it several times, and ended up proclaiming it a national monument in 1908, using the newly established National Antiquities Act. It was also at the Grand Canyon that he made this famous tribute:

> In the Grand Canyon, Arizona has a natural wonder which, so far as I know, is in kind absolutely unparalleled throughout the rest of the world. I want to ask you to do one thing in connection with it

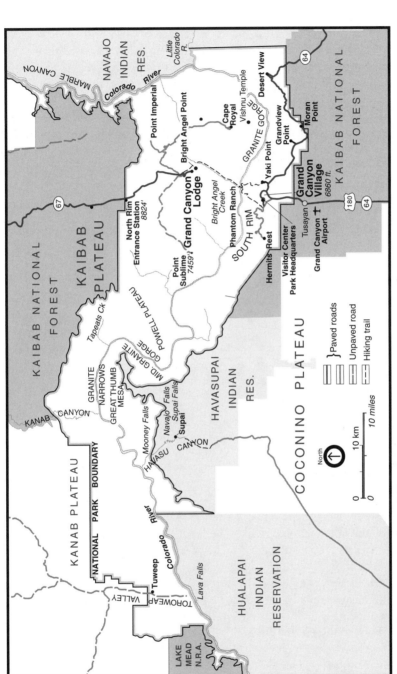

**Grand Canyon National Park**

in your own interest and in the interest of the country—to keep this
great wonder as it is now. . . . I hope you will not have a building of
any kind, not a summer cottage, a hotel or anything else, to mar the
wonderful grandeur, the sublimity, the great loveliness and beauty
of the Canyon. Leave it as it is. You cannot improve on it. The ages
have been at work on it, and man can only mar it. What you can
do is to keep it for your children, your children's children, and for all
who come after you, as the one great sight which every
American . . . should see.[5]

His admonition that the canyon is one great sight which every
American should see has been heeded with a vengeance. "I've never
been to the Grand Canyon" seems a much more reluctant admission
than "I've never been to Yellowstone or Yosemite." The tourists pour
in—4,537,703 in 1996, more than at any other national park in the
western United States.[6] There is every indication that this number will
increase. Most Americans have not seen the Grand Canyon, and most
would probably like someday to see it. In addition, there are enormous
numbers of people outside the United States who would also like to see
the Grand Canyon. Forty percent of the visitors to the canyon now are
foreign, led by the Germans, French, and Japanese. They can afford it—
perhaps someday the rest of the world can.

## PROPOSED DAMS IN THE GRAND CANYON

The Colorado River, which cut the canyon, while not a giant river by
any means, has the potential to create considerable electric power in
its 1,900-foot drop through the canyon. It represents one of the big
untapped hydroelectric potentials in the country. Excellent dam sites
are common in the canyon. There are no roads or habitations to worry
about or purchase. It is all public land. There are large and growing
markets for power nearby in Las Vegas, Phoenix, and Los Angeles. The
recreational potential is high, as heavily used Lake Powell and Lake
Mead, above and below the canyon, seem to indicate. Finally, there was
a rider in the bill establishing Grand Canyon National Park and National
Monument that would allow reclamation projects if they were in the
best interests of the public.[7]

There have been many applications from both federal and nonfederal
sources to build projects in the Grand Canyon, including one that would
have put the entire Colorado River in a tunnel through the heart of

the Grand Canyon. The proposal which came the closest to succeeding consisted of one dam (Marble Canyon) just above the park, and another (Hualapai) below it.[8] Neither dam was in a park then—Marble Canyon National Monument had yet to be established—and the reservoirs and dams would be invisible or "unobtrusive" from the rim. Marble Canyon Dam, however, would have flooded the present-day landmarks of Redwall Caverns, Vasey's Paradise, and Stanton's Cave, while Hualapai Dam would have flooded Lava Falls, and Havasu, Kanab, and Tapeats side canyons. As there were few river trips into the canyon at that time, most visitors would not have noticed the loss of these features.

The dams were to be built by the U.S. Bureau of Reclamation as part of the Central Arizona Project, for the benefit of the state of Arizona. Arizona had wanted to tap the Colorado River for years, but had been unwilling to pay for the expensive canals to deliver the water to central and southern Arizona, where most of the people lived. The underground aquifers which support the main urban areas of the state were beginning to run dry, and a Supreme Court decision in 1963 gave the state part of the water that California had been using.[9] Dams in the Grand Canyon were envisioned as cash registers to pay for moving that water. As opponents were quick to point out, the dams were not connected in any other way with the project. They would not serve the purpose of flood control, irrigation, or water supply.

During the debate on the Grand Canyon many people were discovering for the first time, through photos and trips through the canyon, that the canyon was just as impressive from below, along the living river, as from the rim. The argument that only a few people see the bottom of the canyon, compared to the multitudes that see it from the rim, was changing rapidly. The trip through the Grand Canyon by boat caught the public imagination. When I went through the Grand Canyon in 1962 and the building of the dams seemed imminent, I wrote in my journal: "It is pathetic to think that some one thousand people may be all that will have enjoyed what must certainly be one of the greatest trips on earth." Today, as many as 26,000 people a *year* make this trip, the approximate maximum allowed by park regulations.[10] An eager public has discovered what a boat trip through the Grand Canyon has to offer: hundreds of named rapids, with such evocative names as Lava Falls, Sockdologer, and Upset; dozens of side canyons, some barely explored, with Indian ruins, clear pools, and desert gardens; pleasant sandbars for campsites; and the silence, the beauty, and the majesty of the incomparable canyon.

The reasons that the dams were not built are complex, but two individuals—David Brower and Stewart Udall—probably had the most to do with the outcome. Brower's work with the Sierra Club resulted in an unprecedented flow of mail to members of Congress on the issue, especially after Brower placed a famous ad in the *New York Times*—"Should we also flood the Sistine Chapel so tourists can get nearer the ceiling?"—which resulted in the Sierra Club losing its tax-exempt status and gaining even more political support.[11] Ironically, Brower was fired as executive director of the Sierra Club because of his free use of club funds in fighting this and other battles, without clearing it with the Sierra Club elected board.

Stewart Udall was Secretary of the Interior and a former representative from Arizona. He, and his brother Morris Udall, the Arizona representative who introduced the Grand Canyon dams bill, were also two of the strongest environmentalists in Congress. Opposing a dam in your home state was something unheard of, but Secretary Udall eventually reversed his stand and proposed a revised Central Arizona Project *without* dams in the Grand Canyon.

## IMPACT OF GLEN CANYON DAM

Any thought that the Colorado River through the canyon would remain natural after the defeat of the Grand Canyon dams, however, was soon crushed by the operation of the Glen Canyon Dam upstream. The old river was a very active eroding agent, 300 feet wide and 8 feet deep, dropping 1,900 feet during its trip through the canyon. The river was limited in how much it could cut and carry away, however, by the tremendous load of silt it was already carrying: 380,000 tons per day on average, 27,000,000 tons on the biggest day on record.[12] The Colorado River now runs clear, creating the possibility of losing many of the sandbars of the Grand Canyon, the living space for visitors and the home for much of the flora and fauna of the canyon. Moreover, much of the work of sandbar building in the canyon was done during the river's annual flood stage, which no longer existed. A typical pre-dam flood was greater than 86,000 cubic feet per second (cfs), and a flood of 300,000 cubic feet per second (cfs) has been calculated for 1884.[13]

The disappearance of the sandbars in the canyon was expected, but the way the Bureau of Reclamation operated the dam was not. The bureau virtually ignored the impact of the dam on the canyon by nearly shutting off the flow of the river through the canyon when power

*Operating Glen Canyon Dam, just upstream from Grand Canyon National
Park, for "peaking power" often strands river runners far from the water.
Recent laws require outflow from the dam to more closely mimic natural flows.*

demand in its market areas was low and increasing it to the maximum
when demand was highest (peaking power). The damage being done
suddenly made a quantum leap, as did the reaction to that damage.
The river-running industry, by the late 1980's, was no longer an easily
ignored handful of adventurers, but tens of thousands of often influential people. The water would be so low during low power demand times
(weekends, holidays, nights) that river parties would be stranded, or at
best have to haul boats to the water. Rapids, without the periodic floods
to remove debris dumped from the side canyons, became more difficult
to run.

Pressure from boaters, scientists, and environmentalists resulted in
the Grand Canyon Protective Act, passed in 1992, which requires the
Bureau of Reclamation to operate the dam with regard for the downstream ecosystem of the Colorado River through the Grand Canyon.[14]
A Glen Canyon environmental impact statement was prepared, which
offered alternatives such as operating the dam with a maximum flow
of 20,000 cfs and a minimum of 5,000 cfs (before it was as high as
31,500 cfs and as low as 1,000 cfs). The statement also called for mimick-
ing the large periodic flows of the past, which would leave warmer, safer
waters for native fish (damaged by the clear, cold water) in backwater
canyons, and allow beaches to be rejuvenated by stirring up sediment

below the dam.[15] The first "artificial flood" took place in the spring of
1996 when the dam was opened to allow high water to course through
the Grand Canyon.[16] The long-term consequences are uncertain, but
for the boaters at least the short-term effects of the flood appeared to be
a success, with the creation of many new beaches.[17]

Despite Glen Canyon Dam upstream, the present-day Colorado is
a river which still flows through the canyon—clearer, colder, and with
fewer sandbars—much as it did in the past. I shed far fewer tears on a
trip through the Grand Canyon in 1993, thirty-one years after my first
trip, when there was no dam upstream, than I thought I would. This
is primarily because the first trip was almost a wake; the dams in the
canyon seemed inevitable in 1962. Also, it must be admitted that there
*are* benefits to the Colorado River ecosystem from the dam. The water
that flows out from Lake Powell, now clear, allows sunlight to penetrate
and life in the water to increase. Because of this and the near constant
temperature of the water, the Colorado River below the dam is becoming a high-quality trout fishery. This in turn has led to the return of
bald eagles, which have suddenly appeared in large numbers.[18]

Recently, a drive has emerged to drain Lake Powell. This would solve
all the problems caused by the dam for the natural environment of the
Grand Canyon and would uncover the somewhat tarnished wonders of
Glen Canyon. Adherents claim that draining is inevitable in the future
as the water lost to evaporation and seepage in Lake Powell becomes
more valuable than the power the dam generates.[19] Opposition to the
draining will come from more than power users, however; 2,500,000
people a year visited Lake Powell in 1995 and caused the spending of
$455,000,000 in the surrounding area.[20] The likelihood of Lake Powell
being drained is minuscule, but a complete scientific airing of the environmental and economic consequences of Glen Canyon Dam, built originally because of political pressure, should be fascinating.[21]

## POWER PLANTS AND AIR POLLUTION

Ironically, the defeat of the Grand Canyon dams led indirectly to strong
threats to the canyon from outside the park. Individuals opposing power
dams in the canyon often pointed to the paradox of building expensive
dams for power in an area containing enormous reserves of coal. That
comparison would come back to haunt environmentalists as a huge open
pit coal mine was built on Black Mountain in the Navajo reservation
not far from the Grand Canyon and a coal burning power plant was

built in nearby Page, the new town connected with Glen Canyon Dam. The result was serious air pollution that has lowered the quality of views of the canyon immeasurably. A good picture of the canyon is sharp and clear and vibrant. A bad picture is dull, hazy, and unclear. This describes the difference between the canyon on an average day in the past, when the Colorado Plateau was considered to have some of the best visibility in the country, and a frequently bad day today.

By law, the air quality of the Grand Canyon should not be lowered.[22] The amendment to the Clean Air Act that added this mandate was not passed, however, until the Navajo Generating Plant, the main threat to the canyon's clean air, was already in operation. The Navajo Generating Plant, which produces more power than Glen Canyon Dam and Hoover Dam combined, would never have been allowed in any area with an air pollution problem.[23] By 1999, however, sulfur dioxides from that plant will be reduced by 90 percent in a plan announced by President Bush on his visit to the canyon September 18, 1991.[24] Unfortunately, the problem will not be solved with the clean-up at Page. Some of the pollution comes from another huge power plant at Laughlin, Nevada, and much of the rest from Los Angeles.

## OVERFLIGHTS

For many, the best way to see the canyon is by plane. You certainly see more of it this way, but the detachment from the resource is greater, and improving on the extremely dramatic view of the canyon you can get from almost any viewpoint on the canyon rim is difficult. Still, the flights are quick, easy, and relatively inexpensive.[25] About 800,000 people took air tours over the canyon in 1995. The impact of these flights over the Grand Canyon has been enormous. Finding a quiet spot on the canyon rim to contemplate the awesome view and perhaps achieve the spiritual feelings that some people get from a place like the Grand Canyon is becoming increasingly difficult. Even if you are willing to put out a maximum effort to reach the most isolated parts of the canyon, your chances at serenity are minimal at best. A recent NPS study on aircraft noise showed only 31 percent of the park enjoyed natural quiet.[26]

A midair collision which killed twenty-five people in 1986 focused attention on a controversy that had been building for years. The collision led to the National Parks Overflight Act, which was signed in August 1987.[27] This in turn led to Special Federal Aviation Regulation 50-2, restricting aircraft to a minimum height over the canyon (14,500 feet) and to certain flight corridors, which was meant to assure that almost all the rim visitors and 90 percent of backcountry users were not bothered by overflights.[28] The NPS, however, in a report to Congress in October 1994, said the plan had *not* restored quiet to the canyon,[29] and recommended expansion of flight-free zones from the current 45 percent to 82 percent of the park and phasing in the use of "quiet aircraft technology" with rewards and incentives.[30] A stronger plan, based on recent political activity concerning overflights, seems almost inevitable.[31] Air tour operators, on the defensive, have come up with some suggestions of their own, such as leaving the park free from buses, cars, inflated rafts, and feet, by allowing *only* overflights into the park.[32]

## THE SOUTH RIM AND CROWDING

Virtually everyone who visits the Grand Canyon, even the small percentage that takes the river trips and the larger percentage that takes aerial tours, visits one of the rims of the canyon. Ninety-two percent visit the South Rim and 8 percent visit the North Rim.[33] The portion of the South Rim of the Grand Canyon that extends some 23 miles from Grand Canyon Village to Desert Tower is where most visitors get their first and often only view of the canyon. It is one of the most important places in the National Park System, like the Upper Geyser Basin in Yellowstone National Park, or Yosemite Valley. Unfortunately, we do not treat this section like a national treasure, although the task of doing so does not seem overwhelming.

The preservation of the Grand Canyon benefits from the nature of tourism at the canyon; it is "used" primarily by looking at it from the rim. The attractions at other parks, such as Carlsbad Caverns, the flower fields of Mount Rainier, and Yosemite Valley, require a much closer contact to enjoy. Visitors still need a place to park, however, and a restroom, a museum where they can find out about the geology of the canyon, and perhaps a place to eat and shop for souvenirs. These are all in short supply. On a peak day, 6,500 vehicles compete for 2,400 parking spaces.[34] The parking lot for the visitor center, which every visitor probably wants to visit, offers only "idle and wait" for parking spaces all day long. The shuttle bus system, inaugurated to prevent crowding on the rim, reached a state of overcrowding that no public bus system would tolerate, although current funding should improve this service.[35]

The rules and regulations that have been established to protect the park are not working as well as they could for the simple reason that there is a shortage of enforcement people to carry them out. There are seldom enough rangers to interpret the scenery, provide assistance, and answer questions. The limited number of rangers that the park can afford are often in the visitor center in front of a long, slow line all day, or collecting fees at an entrance station. The rangers walking around, checking out the park, talking to visitors, and acting like the hosts that they really are, are an endangered species.

A solution is at hand, but it will require increased funds. The NPS has just completed a plan that could make visiting the Grand Canyon a vastly improved experience by the turn of the century.[36] Four alternatives are presented in this plan: a "do little" alternative that would still address some of the park's problems, another that would sharply reduce development in the park, another that would expand development, and the proposed alternative that would create the showplace the NPS is hoping for. Once an alternative is selected after public review, then the hard part of getting the $171,000,000 to $383,000,000 in public funds to carry out the program must begin.[37]

The proposed alternative would remove most auto traffic from Grand Canyon Village, expand the shuttle bus system, increase parking, build bike and foot paths, relocate and build much better orientation and interpretive centers, increase lodging and food service (moving some of the lodging away from the rim and the food services toward it), and make life much better for rangers and concessioners by improving housing and community services. A light rail system even seems possible.[38] All this would be done while increasing the environmental quality of the area, reducing crowding, and offering better access to the rim. Similar programs are proposed for Desert View and the North Rim, the other major visitor access points.

All this assumes that Congress will appropriate the funds to carry out a program which would free the South Rim from traffic, which may be wishful thinking. The Grand Canyon Trust, a nonprofit conservation organization based in Flagstaff that has a staff working full time on the environmental preservation of the Colorado Plateau, feels that the NPS should be working on a reservation program now. It does seem that trying to solve a park's overcrowding problems with more money should realistically be paired with the more direct approach of simply limiting visitors.[39] On the other hand, given the tremendous economic value of the Grand Canyon to Arizona, limiting visitors to the canyon may be even more wishful thinking than getting the congressional appropriations.

## RAFTING THE GRAND CANYON

The most spectacular activity at the Grand Canyon is traversing it by boat. Although only up to 26,000 people a year raft the canyon, they spend up to two weeks doing so, compared to the few hours spent by the average visitor on the rim. Not to belittle the experience from the rim or a plane, a raft trip through the canyon can easily be the "trip of a lifetime" for many who take it.

Floating the Grand Canyon has to be one of the world's great adventures. Perhaps the canyon is not as spectacular from the bottom as the top, but it's more interesting. For people who have not traveled down a river, any river, the first revelation is that the river is changeable, moving, and powerful. There are many side canyons, some of which contain clear, beautiful streams. The life is here: trees, flowers, birds, mammals. The river is also tremendously exciting. There is a rapid a mile for most of the trip, some among the hardest in the world run by commercial companies. With only a few rapids in the canyon causes for concern, the guides often look for the hardest routes through the rapids, or at least those which will give the biggest thrill.

Rafting the Grand Canyon offers a good example of the steps taken by the NPS to protect an environment after rapidly expanding numbers make controls necessary. On my first Grand Canyon trip, in 1962, we threw trash in the river, went to the toilet wherever we wanted, had big campfires—and this was on a Sierra Club trip. Today, everything comes out, including human waste. A river tour business, quite lucrative, can be lost through environmental carelessness. In the mid-1970's, trails from the river up to the most popular campsites had become trenches, beaches had become litter boxes with all the insects and animals you would find back home, and a garbage scow went through the canyon annually, trying to keep up with the waste. By 1979 the NPS had set limits on the number of float trips and established rules relating to use of the canyon.[40]

The system in the Grand Canyon, followed with similar goals in most parks with wild rivers, has had only one setback, that of noise. Motors seem totally out of place in the bottom of the canyon, although they do shorten the time for a trip through the canyon. After extensive hearings in the 1970's it looked as if the bottom of the canyon would

*If the scenery through the Grand Canyon were not enough reason to take float trips through the canyon, hundreds of runnable rapids add to the popularity of such trips. (Photo by Gary O'Brien)*

be made wilderness, and therefore motorless, when Senator Hatch from Utah added an amendment to the Department of the Interior appropriations bill which mandated continued use of motors on the river.[41] Soon after James Watt became Secretary of the Interior he took a boat trip in the canyon where he stated unequivocally which side of the issue he was on: "The first day was spectacular . . . the second day started to get a little tedious, but the third day I wanted bigger motors to move that raft out. There is no way you could get me on an oar-powered raft on that river—I'll guarantee you that."[42] There is hope for the future, however. A study was made in 1976 of parties using both oars and motors, and all but 5 percent of the passengers preferred oars over motors.[43] There is also the possibility of much quieter four-stroke motors for the boats, which some operators are already using.

## HIKING THE CANYON

There is a large gap between the "drive up and look" tourist and the full-scale backcountry hiker in the Grand Canyon. In Yellowstone you can spend days driving around the Grand Loop Road in the park and taking hikes to the falls of the Yellowstone, the geysers in the Upper Geyser Basin, and the large number of attractions in the park. This is typical of most national parks. With the exception of short rim walks at the Grand Canyon, however, the action is very much centered on going *into* the canyon, and that's where the trouble starts. You start by going down, the easy part, and the obvious goal is the river, a mile down and at least 6 miles away. During the summer, when most people visit, you deal with the heat, several degrees more for every thousand feet down, and with water, which is nonexistent on some of the trails in the canyon. A number of people are rescued from the canyon every year, and there have been deaths. The NPS has a hard time being ambassadors of good will for the national parks and being tough enough to keep people from doing stupid things, like heading for the river at midday without water.

Ironically, the Grand Canyon is not yet protected by the 1964 Wilderness Act. In 1980 the NPS sent a wilderness proposal to Congress to protect 91 percent of the park as wilderness, a proposal which was ignored.[44] A new proposal would increase wilderness to 94 percent, but the unresolved issue of motors on the river might require another National Environmental Policy Act assessment.[45] The good news in all this is that, for now at least, inclusion in the National Wilderness Preservation System does not really seem to matter for the Grand Canyon. The 91–94 percent of the park that is wilderness can be controlled by permit and is relatively free of problems.

A final note on the Grand Canyon wilderness is a caveat to that last statement—feral burros are not controlled by permits. Burros, which were turned loose by or escaped from prospectors in the canyon, have adapted well to the canyon environment, but the reverse has certainly not been true. The animals can have a harmful effect on the vegetation of an area, especially around critical watering holes, and on all the native wildlife that depends on it. Finding the burros and removing them were difficult enough, and then animal rights activists required the NPS to find homes for the animals and airlift them out of the canyon, at great expense.[46]

## SUMMARY

The defeat of the proposed dams in the Grand Canyon in the 1960's seemed to remove the last barrier to a sustainable future for one of the world's greatest natural features. Visitation to the park was almost entirely to a narrow zone along the rim of the canyon, and seemed easily controlled. Then the national park received a basic lesson in ecology—that all places on earth are interconnected and taking care of *just* the Grand Canyon would not be enough. Smog drifted in from power plants near and far. The operation of a dam upstream from the park threatened life in the bottom of the canyon and made float trips through the canyon, which had grown exponentially in popularity, more difficult. Overflights became one of the most popular ways to see the canyon and were ending the age-old natural quiet of the canyon. Visitation to the canyon was leaving Yosemite and Yellowstone behind as the most popular park in the western United States, and crowding on the rim was reaching epic proportions.

Still, each of these crises was being met in turn, and while their outcome is still problematical, there is considerable hope for a reasonably natural canyon and a sustainable future. The trump card is the love of the canyon by the people in the United States who will not allow it to be less than it has always been. Inevitably, there will be crises in the future, and just as inevitably people will say (paraphrasing Teddy Roosevelt): this is the *Grand Canyon* you're tampering with—leave it alone!

# 6  Wilderness

WHEN the first national parks were established, the landscapes that they protected were considered saved forever. Certainly in the late 1800's when forests were being leveled, landscapes ripped apart by miners, and animals slaughtered without any thought for the future, the national parks were considered heaven on earth by the environmentalists of the time. Low visitation to the parks until the early 1900's allowed road building and tourist development to continue as fast as funds would allow without lasting damage to the parks. The coming of the automobile and visitation that soared, especially following World War II, showed that a natural landscape could be destroyed almost as quickly by tourist development as by commercial activities. The idea of wilderness and its value was increasingly heard among those concerned with the national parks.

## THE WILDERNESS MOVEMENT

The literature of the wilderness movement is extensive and of a high quality. The list of writers is long, including such diverse types as Henry David Thoreau, Aldo Leopold, John Muir, Bob Marshall, Roderick Nash, and Edward Abbey. The list of values assigned to wilderness is also long, including such things as watershed protection, source regions for wildlife and biodiversity, and high-quality outdoor recreation. On this last point, I would like to make a single statement on wilderness values.

In 1964, I was the Wilderness Society representative for a two-week horseback trip into the vast wilderness of southeastern Yellowstone Na-

*An ordinary landscape — meadow, trees, and a mountain — made exceptional by the complete absence of development. There are no roads, phone lines, logged forests, or buildings in this wilderness view of Mount Sheridan in Yellowstone National Park.*

tional Park. On the last night of the trip we camped in a grove of trees at the edge of a meadow that swept up to Mount Sheridan, a few miles in the distance (see photo). Everyone agreed that this was the most beautiful camp of the trip. Looking later at a slide taken of the site, however, it occurred to me that the basic view of forest, meadow, and mountain could be repeated a thousand times in the western United States. What was special about the scene was what *wasn't* there: logged forests, mined hillsides, road scars, buildings, transmission lines—there wasn't even a vapor trail from a high-flying jet. As the years and trail miles have gone by, I have found that many of my favorite scenes are beautiful for no other reason than that they are pristine.

The NPS recognizes this basic truth. To maintain the natural high quality of the areas they take care of, as much land as possible must be maintained as wilderness. The standards for wilderness are fairly simple. Leave such areas as they are. Let nature, which after all is responsible for our parks in the first place, work its wonders "untrammeled by man," as stated in the Wilderness Act.[1] As early as 1923, wilderness values were given as the reasons for limiting road building in the national parks.[2] The policy for some years after that, stated by various directors of the NPS, was to limit development in the national parks to the minimum necessary to allow reasonable visitor access. Despite the considerable latitude allowed by this policy, virtually no new areas were opened for development in the National Park System from the 1920's on. The establishment of the National Wilderness Preservation System in 1964 legally closed the administrative possibility of opening roadless park areas for development in the future.

## NATIONAL WILDERNESS PRESERVATION SYSTEM

The value of wilderness is debated endlessly, but there is little doubt that the vast majority of the American public is solidly for wilderness preservation. This was evidenced originally by the vote on the Wilderness Bill in the U.S. House of Representatives in 1964: the only vote cast against it was admittedly made in error.[3] This doesn't mean wilderness lacks powerful opponents. Mining, logging, and general development interests kept the bill from even coming to a vote for years. The Wilderness Bill was rewritten seventy-six times, and only after endless hearings and debate on the bill was it allowed to pass in 1964.[4]

The Wilderness Bill was originally intended to strengthen the U.S. Forest Service wilderness areas. Aldo Leopold in the late 1920's and Bob Marshall in the 1930's set up a process of saving wilderness in a lumber-oriented U.S. Forest Service. As envisioned by Leopold and Marshall, a large number of "Primitive Areas" were set aside before World War II in the national forests to be studied later and either declassified or put into "permanent" Wilderness Areas. This "upgrading" stopped with the war and was not resumed; some areas were opened to logging, and the only thing wilderness supporters could do was to try and change the law. From the mid-1950's to the mid-1960's the passage of a wilderness bill dominated the energy of the entire conservation movement.

President Johnson signed the Wilderness Bill on September 3, 1964, establishing the National Wilderness Preservation System, and giving wilderness the same congressional protection enjoyed by the national parks. The original system contained only national forest wilderness areas, but procedures were adopted to include the study of all roadless areas over 5,000 acres in national parks, national wildlife refuges, and the public domain. After studies were completed and public hearings held, Congress could then vote to establish wilderness areas. There are currently 88 million acres in the National Wilderness Preservation System, two-thirds of it in Alaska, with the potential for still more.

*Natural boundaries such as the Yellowstone River increase the feeling of
wilderness in this scene above the Upper Falls of the Yellowstone, although a
road and automobiles are just behind the two visitors.*

## NATIONAL PARK WILDERNESS

The national park policy concerning wilderness is very similar to the organic act creating national parks, except for the last two words: the NPS
will manage wilderness areas for the use and enjoyment of the American
people in such manner as will leave them unimpaired for future use and
enjoyment *as wilderness.*

It is hard sometimes to see the importance of including national parks
in the National Wilderness Preservation System, as developed areas and
roads in the parks are highly unlikely to be expanded beyond their present locations. The NPS itself originally opposed the bill for this reason.
The opposition also believed that certain areas, because of topography or
location, would *never* be developed. Both are false arguments for the
parks, as well as for wilderness in general. In 1996 there were attempts to
allow snowmobiles in roadless areas of Voyageurs National Park and to
build highways in similar areas in Denali National Park. Leaving decisions for preserving wilderness to the NPS may have worked in the past,
but without statutory protection, there is no assurance that it will work
in the future.

## PROVISIONS OF THE WILDERNESS ACT

The Wilderness Act defines wilderness as a landscape untouched by development, with no permanent habitations, no roads, and no use of motorized or mechanical equipment. The act establishing the Yosemite National Park wilderness, for example, covers 89 percent of the park, all but a strip 200 feet from the centerline of existing roads and 100 feet from all developed areas in the park; below the 4,200-foot contour in Yosemite Valley; Hetch Hetchy and Lake Eleanor; unsuitable land in the southwestern section of the park; and small areas surrounding the five High Sierra Camps (which are potential additions to park wilderness).[5] The rationale that an area has to be pristine, that it show no signs of ever having been used, has been discarded in favor of *returning* areas to wilderness. Under the ever-present process of entropy this can happen quickly, even in a developed area. In Yosemite, many abandoned roads have been returned to wilderness, including roads that will continue to be lightly maintained to prevent erosion, to allow use as trails, or to meet historic guidelines.[6] Power line locations, old water supply facilities, and old campgrounds will also be returned to wilderness.

The wilderness world is going to be something far different from what a person sees on the outside. There may be a patrol cabin, but then another one won't appear for 20 miles. There may be a road "being returned to the wilderness," but there will be no vehicles on it; not even a mountain bike. Cellular phones are making their appearance in the wilderness (with a potential for aiding mountain rescue), but unless it can be carried, our vast world of TV, computers, and appliances will be left behind. More importantly, the wilderness is one place, almost by definition, where the population explosion does not exist.

### Exceptions to the Wilderness Act

Within the section of the Wilderness Act prohibiting roads and motors there is a thirty-two-word "exception" statement: "except as necessary to meet minimum requirements for the administration of the area for the purpose of this Act (including measures required in emergencies involving the health and safety of persons within the area)."[7] Trails and trail bridges are obvious structures in park wilderness. Not so obvious are the chainsaws used to clear the trails quickly before side trails develop around them and to fell potentially dangerous trees in campgrounds, and jackhammers and dynamite used in trail development to obviate the time and labor that would be necessary without them. Composting toilets are also found in several heavily used wilderness areas for "health and safety" reasons. The small intrusion these buildings make seems to be far outweighed by the benefits gained. Patrol cabins are found where the heavy traffic warrants it, such as Evolution Valley in Kings Canyon National Park. Metal bear-proof lockers, high wire cables for food balancing, and "hanging poles" for food sacks are devices felt necessary for both people and bear safety in the backcountry. Emergency evacuation, fire management, and even cannabis plot searches have been reasons for highly restricted helicopter use in wilderness.

## WILDERNESS USE

An enormous increase in wilderness use came during the period before and after the passage of the Wilderness Act in 1964. Backpacking equipment, almost unavailable up to the 1950's, has reached such a state that

*Multiple trails are often a problem when they traverse a meadow and are heavily used, such as this trail near Tuolumne Meadows in Yosemite National Park.*

*Cascade Pass, in what is now North Cascades National Park, in 1958. The open fire, dog without leash, and even camping at this site were suspended years ago to preserve a popular wilderness area.*

hikers can almost outfit themselves for a major backcountry trip in the local discount supermarket. Damage to backcountry areas was noticeable even before this increase in visitation; wilderness managers now knew that something had to be done, and done quickly. In the past, popular backcountry areas were turned into semipermanent camps by packers and backpackers with such things as large rock-lined fireplaces and primitive tables. Trails, especially through meadows, could develop into six-track wilderness highways as people avoided mud and deteriorated sections of the old trails. Wilderness permits based on carrying capacity had to be instigated.

The first and ongoing task of wilderness managers is to establish a carrying capacity for an area and decide how to limit the use of such areas to stay within that capacity. The carrying capacity can be physical or psychological. Physically, it can be defined as the level of use that will not cause the natural environment to decline in quality, or, if it is in bad shape, the level at which it can recover. Psychologically it is that level where people can really feel they are in the wilderness. Obviously, psychological carrying capacity will be different for almost everyone.

The most crowded wilderness areas, such as those in Yosemite, the Grand Canyon, and the Teton Range, were among the first to require wilderness permits; now almost every NPS wilderness requires them. In some areas they are just a counting device and a means of dispensing environmental education to those picking up the permits. Limits to wilderness access are increasing, however, and driving to an area, picking up your pack, and heading into the wilderness is almost a thing of the past. Along the east side of the Sierras—in Sequoia, Kings Canyon, and Yosemite—it is common for campers to take up position when the wilderness offices close the night before the permits are offered, in order to have a chance at getting a slot the next day.

Permits are issued in a number of ways: in advance by mail or phone, in person the day of the entry, by number entering from a particular trailhead, for a particular geographic area, for sites in a backcountry campground, and so on. The NPS will also set limits on the number in a party (no more Sierra Club base camps with hundreds of participants), on whether or not fires can be built, on the use of horses and pack animals, and on the distance camp can be made from a stream. As onerous as these rules might sometimes be, they virtually insure that when hikers get to their site they will have a true wilderness experience. The permits were free as late as 1996, but several national parks now charge for them, to pay for necessary improvements in wilderness areas.

Wilderness areas, as defined by the Wilderness Act, are simple lines on the map that signify the use, as wilderness, of the areas included within those boundaries. These lines may be on any federal land, and the rules for the agency in charge apply, subject to the regulations given by the Wilderness Act. Hunting is allowed in the national forests, for example, but not, except for national preserves, in the national parks. Essentially this is a rare case of intergovernmental cooperation, because the difference in management between the governmental agencies is very small compared to the similarities. You could get a wilderness permit for the Pacific Crest Trail in Southern California, for example, and it would be good all the way to Canada. You couldn't have a dog or firearms for the national parks you would go through, but the important rules concerning trails and campsites would apply everywhere.

## SUMMARY

I saw my first mountains when I was eleven, was profoundly moved, and then World War II and gas rationing kept me from them for the next four years. During that time I thought and dreamed about the mountains, wilderness, and the national parks. Books on the parks filled the niche and taught me things, perhaps, that I wouldn't have learned through travel.

We can't always get into wilderness areas—for various reasons some people may never get there—but that doesn't diminish their importance. Simply knowing that wilderness exists is perhaps the most prevalent reason for support of these small pieces of the earth where we're willing to let nature be fully in control.

# Case Study:
# Denali National Park

ALASKA is *the* wilderness state, with 59 percent of the dedicated wilderness of the United States. Half of the visitation to that wilderness takes place in Denali National Park, one of the most accessible Alaskan parks. This wilderness is still wilder than that of most of the parks in the lower forty-eight. There are only a few miles of trails in the entire park, and these are around park headquarters. The Denali wilderness is divided into forty-three trail-less units, with a limited number of backpackers allowed in each.[1] Only a third of the park is included in the National Wilderness Preservation System, although this total could more than double under NPS recommendations.[2] The remainder, which is roadless, is open for traditional subsistence use by natives, which may include aircraft landings or snowmobiles.[3]

The Athabaskan Indian name for McKinley is Denali, a name the park service has adopted for the former Mount McKinley National Park. Changing a geographic name, especially of a feature so famous, is much more difficult, but it seems inevitable. The mountain was named by a prospector to honor a presidential candidate of his time, without, I guess, asking the natives what it was called. Insensitivity to the natives was pretty typical then, but it's not something we have to live with. Besides, Denali is a much more beautiful name.

With the mountain as a backdrop, visitors to the park are also treated to one of the Western Hemisphere's greatest wildlife shows. In this once remote and isolated part of the continent no animal has yet been exterminated. From grizzly bear to caribou to Dall sheep to gray wolf, they are all there, in healthy numbers, and easily observable. There are undoubtedly areas in Alaska or Canada where there are greater concentrations of large species of wildlife. There are much larger extents of wilderness. But here people can enjoy all this with little more discomfort than leaving their cars for a bus, or waiting a few days for the mountain to clear.

## ALASKA NATIONAL INTEREST LANDS CONSERVATION ACT (ANILCA)

When Alaska became a state in 1959, 104 million acres of public domain (which included over 80 percent of the 375-million-acre territory) was made available to the state. The state chose timber land, potential settle-

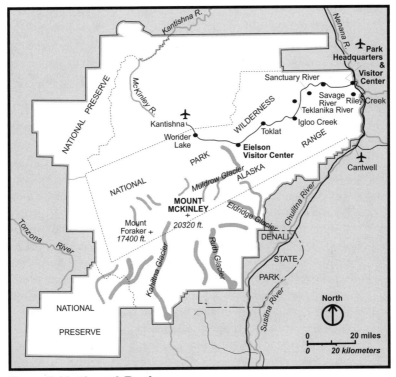

# Denali National Park

ment land, and mineral rich areas. The most desirable lands were those that had oil like Prudhoe Bay, the largest oil field in North America, discovered in 1968. Alaskan natives were also pressing their claims at that time, leading Secretary of the Interior Stewart Udall to put a freeze on the selection of state lands in the 1960's until the native claims could be settled.

The Alaska Native Claims Settlement Act was passed in 1971, allowing natives to select up to 44 million acres of land. In the same act, in what came to be known as the "d-2 section," provision was made for the selection of up to 80 million acres of public domain for national parks, forests, wildlife refuges, and wilderness areas.[4] The fight for Alaska's public land pulled together environmentalists in much the same way as Echo Park in the 1950's and wilderness in the 1960's. Some of the more vocal Alaskans, however, didn't want any land where they couldn't log, mine, or hunt. Until President Carter assumed office in 1977, d-2 seemed to be going nowhere, despite the lobbying efforts of a powerful group of fifty-five conservation organizations known as the Alaskan Coalition. Opponents were able to stall the bill until its deadline approached, forcing President Carter to use the 1906 Antiquities Act to designate 17 national monuments on 56 million acres, and suspend mining claims and logging on all the rest under consideration.

The Alaska Lands Act (now known as the Alaska National Interest Lands Conservation Act—ANILCA) was passed by the House, weakened by the Senate, but finally accepted in December 1980 because of the victory of Ronald Reagan over Carter and the unlikelihood of passing a better bill. The act placed 104.5 million acres under protection, doubling the size of the National Park System and tripling the size of the National Wilderness Preservation System. It allows "traditional uses" to continue in the newly added areas.[5]

Denali was nearly tripled in size by ANILCA, but it created the equivalent of three parks in so doing. The original acreage of the old park—2,108,041 acres—became wilderness, with the exception of a 300-foot-wide corridor along the single park gravel road; 2,616,604 acres of new parkland was opened to traditional subsistence use; 1,334,618 acres became a national preserve where both subsistence use, including trapping, and sport hunting were allowed.[6] All these uses "must occur within the context of managing the area for natural values," according to the NPS.[7]

## THE GREAT ONE

The argument over the most impressive feature of the National Park System is no contest if you limit the debate to outstanding mountains in the system. Mount McKinley is not only the tallest mountain in North America at 20,320 feet, but from base to top, it is one of the tallest in the world. Mount Everest, at 29,028 feet, is certainly impressive, but its base is at around 17,000 feet. McKinley's base is at only about 1,400 feet, giving a "view" of the peak of almost 19,000 feet, a full mile higher than Everest. Mount McKinley's latitude, 63° N, means snow from base to top, adding to its impressiveness. Statistics aside, McKinley is truly one of the world's most spectacular mountains.

One thing the tourist bureaus may not tell you about your visit to Denali National Park is that the odds of seeing the mountain are less than not seeing it. In other words, the mountain is clouded in much of the time. On my trip to Alaska in 1983 I had eight days in the park, making it certain (I thought) that McKinley would be visible at some time during the visit. But as I waited, and worked up the queue toward

*Mount McKinley, snow-covered to its base in August, is the tallest mountain in North America and the centerpiece of Denali National Park.*

93

*Mount McKinley attracts hundreds of climbers a year from throughout the world, despite its difficulty. The base camp at 7,200 feet on the Kahiltna Glacier, accessible by air, is still 2.5 vertical miles below the summit. (Photo by Patti Dodgen)*

my desired campground at Wonder Lake, the closest I would get to the mountain, I started to worry. On my last night in the park it snowed (in August, at 2,000 feet). As I looked out of the tent at 4:00 A.M., however, broad daylight in that part of the world, I could see a faint outline of the peak through the clouds. As I watched in wonder the clouds dissipated, leaving the incredible bulk of McKinley shining in the bright morning sun.

Mount McKinley is considered one of the world's premier mountaineering destinations. The reason for its popularity, besides its being the highest mountain in North America, is paradoxically because it is one of the most hostile environments in the world and an ultimate challenge for mountaineers. To be prepared for what could be a two-week storm on the upper slopes, with temperatures of −50 °F and 100-mph winds, McKinley climbers must carry enormous loads to virtually their last camp at 17,200 feet. That means they must start with 100 pounds, a total which means shuttling loads, or using sleds to drag the load up the glacier from the 7,200-foot base camp. The climber needs a minimum of twenty days of food and the best and warmest tents and clothing available. It is hard to cut the weight and time without extreme hazard, partly because it takes at least seventeen days to acclimatize to the altitude.[8]

The peak is also notorious for danger. The eleven people killed on the mountain in 1992, and twenty-eight since 1986, have led to a $150 fee on each climber attempting the mountain. The money collected has been spent on better rescue gear and more climbing rangers.[9] Sanitation on the mountain is also highly regulated: all garbage and surplus food and equipment must be carried off the mountain.[10]

## WILDLIFE

I stopped wanting to go to Africa about twenty years ago when the stories of the disappearance of wildlife became too intense. I had already said good-bye to Glen Canyon in 1959 before the gates on the Glen Canyon Dam closed, and I didn't want to say good-bye to another part of the world. With Denali, so far, I don't have to worry. The incredible wildlife show available from the window of the buses in the park should be available to my kids and their kids, in the same richness and variety that we enjoy today. No animals have gone extinct in the park, and none has had to be reintroduced.

Problems must be overcome, however. Subsistence hunting in the additions to the park under ANILCA, and sport hunting in the Denali National Preserve, could get out of hand and damage the quality and quantity of wildlife in the park. The expansion of the Denali Park Road and development in the Kantishna area, as discussed below, could also have a negative impact on wildlife. As in all parks, sustainability is only as certain as the level of vigilance by those who love the park.

## ACCESS AND VISITATION

A solid plus for the wildlife of Denali—the grizzlies, moose, Dall sheep, wolves, and caribou—is that they can be seen so easily and in such a natural setting. Ninety percent of the visitors to Denali see all but the wolves on their visit.[11] When the park was established, however, visiting it was quite an undertaking, just like Gates of the Arctic National Park today, but without the planes. With the coming of the railroad in 1923 access improved, but there were still only 6,000 visitors as late as 1950.[12] Alaska, with a state population less than that of any of two dozen U.S. cities, has always relied on foreign and out-of-state visitors (from a practical standpoint, almost the same) for its tourist income, and getting to Alaska has never been a simple undertaking. Only a small percentage of the population was into flying until fairly recently, and cruise ships or ferries seemed a luxury to most people. Driving the unpaved Alaskan Highway in the past was only for the adventurous. All this has changed with better ferry service, the increased popularity of cruises, and the commonness of flying, bringing the flood of visitors we see today. Advertising has also put Denali in a "must see" category, especially for foreign visitors.

The 90-mile Denali Park Road, completed in 1938, was built before the highway to the park was completed (1972), and before there was any pressure to upgrade the road. An attempt to widen the road in the 1960's brought strong opposition from the environmental community.[13] The widening was stopped, and for safety as well as environmental reasons, private cars were banned over all but the first 15 miles. A bus system, free at first, was provided.[14] The major benefit of this system is an outstanding wilderness and wildlife viewing situation.

There are seven campgrounds along the park road and a single development without services—the Eielson Visitor Center. The "wilderness beyond the shoulder of the road," a special feature of national parks, reaches its peak in Denali. If the road were open to traffic the attraction would be much less. The situation of game parks in Africa, with small buses surrounding a pride of lions, would be replaced with an Alaskan version of the bear jams of Yellowstone. Unfortunately, rationing the resources means the visitor might have to plan ahead, or wait, for tours in the park, so not everyone is happy with the present situation. Several critical issues face Denali National Park in the future.

## ACCESS AND DEVELOPMENT AT KANTISHNA

Kantishna is an inholding with a small group of lodges and mining claims, which was just outside the park on the road past Wonder Lake before it was absorbed in the ANILCA expansion. For the last decade it has been the center of pressure to expand the park's access and development. ANILCA provides for access to inholdings, which has led to demands for another road, or rail line, into Kantishna from north of the park, constructing an RV park with privileges to use the Denali Park Road, and even a "day use" of the area, which would also allow the road to be used.[15] A task force assigned to the problem in 1994, made up of state, federal, and private interests, emphasized the importance of the uncrowded wilderness character of the road and suggested several actions to improve the situation. The RV park and "day use" ploys should be prohibited, improved buses provided, a youth hostel established in Kantishna, and inholdings acquired as soon as possible.[16]

## SOUTH-SIDE DEVELOPMENT

Outstanding views of Mount McKinley and the possibility of more visitor accommodations have led to a high degree of interest in the south side of the park.[17] Although the area is off the main highway, it is closer to Anchorage, and state, tribal, and private land are available for development. The potential for wildlife viewing is less than in the north, but the terrain is more interesting and the views of Mount McKinley even better. The tourist infrastructure would have to be developed, and some are concerned with what greater development might bring.

## SUMMARY

Alaska calls itself the "last frontier," which is certainly appropriate as the world fills with people and wilderness disappears. With spectacular landscapes, huge wildlife numbers, and vast tracts of protected wilderness, Alaska will be a prime ecotourism location, which should increase in importance far into the future. Denali National Park holds a privileged position in all this. It not only contains one of the world's most impressive mountains in McKinley, and some of North America's richest assemblages of wildlife, but a truly sustainable situation has developed where visitors can be immersed in this wild scene in relative comfort with minimal damage to the environment.

Visitors have doubled in the last decade, however, opening the question as to just what is going to be "sustained." Some solutions to growth pressures, such as opening the Denali Park Road to more traffic, and allowing development in the Kantishna area, might severely impact wildlife viewing and the serene wilderness contact now available. It is hard to believe that the public would ever let this happen, however. More efficient buses and scheduling, better control over private vehicles now using the road, and limited development south of the mountain might carry the outstanding quality of the Denali visit well into the next century.

# 7  Wildlife

THE area covering the present United States, when it was first settled by Europeans, had one of the richest collections of wildlife to be found anywhere in the world. Bison, elk, mountain lions, grizzly bears, and wolves were found throughout vast areas of the country, the rivers were full of fish, and birds were present in incredible numbers and variety. Wildlife conservation, however, was not even remotely in the picture. We hunted wildlife for food, we hunted for markets, and we hunted for sport, with no thought for the future of wildlife in this country. By the late 1890's, when the frontier was beginning to close, it looked like we were going to lose all that was both big and beautiful among America's original wildlife. Enter Yellowstone National Park, which was not just the first national park but one of the first large wildlife refuges in the world.

## THE YELLOWSTONE NATIONAL PARK RESERVE

Because of a lack of exploitable resources, the wildlife on the Yellowstone Plateau escaped some of the rapid destruction of animals and habitat taking place in the rest of the country. In the mid-1800's the Yellowstone area harbored substantial numbers of large mammals, including herds of elk and bison.[1] When Yellowstone National Park was first established in 1872, the nation was already beginning to feel prickings of conscience about the destruction of its native wildlife, yet without any clear idea of how to combat the problem. Preserving wildlife in the new park was not even a top priority. There was a clause in the Yellowstone Act stating that those in charge would "provide against the wanton destruction of the fish and game found within said park and against their capture or destruction for the purpose of merchandise or profit,"[2] but no provisions were made to enforce protection of the wildlife or penalize its destruction. People continued killing wildlife as if the park did not exist. As late as the 1890's hotel employees were hunting elk for the visitors' meals.[3]

A change in attitudes and behavior toward animals in the parks occurred because of those last few bison. A notorious poacher was caught by army troops in March 1894, systematically shooting bison in this last herd, but because of a lack of specific laws and punishment had to be turned loose. A popular wildlife writer, George Bird Grinnell, fanned the flames of public indignation enough to insure passage, in 1894, of a strong wildlife bill by Representative John F. Lacey of Iowa. Unpunished sport and market hunting were at an end in Yellowstone.[4]

## WILDLIFE REDUCTION AND THE NATIONAL PARKS

Yellowstone National Park was one of the first large areas in the country where hunting was banned, and this has made all the difference in wildlife populations in the park. Wildlife disappears for reasons other than hunting, however—predator control, natural causes, pollution, accidents—with the national parks varying in the extent of their protection. Habitat preservation is ultimately the most important factor in keeping wildlife populations in this country healthy, and in this the parks are preeminent. On the other hand, nonhunting contact with animals is very high in the parks, which can cause special problems, discussed later in this chapter.

Ironically, the Lacey Act of 1894, which first gave protection to animals in the national parks, was applied only to those animals favored by the public and park administrators. Americans have long divided their animals into heroes and villains, with the heroes being the large ungulates such as elk and bison, and the villains the predators, such as wolves and mountain lions. The U.S. Army, in control of Yellowstone from 1883 until the founding of the National Park Service in 1916, started the removal of predators from the park—mainly wolves, coyotes, and mountain lions, but also bobcats, lynx, wolverines, foxes, and hawks.[5] Any method that worked was used, including traps and poisons. Official records for 1904 to 1935 show 121 mountain lions, 4,352 coyotes, and 132 wolves destroyed in Yellowstone.[6] After 1915, two government trappers were assigned to the park's staff just for predator control.

Adolph Murie, who worked for the Wildlife Division of the NPS until it was abolished in 1947, studied the coyote in Yellowstone from 1937 to 1939 and debunked the myth of the coyote as a factor in reducing elk numbers. An analysis of coyote droppings showed half of their diet consisted of mice and gophers; of the 15 percent of the coyotes' diet attributed to elk, it was felt that all of their prey were either carrion or weak and sick animals. With the mountain lion and wolf already exterminated, Murie believed it made little sense to continue the predator control program. Besides, there were now far too many elk. It appeared more predators rather than fewer might be the most pressing need.[7]

The present policy concerning predators, first enunciated as early as 1933, is as follows: "No native predator shall be destroyed, on account of its normal utilization of any other park animal, excepting if that animal is in immediate danger of extermination, and then only if the predator is not itself a vanishing form. When control is necessary it shall be accomplished by transplanting, or, if necessary by killing offending individuals, not by campaigns to reduce the general population of a species."[8]

Hunting still takes place in the parks, however. To allay part of the animosity felt in Jackson, Wyoming, for the creation of an expanded Grand Teton National Park and a reduction of hunting areas, a Faustian bargain was struck which allowed elk hunting in the park. Defending the public law which allows the hunt, officials explain that when elk are blocked by development from migrating south to lower grazing areas, the hunt helps keep the number of elk in balance. The NPS maintains that if population numbers of the elk ever stabilize then the hunt will be unnecessary. The mean number of elk killed was 598 a year from 1963 to 1983.[9]

Hunting is also allowed in national preserves, most of which are in Alaska. In many of the lands considered for new national parks in Alaska in the 1970's, such as Wrangell–St. Elias National Park, hunting was the only use for large areas, with only light tourist visitation ever envisioned. With strong resistance to national parks by many Alaskans, the concessions were made and hunting was allowed in portions of the new national preserves. A further compromise was made to pro-gun groups in 1994 when an area in the California desert was changed from the potential Mojave National Park to Mojave National Preserve.[10]

Poaching was and continues to be a serious problem in parks. As wildlife becomes more scarce in the United States and the world, it seems obvious that the situation can only get worse. Among the incentives for poaching are demands for Asian medicines and greed for trophy animals. A sting operation in Great Smoky Mountains National Park in 1985 yielded

266 bear gall bladders, which are used in Asian medicines. Elk antlers are in demand for the same reason. Hunters also seem willing to spend large amounts, $10,000 for a trophy brown bear and $50,000 for a record big-horn head, to obtain a stuffed animal or head for their den, even if it means breaking laws to do it.[11] The primary problem with stopping poaching is the cost in money and personnel. There are only a few hundred federal wildlife agents nationwide, and assigning a park ranger to a time-consuming and dangerous task is usually not possible in this time of shrinking budgets.

In a natural ecosystem, unaltered by human intervention, animals disappear because of malnutrition, disease, parasites, and predation. In many of our national parks, similar scenarios exist. Some would argue that this natural evolution takes place *more* in the national parks because of a policy of noninterference. Elk numbers in Yellowstone expand during periods of high rainfall and mild winters, for example, and are reduced, mostly through winter kill, during the severe winters. In the past, attempts have been made to reduce winter kills through supplemental feeding, a process which still takes place in the National Elk Refuge in Jackson, but is no longer accepted as desirable elsewhere in the National Park System. Besides preventing the buildup of populations which the range can't support, winter kill results in elk carcasses, which are an important source of nutrition for predators such as grizzlies, black bears, coyotes, mountain lions, and wolves.

Wildlife in the national parks tends to be much less affected by pollution than in areas outside park boundaries. In Yellowstone, for example, streams start in the park, or in adjacent wilderness areas, and flow clean and pure through the park. Industries and cities causing air pollution are mostly absent in the area. There are exceptions to this general statement, but remoteness and protection within the parks have definitely made them cleaner than most nonpark areas. Global pollution sources, such as those which could cause ozone depletion and global warming, may of course affect all of the parks.

Outside the parks roadkills are one of the leading causes of death of mammals. Although occasionally occurring within parks, due to increased numbers of animals and lack of fencing, a generally lower rate of speed on park roads and an awareness of the presence of animals tend to mitigate the danger. Still, an average of 108 roadkills per year occur in Yellowstone, mostly elk and deer, with a federal highway which skirts the northwestern portion of the park accounting for 39 percent of the kill in 1994.[12]

Parks are not free from disruption of habitat—witness the stores, hotels, and roads of Yosemite Valley. Non-native plants and exotic animals also find their way into the parks, usurping native plants and animals from their ecological niches in the process. A gross example of habitat disruption is the illegal introduction of lake trout into Yellowstone Lake, discussed later in this chapter. On the other hand, such disruption is far less than outside the parks, and park goals include active programs to eradicate the non-natives. In time, it is hoped that restoration can lead to an increasingly natural landscape in the parks.

The primary cause of disappearance of wildlife today is loss of habitat. Consequently, the main value of national parks to wildlife is protection of that habitat. Unfortunately, the scenic mountains, canyons, and deserts which make up much of the National Park System, and which are relatively poor economically, are not often the best wildlife habitat. The richest habitats for wildlife are often the places we choose for agriculture, homes, and cities. The expansion of national parks or other protected landscapes into ecologically diverse areas, and the tying together of networks of protected lands—national parks, state parks, national forests, wildlife refuges—including private land, may give the best hope for wildlife in the future. Programs have already begun, using a powerful computer mapping program known as Geographic Information Systems (GIS). It is operated by the National Biological Survey, and if it proceeds as planned, would be a powerful tool for wildlife conservation in this country.[13]

## MANAGING WILDLIFE IN THE NATIONAL PARKS

The benefits of having national parks become evident as people drive through Gibbon Meadows in Yellowstone and see herds of elk grazing along the river, or when they see a grizzly sauntering along the road from a bus window in Denali, or a black bear while hiking along a trail in Kings Canyon. The benefits of being able to see animals within their natural habitats also create some of the most intractable management problems within the national parks. It is one thing to deal with protecting grizzlies from disappearing habitats and hunters, and still another to protect them when they've injured a camper. Unless there is a radical change in the way parks are managed, this volatile mixture of people and animals will continue, and inevitably worsen. Yellowstone, with one of the largest assemblages of wildlife in the National Park System, and with a long record of conflicts between people and wildlife, will be the focus of discussions of some of the best-known and most studied species of wildlife in the parks.

## Black Bears

Black bears are present in virtually all of the national parks. The black bear is not normally a threat to humans, and there has been only one death in the national parks attributed to black bears.[14] Injuries, however, have been fairly common, and as nuisances, bears have few equals. Completing the potential for trouble, they are also the most interesting animals in the national parks. As Paul Schullery put it, talking about Yellowstone:

> I have often been confronted by families who "haven't seen a thing here in the park." Usually I find that they have seen deer, elk, moose, bison, and so on, "but we haven't seen any *bears*." . . . The visitor watching a magnificent bull elk graze in a mountain meadow, even if that visitor has never seen an elk before, will get restless quickly. He's seen horses do the same thing, back home, for hours. The bear is a different matter; it turns over rocks, climbs trees, eats candy wrappers (and elk), hibernates, mauls people . . . now there's an animal a man can appreciate![15]

Bears were both enjoyed and tolerated in Yellowstone until sometime after the entry of vehicles in the park (1915) and the subsequent arrival of masses of visitors, when the "roadside bear" appeared. For the next half-century, every visitor to Yellowstone saw bears, as the bears learned that the easiest way to get food was to simply stand alongside the road, hold out a paw, and let the cubs play nearby. This caused some incredible traffic jams, "bear jams" as they were called, particularly if there were two or three cubs, the road was narrow, and it was midseason. But you saw bears and the trip was a success. In addition to seeing bears, bear stories were a staple topic of conversation for everyone who had ever been to Yellowstone. My favorite story was told to me by a student who used to deliver the *Denver Post* in Yellowstone every day. He drove from Bozeman to Billings to get the papers, around the Grand Loop in Yellowstone to deliver them, and home again to Bozeman: 500 miles a day. This "paper route" gave him a great chance to see a lot of bears, and to get entangled in many bear jams. As he told the story, a tourist wanted to get pictures of a mother bear and her two cubs, so he tossed them a fish. When he started to take the picture, however, he got too close, and the mother shooed the cubs up a tree. The photographer, frustrated and angry, grabbed one cub by the hind legs and pulled it out of the tree. Another incident, which I witnessed, was a bear on his hind legs, with his paws on a man's shoulder, and the man calmly plopping candy in the bear's open, teeth-filled mouth, 6 inches away. When the man ran out of candy, the bear simply dropped down and moved over to another tourist.

The Yellowstone bears went into garbage cans, tents, cabins, cars—wherever food was available—but they usually avoided confrontation. There were injuries—1,883 in Yellowstone overall—mostly minor and mostly incidences of a tourist illegally feeding bears, or unintentionally feeding them when a bear joined a picnic.[16] Yosemite and the Great Smokies also had more than their share of injuries and property damage by bears, resulting in many bears being killed as a way to solve these problems.

By the late 1960's the NPS was becoming much more environmentally conscious. The NPS was preparing to host a world national park conference in 1972, celebrating Yellowstone's one hundredth anniversary. Many in the NPS felt that visitors from parks around the world, driving into the mother of all parks, about which they had heard so much, and having Yogi Bear greet them with outstretched paw, was not the image they wanted to leave with the visitors. Also, recent autopsy tests of the bears, in national parks and in the nation's zoos, had shown some pretty horrifying things. A bear's stomach was equipped to take a wide variety of food, but not broken glass and plastics, which can cause suffering and death. Whatever the reason, the NPS soon "got tough" with people feeding the bears and was forced to remove habituated animals to keep them from teaching more generations of bears to seek human foods. Inevitably, many animals were killed. The park service also converted to bear-proof garbage cans and emptied them daily. This meant an end to the bears wandering between tents and cabins followed, like the Pied Piper, by kids, mothers beating pans, fathers taking pictures, and so on. By the early 1970's the roadside bear was miraculously gone. Although there are detractors, the NPS feels there are as many bears as ever, in the backcountry acting like bears.[17] The roadside bear has been relegated to park lore.

Yosemite, on the other hand, still has its campground bears, and they are still causing problems. In 1997, bears broke into six hundred cars in Yosemite, causing over $500,000 in damage.[18] The NPS has had some success by putting "bear lockers"—cement-based, metal, bear-proof containers—in the camprounds, and is aggressive in requiring that people not leave food out where the bears can get to it.[19] The problems occur when, according to a Yosemite park biologist, "the smarter bears and the dumber visitors intersect."[20]

Some parks (Kings Canyon, Sequoia) have placed bear-proof lockers in

*Counterbalancing food bags from tree limbs is one method, occasionally successful, of keeping bears from food in national parks in the Sierra Nevadas of California.*

the backcountry and they work very well, but in other backcountry areas the battle of wits over the backpackers' food continues. I tend to be pessimistic, feeling all the natural methods of keeping food from the bears— hanging it from trees and cliffs, immersing it in water, hiding it—are all doomed to fail for most hikers (at least in the Sierras). The Wilderness Act allows minor development for the public's health and safety, and a single 6' × 3' × 3' dark brown "bear box" in each of the popular backcountry campgrounds seems a minor enough exception to the rules to allow returning the bear to nature. "Bear poles," unclimbable by bears, with provisions for hanging food, and "bear cables," which simplify the counterbalancing act, are also found in the backcountry in some parks. Lightweight bear-proof food containers which fit in the pack and hold three or four days' food may obviate even this concession.

Solutions to bear problems can vary from park to park. The Yellowstone black bear, for example, is not as aggressive in getting to food as the Yosemite bear, and leaving food locked in a car trunk will not result in a

*Leaving food on a picnic table can lead to a disastrous outcome for both humans and bears. This grizzly bear is inspecting a campground in Denali National Park, Alaska.*

damaged automobile. You'll find "bear boxes" in Yosemite, therefore, but not in Yellowstone. It is also not necessary in the Yellowstone backcountry to go through the work of counterbalancing food from a tree; hauling it out of the bear's reach and tying it to a tree are usually good enough. Big Bend, with newly arriving bears from Mexico, Great Smoky Mountains, with major bear food sources just outside the park, and all the other parks have bears with their own personalities. Reducing human-animal contacts, however, is always basic.

## Grizzly Bears

Besides being a larger, more impressive animal, the grizzly is also considerably more dangerous than the black bear. The individual in Yellowstone who was feeding the black bear and pulled the cub out of the tree would have become food if that had been a grizzly. Yet grizzlies were showpieces even before the black bear, with people watching them eat kitchen scraps on a floodlit "table" from bleachers at Canyon in Yellowstone. These grizzly bear shows continued right up until World War II but were not reopened after the war. They were still being fed, though, unofficially, in the large open dumps which existed south of Canyon and near Old Faith-

*Grizzly bears are found only in Glacier and Yellowstone National Parks in the conterminous United States, and their survival is still in doubt despite a massive effort mandated by the Endangered Species Act. (National Parks photo)*

ful in the park. The grizzly became big news in Yellowstone in 1970 when the last and largest of the park's open dumps was closed. Grizzly researchers in the park warned that the bears, used to free meals, should be "weaned" from the dumps by closing them slowly and by moving food such as elk carcasses into the backcountry. Park administrators, supported by other grizzly experts, argued that the bears did fend for themselves before and after the tourist seasons and quick withdrawal would work faster than slow withdrawal.[21] Besides, the park service was just starting its "natural" program, and it wanted proof of the program's efficacy.

The results are still being argued, but it appears that the NPS was right. Property damage from all bears dropped from an average of 261.5 incidents per year before the dumps were closed and other human food sources reduced, to 99.3 per year in the 1970–1972 period, and to 14.3 between 1983 and 1993. People injured by grizzly bears dropped from 4 per year between 1960 and 1969 to 2 per year between 1970 and 1972, and to about 1 per year thereafter. Many of the bears resisted being separated from human food, of course, and were either translocated or removed. Thirty-nine nuisance grizzly bears per year were translocated between 1970 and 1972 and 12 per year were removed. Critics of the NPS would point to that figure as one of the reasons for the grizzlies being endangered, but it did seem to take care of the problem: only about 5 grizzlies per year have had to be translocated since 1973 and less than 1 per year removed. They are, however, still on the endangered species list, despite pressure from ranchers and loggers around the park to delist them.[22]

The grizzly *has* returned to the natural environment in the Greater Yellowstone Ecosystem, and there is some reason for optimism for its future. The remaining grizzlies are relearning many survival techniques which might have been discarded while feeding at the dumps. Fish seem to play a more important part in their diet than before, and the NPS is beginning to adjust campground openings and even the total operation of Lake, Fishing Bridge, and Grant Village because of the small spawning streams there. When the original sites for visitor development in Yellowstone were chosen we knew far less about the grizzly than we do today. One such area, Fishing Bridge, at the outlet of the Yellowstone River from Yellowstone Lake, became a major development, with cabins, stores, and campgrounds, including one of the few full-service RV campgrounds in the National Park System. When the dump was closed and the bears moved into developed areas, Fishing Bridge, only 10 miles from the Trout Creek dump, suffered the worst. It had the highest degree of grizzly incidents, and so many bears were removed, mostly by killing, that it became known as a "population sink."[23] Fortunately, the decision had already been made to close Fishing Bridge because of its importance to all wildlife, and because another development, Lake, was only 2 miles away. The bear problem lent urgency to the closure.

The NPS had not reckoned with political pressure. Even though the NPS was adding even more development by establishing Grant Village at another spot on the lake, the closing of Fishing Bridge would remove the park attraction closest to the tourist town of Cody, Wyoming. That tourists would use Cody and the East Entrance to Yellowstone National Park, just to go by Fishing Bridge, seems a stretch, but Wyoming politicians have held up the removal of Fishing Bridge for years. Although many of the facilities at Fishing Bridge have been closed, the RV campground, a large store, and a small visitor center remain. The final irony came when further research showed the grizzlies utilizing not only the Fishing Bridge area for their fishing but also several spawning streams in the Grant Village area, picked for expansion as a replacement for Fishing Bridge. Delaying the opening of the campgrounds in Grant Village until after the spawning season has taken care of some of the problem, but few feel the problem will go away as long as the developments at Fishing Bridge, Lake, and Grant Village remain.

Human contact with the grizzly remains the most important consideration.[24] Although present policy is to spare bears that injure people in defense of their cubs or food, bears that become habituated to humans may be seen as a hazard necessitating removal.[25] Methods of securing food from animals, discussed above, become even more important for the grizzly. Fines are levied for leaving food out in park campgrounds and picnic areas, as the rangers know the lives of both the visitor and the bears may depend on it. Without exposure to the visitor's food, most of the grizzly's interest in the visitor is removed. One of the first two deaths by grizzlies in the National Park System occurred because grizzly bears were fed table scraps near a backcountry chalet in Glacier National Park in 1967, and a hiker made a camp near the feeding area.[26]

Reducing food odors by keeping a clean camp and never leaving behind garbage which will allow bears to associate campers with food are obvious points. Never surprising a grizzly on the trail is another, leading to the bizarre picture of hikers rattling rocks in tin cans or whistling loudly as they walk along. Park rangers run a surveillance of the location of grizzlies through hiker sightings and often close areas where the bears are found, especially if a bear is feeding on a carcass. The closure will last until the carcass is consumed and the bear moves on.

The ultimate goal in managing wildlife in the national parks would be no management at all; that is, to interfere with the wildlife as little as possible.[27] The difficulty is knowing at what point "leaving them alone" will lead to disaster. In a way, observing the mob scene around Old Faithful in midsummer at eruption does make the assumption that Yellowstone is "natural" appear pretty naive. However, all the manipulation of wildlife in the national parks in the past—the bear shows, predator control, removing grizzly bears—leads to the feeling the NPS can't do worse by just leaving them alone. No matter what the NPS does, the fate of the grizzly is ultimately going to be out of its hands. Only greater tolerance and support for the grizzly by those who live, work, and play in the area are going to insure survival.[28]

## Elk

The original slaughter of predators in Yellowstone was to improve the viability of one of the public's favorite animals: the North American elk, or wapiti. This succeeded so well that by as early as 1919 NPS officials were beginning to talk about too many elk and the destruction of rangeland in the northern part of the park. To correct this supposed overpopulation the NPS conducted a large-scale elk reduction program between 1935 and

*Elk in a meadow near a road often attract a crowd in Yellowstone National Park.*

1968, removing through live trapping and shooting a total of 26,241 elk.[29] In the winter of 1961–1962, with the backing of the Secretary of the Interior, 4,215 elk were killed by professional hunters with the aid of helicopters, as quickly and as humanely as possible.[30] The meat was given to the poor. The outcry was immediate and vociferous. Hunters who had perhaps wanted to shoot an elk for years and been unsuccessful were especially outraged. The NPS stood its ground for a second and much smaller hunt, then relied on rounding up and shipping the animals elsewhere to reduce the numbers within the park. This also involved the expense of building corrals and dehorning and vaccinating animals, and was eventually stopped also.

At the peak of the elk controversy a blue-ribbon committee of wildlife experts, headed by A. Starker Leopold, was chosen to study the elk situation. Its report has become a classic in national park management because it synthesizes a commonsense goal for park management: "A national park should present a vignette of primitive America."[31] In other words, we should try to reconstruct the landscape and its wildlife assemblage in approximately the same natural conditions as those found by Europeans when they first arrived on the scene. It gives direction and puts emphasis on preserving and enhancing a landscape where all living things have a place, rather than one which contains only those animals that some prefer seeing.

After three decades of studies the NPS feels that the northern range is in reasonable shape and there is no reason to reduce elk numbers.[32] All the elk's predators—wolves, mountain lions, grizzly and black bears—are back, which along with severe winters, should provide all the regulating influences needed for the elk. Finally, 70,000 acres of private land in the Gallatin Range north of Yellowstone has been purchased for the elk, a step toward reinstating winter range.[33] Detractors, however, still maintain that the NPS is simply reacting to a public which loves to see the animals and would decry the killing necessary to reduce the herd, and to hunters who love to see all the elk flow out of the park in the winter. The range, in the detractors' opinion, is still in terrible shape.[34] A final answer to this ongoing controversy that would satisfy everyone doesn't appear likely for some time to come.

## Bison

As mentioned in the beginning of this chapter, a small herd of bison in Yellowstone had escaped extinction in the 1800's. Not trusting the odds for survival, the NPS bought a few bison from private herds and used them to augment the herd in the park. These bison were managed like cattle from 1907 to 1936 and fed through 1952 at the "buffalo ranch" in the Lamar Valley of Yellowstone. From these semidomesticated beasts several hundred bison were raised and eventually turned loose to mix with the surviving herd.[35] The "unnaturalness" of this approach never occurred to rangers in the early 1900's, and they closed down the ranch only when it was obvious the bison could survive on their own. Numbers of bison grew until there were perceptions of overpopulation, especially after the predators were eliminated. This problem was met quietly by removing animals above a number considered reasonable for the environment. This program stopped in 1966. Then in the 1980's the number of bison increased,[36] and for several reasons (including severity of winters, and plowed roads) the animals started to move to lower ground in the winter.[37] Unfortunately, bison carry brucellosis, and though it has never been proven that it has been passed to domestic cattle, the state of Montana stopped the migration by passing out hunting permits for all the bison that left the park. Hunting the Yellowstone bison is not a very sporting proposition—you just walk up and shoot them—so the outrage of

*Mixing people and wildlife in the national parks makes them special, yet gives nightmares to rangers in Yellowstone and other parks where the bison is found, because of its size, unpredictability, and seeming harmlessness.*

animal rights activists and the general public was enormous.[38] The result was an end to the hunting, replaced by systematic slaughter by the Montana Department of Livestock. Winter residents and tourists are just as unhappy with this situation, where up to 83 animals are killed a day, with all the blood and gore that this represents.[39]

The winter of 1996–1997 proved to be the ultimate nightmare for the bison. Heavy rain around the first of the year saturated heavier than normal snowfall and created a thick ice layer which the bison could not penetrate.[40] Nearly two-thirds of the Yellowstone herd died, including over 1,000 which were either shot by the Montana Department of Livestock or captured and sent to be slaughtered by the NPS.[41] The public revulsion at the situation, compared by some to our original slaughter of bison in the 1800's, may force cooperation by the state of Montana in coming up with a solution. Tourism is, after all, as important to the state as its cattle, and up to now the bison has had to pay the full price for a bad situation.

The winter of 1997–1998 is unlikely to be as bad for the bison as the previous winter, because there are far fewer bison and the weather conditions are unlikely to be repeated. The bison that made it through the winter seem to be in good shape, delighting the visitor as usual. Whether the reduced numbers will separate the bison from visitor concentrations is doubtful, and the NPS continues to worry about injury and death to the visitor who approaches too close to the bison. The bison, lord of the range, goes wherever grass is to be found, whether it is in a busy campground or a hotel lawn.

## Trumpeter Swan

The trumpeter swan, North America's largest waterfowl, was once down to 35 birds in the conterminous United States, mostly in and near Yellowstone National Park.[42] Despite a recent setback, the freezing of the Henry's River southwest of the park boundary due to low irrigation flows, and subsequent starvation of the swans, the trumpeter is one of the few species that has been removed from the endangered species list. Part of the success has been a recognition that nesting swans and human traffic of any sort just don't mix. Curtailing fishing along parts of the Yellowstone River where the swans nest and putting up "do not approach" signs near certain lakes have been some of the methods used. Cooperation with private landowners along the Yellowstone River north of the park who have replaced mute swans with trumpeters on their ponds seems to have been successful also.[43] Nesting failures in 1997, however, and a census that revealed only 23 adult trumpeter swans in the park, show that vigilance in protecting the swans must not be reduced.[44]

## Fish

Fishing seems to be the last refuge of wildlife exploitation in the national parks. We have come a long way in Yellowstone, however, from unlimited catches and stocking "catchables" from a fish hatchery operated in the park. Yellowstone has perhaps had more problems with fishing than most parks, because a fishing license was unnecessary until recently (Yellowstone was a park before Montana, Wyoming, or Idaho were states) and the fishing is among the best in the country.

The recognition of the uniqueness of the Yellowstone River and the endangered status of the trumpeter swan and bald eagles led first to the protection of the streamside environment for nesting swans and then protection of the fish themselves so that eagles, pelicans, grizzly bears, and other animals could utilize them. The infamous Fishing Bridge over the Yellowstone River was the first to go. The bridge was once packed with anglers, and there was a flotilla of boats upstream, also utilizing this fishing Valhalla. Downstream, and elsewhere in the park, an angler must now read the regulations carefully, as some areas are permanently closed, some are periodically closed, and some are for fly fishing only.

The fact that nature can never be completely left alone as long as humans are around was underlined dramatically by the discovery of lake trout in Yellowstone Lake in the summer of 1994. The fish were undoubtedly illegally stocked, an act of vandalism which could have a monumental impact on park wildlife. If left unchecked the lake trout could wipe out the native cutthroat population, on which some 42 species of mammals and birds depend (the lake trout spends most of its life in deep water, out of the reach of predators).[45] The cutthroat is also the basis for a multimillion dollar sport fishing industry in Yellowstone, which could also be hurt by the invasion. Discovering the spawning beds of the lake trout and selective gillnetting are partial solutions to the lake trout invasion, part of an estimated $9 million control program which will be paid for by doubling the cost of park fishing licenses.[46]

## Cougar

Mountain lions were removed from Yellowstone along with the wolves, in the park's predator control program.[47] Because lions are secretive animals there is some doubt that they were exterminated; at any rate they are back in fair numbers now, which is no surprise considering the vast number of elk around, a veritable lion supermarket. Contact of visitors with the lions has been almost nonexistent in the past in the national parks, a pattern which seems to be changing dramatically. The NPS recently started a study of lion-human interaction in Yosemite National Park, where one lion reportedly slept in a busy campground, and another stalked a man walking his pet.[48] In Big Bend National Park a young mountain lion confronted a mother and her five-year-old on a popular park trail in 1990, leading to closure of the trail for a period, and increased research into lion behavior.[49] In the summer of 1997, a young boy's death in Rocky Mountain National Park was attributed to a mountain lion attack, the first in the National Park System.[50]

## Wolves

Until recently, the Greater Yellowstone Ecosystem was called one of the largest relatively intact temperate ecosystems in the world. The "relatively" refers to the fact that one of the major predators in the original system, the gray wolf, was gone, exterminated in the early years of this century under the predator control program discussed above. From time to time, a rumor would surface that a few wolves had been able to survive, then one was killed near the park and another captured on videotape in 1992. Whether these were escaped or abandoned pet wolves or dispersed from Canada, the fact was that if the Yellowstone visitor were to hear the howling of wolves in Yellowstone in the foreseeable future, there would have to be a reintroduction of several animals. This reintroduction was the focus of a virulent debate for at least a decade.

Some facts are unarguable. Wolves were once in Yellowstone. There are plenty of wolves in Alaska, Canada, and Minnesota that could be captured and released in the park. Most people, according to numerous polls, would like to see the wolf back in Yellowstone. Just as unarguably, most ranchers *don't* want the wolves back. Wolves will eat various farm animals, although the amount and impact are disputed. To counter this threat, two concessions were made: conservation organizations have created a fund to reimburse ranchers for any animals lost to wolf predation, and because the wolves are classed as nonessential experimental animals, individual wolves can be removed if they do prey on livestock. Ranchers, who felt their whole way of life was being threatened, were in no mood to compromise. Politicians in the states surrounding Yellowstone National Park, perhaps sensing the pro-cowboy bias of their constituency, have formed an almost solid block of opposition to reintroduction. Some of them made far-out statements on the bloodthirsty nature of wolves, familiar to all of us from fairy tales and movies, but unsupported by scientific research.[51]

The election of Bill Clinton in 1992 and the appointment of Bruce Babbitt as Secretary of the Interior lent support to the final push for reintroducing wolves into Yellowstone. There were environmental impact statements and interminable lawsuits seeking to block the reintroduction. Finally, on January 12, 1995, with school children and park employees lining the road, a caravan containing 15 wolves and accompanied by Babbitt and former Fish and Wildlife Director Mollie Beattie passed under the stone arch at the south entrance of the park on its way to temporary holding pens in Lamar Valley.[52] To the rangers and others who worked so hard to return the wolves to Yellowstone it must have seemed, after such an incredible uphill battle, a dream come true.

The wolves' first year was very successful, with the animals hunting and raising families as if they had never left the park. As of late October 1997, there were 85 wolves in the park, including 43 pups born in nine packs in the spring.[53] The program needed this original success, as funding has been cut, the animals have gotten into trouble with local ranchers, and in December 1997, a federal judge ruled that the wolf reintroduction program was illegal and ordered the wolves removed from the park.[54] Appeals will prevent the wolves' removal for some time to come, and the pups born in the park may not be affected.[55] All that appears certain is that the wolf reintroduction, like the health and survival of the grizzly and bison, is going to be news for the foreseeable future.


## SUMMARY

If fishing is someday phased out, we will have come full circle in wildlife management in the national parks, from total exploitation to total protection. Fishing without limit has already changed to sport fishing only and may eventually result in leaving the fishing to the birds and the bears. From total manipulation—killing predators, raising bison, and producing fish in hatcheries—we may one day move to an ecosystem where humans can observe and learn and perhaps feel humility in watching the wonders of the natural system unfold. The whole movement toward more natural parks and more natural park experiences will enhance the observation of wildlife. I'll leave it to John Muir, in words he penned after a visit to Yellowstone, to explain this obvious point:

> Nothing can be done well at a speed of forty miles a day. The multitude of mixed, novel impressions rapidly piled on one another make only a dreamy, bewildering, swirling blur, most of which is unrememberable. Far more time should be taken. Walk away quietly in any direction and taste the freedom of the mountaineer. Camp out among the grass and gentians of glacier meadows, in craggy garden nooks full of Nature's darlings. Climb the mountains and get their good tidings. Nature's peace will flow into you as sunshine flows into trees. The winds will blow their own freshness into you, and the storms their energy, while cares will drop off like autumn leaves. As age comes on, one source of enjoyment after another is closed, but Nature's sources never fail. Like a generous host, she offers her brimming cups in endless variety, served in a grand hall, the sky its ceiling, the mountains its walls, decorated with glorious paintings and enlivened with bands of music ever playing.[56]

# 8   Visitation

THE popularity of the national parks is overwhelming. In 1996 there were 265,796,163 visits to the National Park System, a number which has steadily increased since figures were first counted in the 1800's.[1] In 1916, when the National Park Service was founded, there were half a million visitors to the national parks, a figure that doubled in three years and has doubled again eight more times to the present figure.[2] Visitation growth shows no signs of stopping, and why should it? A majority of people in the United States still have not seen Yellowstone, or Yosemite Valley, or the Grand Canyon. Foreign visitors to the national parks, whose numbers have also been increasing, may someday include the enormous potential visitation from the developing two-thirds of the world.[3]

The increase in visitation to the national parks is more often associated with problems than benefits, but the benefits are there, too, starting with the economic value of national parks. Tourism is one of the world's largest industries,[4] and the National Park System is one of the world's greatest series of tourist attractions. This is no news to most Western states, where tourism may be the leading money earner in the state and where national parks are usually key attractions.[5]

"Ecotourism" is the word used to describe one of the fastest-growing parts of tourism.[6] One definition is: a nature travel experience that contributes to the conservation of the environment while maintaining and enhancing the integrity of its natural and cultural elements.[7] Ecotourism can also be defined as an ecologically benign form of tourism. It is often touted as the best hope for saving many beautiful, but threatened, parts of the earth.

117

Using tourism as a means of saving an area might have started with Yosemite and Yellowstone National Parks. It is not difficult to imagine what those areas would be like today if they were not protected as national parks. Tourism to the parks as we used to know it, however, no longer works. Tourism must exist in such a manner and with such numbers that it will not destroy what it is trying to save. Even in wealthy countries like the United States we usually need economic justification for saving an area, which means greater numbers of travelers and greater demands for development in the area. Ecotourism will only work if people behave in an environmentally restrained way.

Responsible behavior follows education, which is both an essential element and one of the greatest benefits of ecotourism. Beautiful places in the world have disappeared almost by default when no one cared. John Muir saw this over a hundred years ago when he founded the Sierra Club to get people into the mountains, where he knew they would become activists once they saw what they were about to lose.[8]

The most important reason for visiting national parks, however, is simple enjoyment. People love the national parks, and keeping them away, even in the face of overcrowding, should be a last resort. Rationing should begin when the natural environment starts to suffer and the NPS has done all it can do, from influencing human behavior to seeking the minimal development consistent with park enjoyment, to solve the problem.

## VISITOR NUMBERS IN THE NATIONAL PARKS

To say 265,796,163 people visit the parks each year tells us nothing about which parks are receiving the visits, what the people do when they get there, how long they stay, and ultimately, how much damage, if any, they might do. There is obviously far more impact from an individual who shows up in Yosemite Valley on the Fourth of July, pulling a huge trailer and spending the whole time in the most popular areas, than from the same individual walking down a little-used trail in the backcountry of Yosemite in October. The parks are used very unevenly, with certain parks used heavily all the time and some used hardly at all. Great Smoky Mountains National Park received 9,265,667 visitors in 1996, for example, while Kobuk Valley National Park in Alaska recorded an annual total of only 2,781, about an hour's worth for Great Smoky. The 10 units in the National Park System with the largest visitor totals account for 22 percent of all visits to the national parks. The 10 leading parks in visitor *days*, which

*A significant and rising percentage of visitors to the national parks come from overseas. These German tourists are posing for a picture on the Oak Flat Road (since converted to a trail) in Yosemite National Park.*

counts how long each individual stayed in the park, account for 43 percent of the total.[9]

Visitor use is also very uneven *within* the parks, especially the larger ones. Most of the visitors to the Grand Canyon, for example, go to the Grand Canyon Village on the South Rim. While there, a tiny percentage will take a hike on the Bright Angel Trail, which is still one of the most heavily used trails in the country. Lesser trails in the park get far less use than this, and the trail-less parts of the parks might never see a visitor from one year to the next.

Time of the year also has a lot to do with park visitation. Just under half of all visitors to the National Park System come during June, July, and August.[10] In some parks, particularly in Alaska, nearly all the visitors come during the summer. There has, however, been an increase in "off-season" visits as year-round schools increase, the retirement population increases, and people try to avoid summer crowding. Visiting during the summer months still takes advance planning and means putting up with extreme crowds. For twenty years I have been taking students to Yosemite National Park in early May, when the falls are booming, the weather is usually perfect, and crowding would only seem bad to a non-Californian.

Time of day has a lot to do with crowding. The sun is up in the summer while most of the visitors are still asleep. The sun is also up for hours after people start to leave the park, or settle into their campsites. Both times are among the most beautiful times of the day and the most active for wildlife.

## CARRYING CAPACITY

Overcrowding is a relative term. I remember a cartoon of two trappers on snowshoes overlooking a remote valley with a single cabin in it and one of them saying, "It's good to get back to civilization." Visitors from Tokyo, on the other hand, would be unable to comprehend our calling Yosemite overcrowded, with more open space around the valley than they might see in a lifetime at home. A tool used to establish parameters for the degree of crowding is "carrying capacity," a sustainable use level that does not cause environmental deterioration. This goal is met fairly easily in wilderness, but most parks also include roads, buildings, cars, and many people. Planning in the national parks accommodates use with an *acceptable* level of development. Ideally, the NPS will continue to reduce that development, even as the number of visitors increases; otherwise, visitation must either stabilize or come down. There are several ways to measure the impact that visitors have on the environment, with physical changes being the easiest to measure.

Soil erosion and vegetative changes are obvious to most visitors. As grass and trees disappear in popular areas and erosion gullies appear on hillsides, the number of visitors to those areas must be reduced, or the pattern of use must be changed. Pollution is another measurable quality, whether it is the amount of bacteria in water, sulfur dioxide in the air, litter on the landscape, or decibels of noise pollution. Ideally, the numbers of people and/or their impact are reduced until erosion, vegetation damage, or pollution lessens.

Much depends, however, on the perceived value of an area. More people and development would be tolerated in an ordinary lodgepole forest in Yellowstone than in the Old Faithful area, for example. Unfortunately, in the past, facilities were located as close as possible to the feature(s) people wanted to see. Old Faithful Inn is only a few hundred feet from Old Faithful Geyser, Bright Angel Lodge is on the rim of the Grand Canyon, and nearly all the hotels and lodges of Yosemite National Park are in Yosemite Valley. The NPS has tried for several decades to correct the situation, but once a facility is in place and heavily used, it is hard to move. After years of effort it looks as if at least some of the overnight accommodations in Yosemite Valley will be removed. The NPS has removed campgrounds from Old Faithful and Fishing Bridge. Unfortunately, day use usually fills the vacuum and the overall improvement may be slight.

Psychological carrying capacity is much harder to measure than observable physical changes. At what level do people consider there are just too many other people around for them to enjoy the national parks? Calculations must include not only the people currently using the area and the levels they would choose but also the people who do *not* visit the area because it is too crowded. Bedlam could exist twenty-four hours a day in Yosemite campgrounds in the 1960's, for example. The ordinary tourist would probably not have stayed around long. Today, the campground numbers in Yosemite are less than during the '60's, and the situation is much more tolerable.

## REDUCING IMPACT THROUGH INFLUENCING BEHAVIOR

In one of my old geology textbooks there was a photograph of an amazing sandstone tower called the Goblet.[11] It rose from a tiny base to a top several times larger than the base. Theoretically the number of people who could walk around and view that object was infinite. Then one person, or maybe a few, attached a chain and pulled it down with a vehicle.[12] This is an extreme case of the varying impacts of individuals according to their behavior, unfortunately replicated at the Eye of the Needle Arch in Montana in 1997. We're also aware of the one noisy generator which can spoil the ambience of an entire campground, the loud party next door to your cabin on the first night of a vacation you've been waiting for all year, and the film wrapper on a trail which upsets you far more than you would have thought. I once had a student who took his bongo drums into the wilderness because wilderness to him was "being able to do what I want to do," and took his Australian sheepdog into the country to chase cows, because "that is what they're bred to do." Such rationales demonstrate that there must be rules and regulations.

The NPS's basic rule for park visitors is to take only memories and leave only footprints. Even footprints are no longer acceptable in some areas. Staying on the trail in some desert or alpine areas is of the utmost importance. The actual regulations are so numerous that, more and more, there are only signs saying that the regulations are available at park headquarters or the visitor center, and that the visitor is responsible for knowing and following them. Unfortunately, as more people come to the parks

*Preserving this fragile high-mountain meadow in Rocky Mountain National Park from visitors' feet is done by sacrificing part of the meadow to asphalt, limiting the number of such paths, and forbidding off-trail use.*

expecting a pristine scene, we cannot help having an even greater number of regulations. This will also probably mean more police.

Rangers through the 1960's carried no guns, and most of them had no police training. A riot in Yosemite in 1970 helped change that, and park rangers now go through a police academy and train in a variety of weapons. Training is at the Federal Law Enforcement Training Center at Glynco, Georgia, lasts four hundred hours, and includes everything from communication skills to rape investigation to firearm techniques.[13] The usual crimes—rape, robbery, murder—all take place in the parks, and the rangers must be able to cope with them. There are also the crimes against nature with which the NPS is uniquely concerned and which might not even be crimes outside the parks.

When I was a ranger at Mount Rainier National Park in the late 1950's, one of my duties was to prevent picnicking in the flower fields of Paradise Valley. The NPS had closed a nearby picnic area to construct a new road, and people would appear with their lunches and nowhere to go. It helped me appreciate the almost apologetic tone you hear from rangers when they try to explain why you can't take part in what outside the parks would be a positive activity: walking off-trail, picking flowers, exercising your dog, going for a mountain bike ride, or having a picnic. Most of the people at Rainier understood why they could not picnic or pick flowers

*Cliff dwellings in Mesa Verde National Park, such as the Cliff Palace shown here, are especially vulnerable to damage by visitors. Preserving them entails opening only a few of them to the public, always having rangers present, and "hardening" the areas accessible to the visitor.*

there, once the reason for the rules was explained. Without such rules, the thousands of visitors to Paradise Valley each weekend would eventually have destroyed the flower fields they came to see.

Education seems to have made one of the basic problems of the national parks—littering—almost a thing of the past. It is no longer necessary to have a ranger nearby to tell a visitor not to throw down a candy wrapper; another visitor will quickly do so. I have walked hundreds of miles of backcountry trails in the national parks during the last few years without seeing a scrap of litter. The same thing is true of other antisocial acts, such as carving names on trees or rocks or defacing a sign.

Vandalism still exists, however, particularly if park regulations have changed. In Yosemite fires have always been part of the camping experience. They are still allowed, but during the summer, only from 5:00 P.M. to 10:00 P.M.[14] Air pollution in Yosemite Valley was not going to get better without what were, to some people, draconian measures. In Yellowstone you can now get a ticket for leaving your cooking gear on the camp table if you are not using it. Dissociating bears from humans' food is the only way they are going to be saved, according to some experts. Riding mountain bikes on the trails has never been legal in the national parks, but people buying the bikes and noticing the advertisements for the bikes

123

figure that bikes and trails go together. Some rock climbers feel it puts them in extreme danger not to drill holes for bolts, even with electric drills. And so on. Fortunately for the natural environment, some three-quarters of all vandalism is directed at facilities, rather than the environment.[15]

There is also the problem of rowdyism. People come to the park from the city and often feel a wonderful release, which unfortunately, sometimes, means drinking, partying, and noise until all hours. The solution is no different from what happens next door in the city: you ask the people to be quiet and nearly always they will. If not, you call the ranger. I take up to fifty people in my national parks course to Yosemite each spring, preceded by a little lecture about behavior that I started because of something that happened a couple of years ago. All students are on their own for camping arrangements, and one group of students put a keg of beer in a nearby creek, played their stereo loud, rode mountain bikes off-trail, and were too hung over to attend the field trip which I thought, naively, was the purpose of their visit.

The propensity toward litigation in the United States has definitely affected the national parks. National parks are not Disneylands, and people do fall off mountains, drown, get hit by lightning, or gored by bison. They often sue. A well-known case took place with the first known death from a grizzly bear in Yellowstone National Park. A camper, Henry Walker, was killed by a grizzly as he returned to his illegal camp near Old Faithful, where a grizzly was eating food Walker had left in camp.[16] His parents sued, claiming that since Walker was a hitchhiker he had not seen the literature handed out at the entrance station and was thus not adequately warned of the danger of bears. The NPS won that case and many like it, but the threat of lawsuits might still threaten the legality of risky pursuits like mountaineering in the national parks. It almost certainly will mean more rules and regulations.

## REDUCING IMPACT THROUGH
## TRANSPORTATION CHANGES

The more development you have, the more impact you will have, often making the number of people and their behavior of secondary importance. Converting a park from overnight to day use, for example, frees an enormous amount of land from hotels, campgrounds, and visitor services. Switching from individual cars to buses and from buses to trains also has the potential of allowing the most people to enjoy the parks with the least impact. Overall, I feel that what we do with transportation has more to do with sustaining the quality of our national parks than almost any other issue.

## Auto Travel

We are a nation of car users, with the vast majority of visitors to the national parks arriving by automobile. In Yellowstone, for example, 97 percent of its visitors come by car.[17] Trying to cure the national park overcrowding problem by shifting from private to public transportation is laudable, but realistically, improving the use and design of existing park roads may pay greater dividends in the years ahead. Saying we enjoy the national parks and want to protect them is based largely, for most people, on visits they have made to the parks by automobile.

The importance of experiencing a road system may seem incongruous to many park visitors, but the scenic quality of park roads allows the experience to be one of appreciation and wonder. For example, the road along the South Rim of the Grand Canyon winds into the sheltering forest and then bursts out into the open sky with the chasm below and nothing but a retaining wall between the car and what seems to be infinity. In another case, the approach to Jenny Lake from the northeast offers impressive views of the Cathedral Group of the Teton Range, which seems to increase in size as the lake is approached, until the mountains appear to hang directly overhead at an incredible height. The road above the visitor center in Arches National Park wanders along the front of a red-faced cliff until it reaches the top and the senses are assaulted with rolling rimrock country pocketed with buttes and mesas as far as the eye can see. Trail Ridge Road in Rocky Mountain National Park carries the visitor from the deep forest up into the alpine tundra, reminiscent of the summer Arctic. The road seems to wander aimlessly, following nature's curves and contours, over a bleak but exciting landscape with views into deep canyons on one side and onto mountaintops on the other. Upon entering a park, visitors may not be aware of the unique characteristics of the roadway, but they will have a pervasive feeling of closeness, comfort, or contrast. It is these qualities that make park roads beautiful.

Park-type roads can be described as roads which try to maintain a balance between safe, comfortable travel and closeness to the natural environment. Commercial concessions, accommodations, and services are severely limited along the roadside. No advertising signs are allowed. There are few telephone or power lines and these are screened wherever possible. The highways are designed with aesthetic sensitivity to the landscape. Attention is given to minimizing cut and fill, and there are a great number of scenic turnouts, trailheads, and picnic areas.

The most exceptional thing about park-type roads, however, is that they are roads in the wilderness. Beyond the shoulder of the road the landscape is natural. Outside the national parks there are either dedicated wilderness areas, in which case there are no roads, or inhabited landscapes with buildings, cutover land, and commercial development. There are obviously exceptions to this, but as the years go by, the exceptions become fewer. Viewing a totally natural scene from the auto, most motorists are intuitively aware that they are seeing a very different landscape than that with which they are familiar.

Unfortunately, national park roads are increasingly crowded, some extremely so. Not that crowded roads are rare in the United States—the commuting public twice daily confronts worse conditions than anything they are likely to find in the parks—but a paradox does occur. Consider a family driving to Yellowstone from Chicago, for example, going through increasingly depopulated areas at a high rate of speed, until they hit Yellowstone. The traffic may be backed up at the gateway, and when they get inside they may find a real traffic jam. Such visitors will feel the contradiction between the surrounding wilderness and the jammed roadway and will resent rather than appreciate this type of road.

## Park Road Overcrowding

The quality of park visits that I described at the start of this section was due to the juxtaposition of great scenery and park-type roads. Like a backpacking trip, which can go from heaven to hell with a cold rain, however, park-type roads can be a pain with heavy traffic. Park roads wind, rise, fall, and twist according to the terrain, in contrast to nonpark roads that are straight and flat in order to obtain greater speed, safety, and capacity. A winding road slows all traffic, limits passing, and tends to back cars up behind slower vehicles. The composite effect is crowding. Unfortunately, there are other factors that limit the capacity of these roads even more.

Park roads are similar to city streets where stores and shops line the streets and cars are continually pulling into and out of parking places and drives, thus markedly slowing traffic in the outer lane. In the parks, along any given stretch of roadway there are many reasons to stop: scenic turnouts, historical areas, fishing access, and the big deterrent to smooth traffic flow, wildlife. The NPS has anticipated this problem to some extent by the placement of scenic turnouts. With wildlife, however, there is no way to predict just where an animal will show up and lead to a screeching of brakes.

The increasing numbers of recreational vehicles, house trailers, tent trailers, and pickup campers are adding disproportionately to traffic congestion in the parks. They generally move slower than regular cars because they are less maneuverable on winding or narrow roads or on a grade. Being larger, they are also harder to pass than the average vehicle. It has been estimated that in mountainous terrain a recreational vehicle will take up the same amount of space as eight passenger cars.[18] To help counter this, few commercial trucks jam park highways, because commercial vehicles, other than those serving the parks, are banned.

## Public Transportation

Getting people out of their cars and into buses is the logical way to cut down on the number of vehicles, reduce parking areas, and increase both the education of the visitor and protection of the park. The problems are the same as with public transportation anywhere in the country: it is expensive and the public doesn't switch willingly. But it can work, as shown by Yosemite.

The events leading to the creation of the Yosemite Valley shuttle service were mentioned in the preface: intolerable crowding and the turning of one of the most beautiful valleys in the world into a parking lot. The move by the NPS and the park concessioner was a bold one—close the upper end of Yosemite Valley to cars, design and build attractive and interesting buses, and pay for it with taxes on souvenirs sold in valley stores. As people readily take buses only when they are free, are attractive, operate on an exact schedule, and go places inaccessible by cars, these buses met all four requirements. They have been highly successful, and the possibility of an auto-free valley, discussed later in the case study on Yosemite, seems attainable in the not-distant future. The case studies on Denali, Grand Canyon, and Yellowstone also treat the inevitable, but difficult, switch to public transportation.

## REDUCING IMPACT THROUGH PRICING

It has been decades since the parks have been considered overpriced. On the contrary, the experts have looked at overcrowding, particularly in conjunction with the dire financial straits the parks have always been in, and said: "Raise the entrance fees and solve both problems at once." Attempts at raising fees, however, have run against a stonewall of opposition from every travel or age-related interest group. Only recently was *any* charge made for seniors to visit the national parks; there is now a one-time fee of only $10. Overall fee raises are finally happening in a few parks, as will be discussed in Chapter 11. Regardless of whether fees will be raised or not, they represent such a tiny percentage of the visitor's expenditures on a trip to the parks that they would probably have little effect on limiting overcrowding. Reports on visitation for the summer of 1997 show an increase in visitation, despite higher fees.[19]

## REDUCING IMPACT THROUGH RATIONING

The simplest way to prevent overcrowding is simply to cut down on the number of people in an area, but it is the solution the NPS has been the most reluctant to use. The national parks depend in a real sense on the goodwill of the public. Turning people away at park entrances is not the way to enhance that goodwill. Still, there comes a time when there is no other choice.

No one was surprised when Yosemite became the first national park to say that it was going to close the park after a certain number of people entered. The park closed for the first time in history, due to congestion, May 22, 1993.[20] It lasted three hours and 750 vehicles were turned away.[21] Usually, however, the threat of closing the park prevents it from happening. Who wants to go to a park that crowded, especially when you may not be able to get in anyway? The specter of rationing, which is bound to get more attention as the years go by and the number of visitors goes up, will be self-limiting to a degree. Just as the visitors don't come when they are afraid they won't get in, they will also, it is reasonable to hope, reschedule the trip for a less crowded time or go to a less crowded park.

## SUMMARY

I keep hoping that someday we will value the national parks as the true irreplaceable treasures they are, in deed as well as words. This will mean spending money to take care of them properly, and it will also mean restraint. The NPS can do everything in its power to lessen the impact of people on the national parks, including building major public transportation systems, but eventually the public will have to quit loving the parks quite so much.

# 9   Recreational Land Use

NATIONAL parks, containing some of the most beautiful and interesting landscapes in America, naturally lend themselves to outdoor recreation. One has only to think of rafting through the Grand Canyon, climbing Mount Rainier, or cross-country skiing in Yellowstone to recognize the high-quality recreational resources available in the parks. In addition, with large concentrations of people during the tourist season, concessioners know that whatever form of recreation they offer, from bike rentals to horseback riding, will do well. On the other hand, how much sense does it make to offer forms of outdoor recreation that are easily available outside the parks, while the parks are suffering from overcrowding? The debate over recreational land use is crucial in attempting to provide a high-quality sustainable landscape in the national parks.

People tend to be very protective about their favorite sport, feeling that while off-road vehicles, for example, certainly should not be allowed in the national park backcountry, mountain bikes would fit in perfectly. It must be hard for park rangers to tell visitors that their favorite sport, healthy and perfectly acceptable outside the parks, is not acceptable here, or it used to be all right, but isn't anymore. In the early days almost anything that would attract people to the park was not only allowed, but encouraged. Hot springs were tapped for a swimming pool in Yellowstone, a ski lift was built in Rocky Mountain National Park, and a small golf course was provided in Yosemite Valley. Concessioners offered a wide variety of entertainment at their hotels. The policy of the NPS for most of its early history reflected the Mather-Albright policy that the main threat

*A perfect recipe for a national park: spaciousness, wilderness, and great beauty. The southern portion of Sequoia National Park near New Army Pass.*

faced by outstanding areas was simply not being a park. Anything that was done to make park visitors happy, increase their numbers, and lead to the establishment of more parks was the preservation goal with the largest chance of success.

Eventually, recreational activities that had little direct relationship to the uniqueness of the park, and that could cause damage to the landscape, were removed. The decision on what to keep and what to remove can be found in the following guideline:

> The Service encourages those recreational uses which draw their meaning from association with, and direct relation to, park resources, and which are consistent with the protection of such resources.[1]

This is a good general statement, but what about something that may not fit that definition, but which is popular and does very little harm to the environment, such as swimming pools at hotels? That is in the regulations, too.

> Certain outdoor recreational activities which are not necessarily dependent upon park resources for their realization, and which do not constitute traditional or customary park uses, may be permitted when they do not:
> —interfere with normal park usage;
> —constitute a consumptive form of use;

130

—have an undesirable impact on park resources;

—compromise the historic or natural scene; or

—present a danger to the public welfare and safety, including safety of the participants.[2]

This opens the door to just about anything, but it also allows the criticism of almost anything. At what point does an "undesirable impact on park resources" take place? This question is at the heart of the preservation/use conflict. The following discussion illustrates the problems the NPS has in balancing this conflict in virtually every form of outdoor recreation found in the national parks.

## RECREATIONAL TRAVEL

The primary use of the national parks is *sight-seeing*, and the primary method is by driving. Unfortunately, much of the deterioration of the natural landscape is caused by automobiles, discussed in other sections of this book. In some parks cars have been, or someday will be, banned and replaced by buses or rail. For most of the parks, however, the automobile will still be the overwhelming choice for sight-seeing for years to come. People also walk, bike, sail, run rivers, and climb mountains with the overall goal of seeing the park.

### Walking, Hiking

A scene that has stuck in my memory through the years is in an environmental film where a speaker at a hearing was defending a proposed highway in the redwoods. It was needed, he said, to see the scenery: "People have to have roads. They won't walk, they won't hike; that's why they build big parking lots in front of all the supermarkets." I wonder what he would think if he walked up the trail in Yosemite Park to Vernal Falls. On a fine summer day the gaps between individuals walking the 1.6-mile round-trip to the falls are only a few feet wide. Day walks to popular sights in the national parks are almost as popular as some of the roads.

Locating, constructing, signing, policing, maintaining, and preserving trails have a strong claim on money and labor in the national parks, although trails will probably never receive more than a fraction of the attention given to roads. An endemic shortage of funds has hurt trails in the parks, and the "completing" of trail systems in line with increasing visitation is years in the future. Fortunately, national parks don't have to ac-

*The major form of outdoor recreation in the national parks, besides sight-seeing by car, is simple walking. The West Rim Trail in Zion National Park serves as a moderate day hike or as an extended backpack trip into the wilderness.*

cept the brunt of the increasing popularity of hiking in this country. Trails are constantly being built, especially those in natural areas close to our cities. There is also the National Trails System, which has 800 trails totaling 9,000 miles in length, found in every state in the union.[3] The trails are mostly located on federal lands, but some are on state, local, or even private lands. Of the 19 long-distance trails in the country, the NPS administers 14 of them, including the famous Pacific Crest Trail and Appalachian Trail.

As more and more people get into hiking or backpacking, the boundaries for a true wilderness experience recede. Some try to reclaim that experience by venturing off-trail. The desire is laudatory, unless too many people do it (which in a way makes it an oxymoron: too many people trying to avoid too many people). The dilemma is that the incidence of damaged landscapes from off-trail experiences is proportional to the increase in the need for that experience. The admonition "stay on the trail" is heard most frequently in areas close to the trailhead in highly popular backcountry areas. Potential damage from off-trail use depends on the terrain and the availability of trails. On the high desert plateaus of the Colorado Plateau, for example, cryptobiotic soils dictate real expertise in off-trail hiking, while in many parts of Alaska, trails are almost nonexistent and off-trail use is standard.

## Bicycling

Bicycling is an alternate form of transportation on many park roads, as well as being one of the most rapidly increasing forms of outdoor recreation. A problem is that bikes travel slower than cars, making them dangerous on many roads, and faster than pedestrians, making them dangerous on paths. Separate bike paths are the best solution, but they are expensive, they conflict with natural areas just as auto roads do, and pedestrians use them anyway. The future seems to lie with replacement of cars by bikes in areas like Yosemite. It's hard to imagine a level of bicycle tourism where the ordinary roads used by automobiles wouldn't suffice when bicycles replace autos. Also, in recognition of the popularity of bicycling, new highways in the national parks are often built with wide shoulders, making cycling in parks like Grand Teton National Park very popular.

Mountain biking has caused real problems on public lands because of its potential for causing soil erosion and because of conflicts with other users of the land, especially hikers. Mountain bikes have not proven to be that much of a problem in the national parks, however, because the parks had a "no bikes on trails" rule before mountain bikes became popular. Bicycles are vehicles and vehicles are allowed only on roads, or bike paths, provided for them. From time to time attempts at opening the trails of the national parks to mountain bikes are made, often in conjunction with opening the National Wilderness Preservation System to bikes also. Such attempts have always failed because mountain bikers themselves are often strong environmentalists.

## Horseback Riding

Horses yield yet another "closer to nature" alternative to vehicles, yet are just as problem-prone as bicycles. Horses are accepted in the wilderness and on dirt paths, and they move at a speed more akin to walkers. Yet they do impact trails, by pounding and despoiling them, and many walkers are not comfortable sharing trails with them. Consequently, more and more trails in the National Park System sport "foot traffic only" signs.

## Adventure Travel

"Adventure travel" can be defined as going to places difficult to reach by reason of remoteness, harshness of weather, difficulty of terrain, or danger. Travel to the polar regions or the great mountains of the world comes to mind, or to countries with unstable political situations. Many of our national parks, particularly those in Alaska, have areas which easily entail some adventure in reaching them. I doubt if many people climb McKinley, raft the Grand Canyon, or visit Lechuguilla Caves without feeling that they have definitely left the beaten path. Travel which is totally blasé to some can also be the adventure of a lifetime to many.

Difficulties because of the climate, or at least the weather, are definitely part of adventure travel. There is no Antarctica or Saharan Desert in the United States, with even the Alaskan parks being relatively benign during the normal tourist season. What we used to call stupidity, however, like going to Death Valley in midsummmer or the Brooks Range in Alaska in midwinter, is being duplicated by a small but growing number every year. I can think of two examples. When I walked to the bottom of the Grand Canyon a few years ago, with the temperature at 110°F at the bottom of the canyon, the Bright Angel Trail was positively crowded. In 1983, on a ski trip to Yosemite in midwinter, I walked through the snow up to the base of the Lower Yosemite Falls at midnight to see the "moonbow." There were at least a dozen people there.

People are going to the park during the off-season, and are going to remote hard-to-reach places like most of the Alaskan parks in growing numbers. It makes sense. A major drawback in visiting the national parks today is crowding, which can be avoided by going to the remote parks or going off-season. Besides, new equipment makes off-season travel much less of a task than it used to be. If a person has the money, making a trip to a remote part of Gates of the Arctic National Park can be comfortable and safe. Difficulty of terrain is the heart and soul of adventure travel. There are roads into the alpine country, like Trail Ridge Road in Rocky Mountain National Park, or to the bottom of a canyon in Zion National Park, but to visit many of the most spectacular parts of the national parks you are going to have to walk, or climb, or run rapids.

## Air Travel

Air travel can represent the ultimate in sight-seeing, but it can also be disruptive. It is surprising that the current debate on overflights didn't happen years ago. Taking flights to see the parks—Mount Rainier, Yellowstone, Grand Tetons, Canyonlands, the Grand Canyon—is something I have been doing for years to get the best possible view of the geography of the parks. Canyonlands, for example, is unbelievable from the air. Some parks in Alaska can only be reached from the air. There are few laws restricting overflights, even over wilderness areas, only the landing of aircraft. Overflights became a problem only after the explosive increase in the popularity of flying over the Grand Canyon in the 1980's. The debate, now found mostly at Canyonlands, Hawaiian Volcanoes, and Rocky Mountain National Parks, will probably intensify in the years ahead.[4]

Hang gliding, parasailing, and skydiving are air-oriented recreational activities which came out of nowhere to become highly popular. Yosemite, with some of the sheerest and tallest walls in the world, has felt the brunt of this new airborne activity. Being able to drive to the tops of some of the walls and be picked up in Yosemite Valley below has added to the popularity. The first hang gliders took off from Glacier Point in the 1960's and immediately caused a sensation on the valley floor. The park service first banned the flights as inappropriate and disruptive, and then reconsidered. They are now stringently regulated in number and required expertise, and takeoffs must be completed by 8:30 A.M.[5]

Parasailing, or its relative skydiving, also received much of its notoriety from the cliffs of Yosemite Valley. El Capitan is one of the two or three highest sheer walls in the world and is a natural for parasailing or skydiving. The first person to go off the top of "El Cap" did so on skis, to get well out from the face. The NPS agonized over this one for a while. It was definitely dangerous, and if it became popular, as even the most outlandish sports have a way of doing, the NPS would be faced with a crowd builder of significant proportions. It was definitely tied to park resources, however, and the NPS has always had a problem saying no to recreational activities. In time various skydiving/parasailing organizations withdrew their support for the El Capitan dive, and the NPS found an ecological reason to bar the activity—the harassing of an endangered species, the peregrine falcon, by the bodies sailing by.

## OUTDOOR LIVING

Camping, picnicking, and wilderness travel are all complete and proper uses of national parks and are discussed separately elsewhere in the book. There are definitely limits to camping, however. Camping takes up space and, with the arrival of travel trailers and campers, is often no more compatible with the landscape than buildings. There have been no new camp-grounds built in the National Park System in years except as replacements for those which have been closed. I must admit to a strong prejudice to-ward this form of outdoor recreation, however, as some of my fondest memories of the national parks have come in the "campgrounds I have known": the Manti La Sal Mountains and the slope down to the Colorado River under a full moon, seen out the opened rear end of my pickup shell in Arches National Park; a herd of elk on the hillside back of my camp in Yellowstone as I sat in front of a campfire; Yosemite Falls seen through the window of my tent on a balmy May afternoon; and listening to the rain on my tent as I lay snug in my sleeping bag after a hard but beautiful day backpacking. The list is endless.

## WATER-ORIENTED RECREATION

When the Outdoor Recreation Resources Review Commission completed its monumental study of outdoor recreation in 1962, it pointed out the ex-treme importance of water in recreation: "Most people seeking outdoor recreation want water—to sit by, to swim and to fish in, to ski across, to dive under, and to run their boats over."[6] The cleaning up of polluted waters and the preservation of wild rivers were important points in its recommendations. This popularity also indicates why various forms of water-based recreation are not allowed in park waters. Motorboats and people water skiing are not what you want to see as you walk, or drive, or camp, or picnic, or climb near a mountain lake.

### Boating

Yellowstone Lake furnishes a good example of the difficulties of remov-ing motorboats from an area where they have become established. In the late 1950's it was clear that powerboats in the southeastern arms of Yellow-stone Lake were disturbing nesting gulls and other wildlife, yet when the NPS proposed closing the three southern arms, boating clubs and indi-viduals in the surrounding states fervently objected.[7] While 110 square miles of the lake would still be open to motors, the 29 square miles closed were admittedly the most interesting. The boaters raised the cry of elitism, frequently heard any time motors or development is kept from an area because of wilderness preservation. The closure was upheld—currently only hand-propelled craft are allowed in the three southernmost arms of

Yellowstone Lake—but a new marina was built in one of the most beautiful sections of the lake, Bridge Bay, seemingly to mollify the boaters.

Nearby Grand Teton National Park still has motorboating and water skiing on Jackson Lake, and a hiker transport service on Jenny Lake. Other lakes in the park can only be used by hand-propelled craft. Canoes, kayaks, rowboats, and sailboats are only a problem when the numbers become very high. A relative new problem concerns personal watercraft (jet skis), which have brought the noise and disruption of motorcycles and snowmobiles to lakes and streams. On Jackson Lake in 1997 I followed the Hermitage Point Trail to a beautiful spot on the lake, with a sandy beach and spectacular views of the Tetons, and got ready to eat my lunch. The whine of a jet boat dominated the environment even before it came into view. The time I sat on the beach, shortened by the noise, was dominated by this intrusion. The rider might be having a wonderful time, but I thought of all the people I had passed on the trail and how their rights to a serene natural environment were being trampled. The watercraft was perfectly legal on Jackson Lake, but several national parks have banned them, including Everglades, Dry Tortugas, Virgin Islands, and Yellowstone, and several others are considering bans.[8] Besides the noise and safety problems, most jet skis emit smog-generating pollutants and discharge unburned fuel in the water.

River running started as a form of transportation, used to visit inaccessible canyons in the national parks, and grew to become a popular sport. On my first trip through Cataract Canyon in Canyonlands National Park in 1955 we used a surplus Air Force life raft, and in the Grand Canyon a few years later we used U.S. Army Corps of Engineers floating bridge pontoons. Now there are sophisticated, self-bailing rafts and an increasing number of boaters who do nothing else but run rivers. Not only has the number of recreational boaters increased exponentially, but every park with good white-water rafting has concessioners specializing in it, some of them multimillion dollar operations. River running certainly fits all the criteria for recreational use in the national parks; the only problem is how to control it. Float trips in the Grand Canyon, discussed earlier, illustrate how controls can work.

## Swimming

The national parks, with all their seashores, lakeshores, and rivers, are outstanding locations for swimming. It is the simplest of sports, with the

*Two methods of enjoying Glacier Bay National Park in Alaska: by cruise ship or by kayak, which was used by the campers.*

*River running doesn't have to be strenuous: a tranquil moment on a float trip through Utah's Glen Canyon in 1959.*

simplest of equipment. Those who cannot swim can wade and play in the water, which is what swimming is mostly about anyway. The drawbacks concern safety—along with car accidents, drowning is a leading cause of death in the national parks—and occasionally, harm to the environment. Yellowstone is one area where the potential for both danger and damage is great, with the almost irresistible lure of hot springs and spring-warmed rivers, combined with the beauty of the park's thousands of thermal features. Nineteen visitors have been killed in the hot springs of the park.[9] Presently, the NPS at Yellowstone allows the use of only one thermal area for bathing, where hot springs enter the Gardner River not far below park headquarters.

The major problem with water and safety is not in hot springs but in rushing waters. Mountain streams can be treacherous, and even those who know exactly what they are doing run a risk. In Yosemite they have signs above both Nevada (594 feet) and Vernal (317 feet) Falls warning against swimming in swift waters above the falls. This seems an unnecessary admonition until you read of someone getting swept over the falls, as happened in the summer of 1997, and several times in the past.

Swimming in pools seems to add nothing to the natural enjoyment of national park features, but neither does it consume much space nor cause an increase in visitation to the parks. In the NPS's studies of Yosemite, swimming pools seemed an obvious target for removing unnecessary developments in Yosemite Valley, such as the pools at the Ahwahnee Hotel, Curry Village, and Yosemite Lodge. The swimming pools had strong support, however, particularly among people who came to the park with small or teenaged children, and the pools were allowed to remain.[10]

## Scuba Diving

Channel Island, Dry Tortugas, and Biscayne National Parks (all upgraded from national monuments and enlarged) illustrate our increased interest in underwater areas. The majority of the acreage in all these parks is water—all but 39.28 acres in Dry Tortugas and all but 4,373 acres in Biscayne.[11] Scuba diving shares the tactile pleasures of water with swimming but also requires considerably more expertise and equipment. The interest in scuba diving has increased in recent years, and protection of underwater landscapes is becoming an important part of the national park environmental agenda.

## SNOW-ORIENTED RECREATION

Snow play is the most important single form of snow-based outdoor recreation. Other than perhaps a sled, nothing is required to participate and no expertise is required. Keeping roads and parking areas open to the visitor is the major requirement for the NPS. Skiing, however, is also an important goal for visitors, and here the level of involvement for both visitor and the NPS is considerable. In the national parks, only Yosemite National Park is involved with fixed skier moving equipment. The Hidden Valley ski area in Rocky Mountain National Park was closed recently. There are no signs that Badger Pass ski area in Yosemite will close, as the winter-use road and parking lot are increasingly used by cross-country skiers. Cross-country skiing fits well into the national parks. It gives the best possible look at the natural scene within the parks during winter and has little impact on the environment. The use of an area by cross-country skiers also furnishes the best defense against snowmobiles, which may have an immense impact on the environment.

The breaking of "winter's silence" is perhaps the main criticism of snowmobiling. Many of the northern or mountain national parks are closed during the winter months, where the park can heal for half a year or more. In a place like Yellowstone, where many animals hibernate, this is especially important. The silence is no longer there. West Yellowstone, the primary entrance into the park for winter recreation, touts itself as the "snowmobile capital of the world." The roads into the park are flat, the hot springs add a note of warmth and interest to the wintry landscape, and the bison and elk are still there. The bison have also found that walking down the road that has been plowed for the snowmobiles is easier than plunging through the snow, and they coexist with the noisy machines. The recreational use of Yellowstone National Park during the winter season has gone from nearly zero to 141,510 visitors since the development of the snowmobile and the increased popularity of cross-country skiing.[12]

The reaction of the NPS to the onslaught of winter use in Yellowstone has been to haul in winterized trailers to serve as warming huts, provide vault toilets as restrooms, and keep open overnight accommodations at Old Faithful. Several ski trails and snowmobile trails in nonwilderness areas are groomed, as are all park roads except Tower Junction to Canyon (avalanche danger) and the Mammoth to Cooke City road that is kept open to auto traffic in winter.[13] Assessments have been made of the amount of damage done to animals in the park, and the amounts of air pollution attributed to snowmobiles. According to one study, the 1,239 snowmobiles entering the park in February 1995 produced fumes equal to those emitted by all the cars entering Yellowstone in a year.[14] The NPS has agreed to do an environmental impact statement on winter use of Yellowstone starting in 1998.[15]

## WILDLIFE-ORIENTED RECREATION

The movement in this country from exploiting wildlife to simply observing it has been steady and might someday, perhaps, be complete. Hunting is illegal in the National Park System, with the exception of Grand Teton National Park and the national preserves. There are good reasons for allowing hunting to continue in this country, but asking that less than 5 percent of America be kept free from high-powered rifles and the killing of animals seems reasonable. I lived in Bozeman, Montana, for a number of years, and during the hunting season you ventured into the mountains at the risk of your own life. I was thankful that Yellowstone National Park was only a short distance away.

Is fishing any more legitimate in the national parks than hunting? As we have moved in the parks from releasing hatchery-bred fish for the bait angler to barbless or catch-and-release fly fishing, we have almost reached the stage of a pure sport.[16] People fishing in the park today have to be conversant with the regulations. They even have to know their park geography. For reasons of conflicts with animals, disturbance of thermal areas, and impact on the natural environment, many areas are closed permanently or seasonally. Bait fishing is illegal (except when done by children in certain areas), several streams are catch-and-release only, and limits and size and types of fish are regulated.

I feel someday we will make the transition from taking the fish to simply enjoying them. Fishing Bridge in Yellowstone Park, across the Yellowstone River near its outlet from Yellowstone Lake, was once just that: a bridge on which you stood to fish. It was fun. Fish were caught, and with the mob on the bridge, the tangling of lines could be hilarious. You can no longer fish there, but it's one of the best places in the park to watch fish. The big lunkers lie there, waiting for food that floats in from the lake. Watching a bald eagle lift a large trout from a stream, which often happens, should make anglers forget the loss of their own caught fish.

## MOUNTAINEERING

Mountaineering could easily be discussed under recreational travel, as traversing and exploring the landscape to reach some lofty summit is the goal of many climbers. Simply reaching a summit is still important, but how it is done, particularly in rock climbing, has spawned a whole new field of recreation. The National Park System contains the most impressive mountains in America, in size and in challenge. Mount McKinley stands at the top of the list, and all fourteen of the highest peaks in the United States are in national parks. Mount Rainier is the most impressive of the great volcanoes in the Cascades of the Pacific Northwest, and Mount Whitney, in Sequoia National Park, is the highest of the Sierras. The Teton Range in Grand Teton National Park is probably the most spectacular range in the conterminous United States. The immense cliffs in Yosemite National Park made it one of the most sought-after goals of climbers anywhere, while some maintain that Joshua Tree National Park is the most popular climbing area in the world.[17] Mountain climbing is an important, and legitimate, recreational pursuit in nearly all the large national parks.

Environmental problems relating to mountaineering are relatively minor in most parks because of the small numbers involved. While as many as a thousand people a year climb Mount McKinley, an enormous number for a mountain as tall and difficult as McKinley, this represents only a fraction of the half-million people who visit Denali National Park each year. The same is true of Grand Teton, Rocky Mountain, and Mount Rainier National Parks. On the other hand, where the number of climbers is high, such as in Joshua Tree National Park, vegetation is trampled, archaeological sites are disturbed, social trails are established, bolts are placed in the rocks with noticeable slings hanging from them, chalk used to keep hands from slipping discolors the rocks, and trash is left behind. Climbing groups have organized extensive clean-ups, however, and in Joshua Tree even paid for the installation of three outhouses at popular climbing areas, surely a first for recreational users of the national parks.

The major problems relating to mountaineering have to do with safety. Mountaineering is one of the most dangerous of all forms of recreation. In the past, before the increased popularity of climbing, the NPS exercised tight control over mountaineering on major peaks such as Mount Rainier and the Grand Teton. I climbed in the Teton Range during the early 1950's, when you had to convince the NPS that you were experienced and had good equipment in order to obtain a climbing permit. An itinerary was required for each climb, and solo climbing was prohibited. Now, in the Teton Range, you just go ahead and climb; even registration is optional. The reason is potential litigation. By "approving" people for a climb the NPS

*Mountain climbing in the national parks ranges from a long hike by trail to the top of Mount Whitney, seen in the distance from the top of Mount Langley, to some of the most difficult rock climbing in the world in Joshua Tree or Yosemite National Parks.*

also took responsibility for them. Regulations, however, vary from park to park, including a "mountaineering fee" for Mount Rainier and Denali National Parks.

In May 1992, eleven people were killed on Mount McKinley, topping the previous record years of eight for 1967 and 1980.[18] The NPS in Denali National Park, spending a disproportionate amount of its resources on rescues, $607 average per climber in 1992, placed a $150 fee on each climber. The first year of the program, 1994, $160,000 was raised, which was spent on mountaineering-related items: rescue gear, radios, more climbing rangers stationed on McKinley, safety brochures in seven languages, and a multilingual phone system. Out of 1,200 climbers on the mountain in 1994, only twelve verbal complaints were received, according to the NPS.[19]

A number of problems have resulted from the increased popularity of rock climbing, especially in the climbing Mecca of Joshua Tree National

*The NPS has tried to solve a conflict between rock climbers and Indians, who consider Devils Tower (National Monument) in Wyoming a sacred mountain, by asking climbers for a voluntary ban on their activities during one month a year.*

Park, where approximately 37 percent of the visitors are climbers.[20] The biggest controversy between the climbing community and the NPS concerns bolting. To increase the safety of "extreme" climbing as it is practiced today, climbers drill holes in the rocks and affix permanent bolts. When the NPS first banned electric drills in the 1980's there was an outcry, which quickly disappeared. New regulations, however, ban all bolts in the wilderness, no matter how they are put it. The NPS claims safety dictates not depending on "permanent" bolts anyway, while climbers maintain this would put much of Joshua Tree's 28,000 acres of climbable terrain off-limits.[21]

Various Indian tribes consider certain mountains sacred, such as Denali and Rainier (Tacoma to the Indians). Devils Tower has been a sacred site for many tribes for centuries. The Dakota, Nakota, and Lakota Indian nations issued a formal resolution demanding that climbing the tower cease, particularly during June, the month of the summer solstice. The NPS instigated a voluntary closure for climbing Devils Tower for June of 1995, which was 85 percent successful. The closure has continued, although one lawsuit objecting to the closure has been made.[22]

## MISCELLANEOUS

In a park system with possibly the world's largest cave (Mammoth), one of the most famous (Carlsbad), and one of the most beautiful (Lechuguilla), it would be expected that *spelunking* would be a major sport. The possibility of environmental damage is so great, however, that strict controls are necessary, especially for pristine caverns like Lechuguilla. Any *outdoor sport* is possible in the national parks if playing fields are provided for them—softball, tennis, golf, basketball, and so on. With the exception of providing for employees who may spend months in the park, such facilities are not provided, as they are easily available outside the park, would take up space, and add little to the enjoyment of the parks. Various activities such as road runs, organized walks, bicycle races, and orienteering are possible as long as they do not interfere with normal use of the parks and if they are put on for charitable organizations. *Concerts and plays* are other activities that could fall under the heading of allowable outdoor recreation if all the criteria are met. Wolf Trap Farm Park near Washington, D.C., is an open-air pavilion operated by the NPS entirely for the performing arts.

## NATURE STUDY AND OUTDOOR EDUCATION

The ultimate aim of visiting a national park is, to many people, the study and enjoyment of nature. The setting is perfect. The visitors come to a place where the environment is in relatively good shape and the possibilities for nature study are outstanding. Nearly all units in the National Park System have visitor centers, where exhibits, publications, slide shows, or movies, and rangers to answer questions, are available. National parks are unique and well-known natural or historic areas; the literature is usually copious and of a high quality. Books on the wolves of Yellowstone, for example, almost beat the wolves to the park; four books on wolves were reviewed in the latest *Yellowstone Science,* out of the many that have been published.[23] The number of exhibits and informational signs might have increased in recent years as personal contacts have decreased because of budgetary restraints. The rangers are still there, of course, including ranger-naturalists and park historians, even if the numbers are smaller. The lineage goes back over a hundred years to the first "cone talks" given in front of Old Faithful.[24] The expertise of almost every ranger I've encountered has been impressive; the possibilities of tapping this potential

145

gold mine of knowledge with greater funds for ranger talks, nature hikes, and creative programs are enormous. There are also numerous nature and historic courses being offered in the national parks. The catalog of Yosemite Field Seminars, for example, is beginning to look more and more like a small college catalog, and the Yellowstone Institute, which offers summer classes in the park, has its own "ranch house" in Lamar Valley in Yellowstone.[25]

## SUMMARY

The national parks are so well known and attract so many visitors that almost any form of outdoor recreation allowed will claim adherents. Because the parks claim much of the nation's beautiful and interesting landscapes, it is natural that resource-based forms of outdoor recreation such as hiking and climbing would occur there. The goal of the NPS is to allow as much outdoor recreation in the national parks as possible, as long as it is directly related to the parks, harms no resources, and doesn't interfere with others' enjoyment of the parks. This is difficult enough in itself, but new forms of outdoor recreation continually appear to complicate the situation. With some of them, like mountain biking, the NPS seemed well prepared for the onslaught; for others like snowmobiling, it was overwhelmed. For the years ahead the NPS has few more serious tasks than staying current with the various forms of outdoor recreation and making sure that the national parks are for "the use and enjoyment of all people," not just the favored few.

# Case Study:
# Canyonlands National Park

I N 1955, a companion and I decided to try to repeat Major John W. Powell's trip through Cataract, Glen, and Grand Canyons. We didn't have the equipment or experience to run the rapids through the canyons, but with a lightweight rubber raft we felt we could portage every major rapid. Unfortunately, we got carried away with the excitement of the rapids and ended up capsizing, losing most of our food, and completely losing our desire to complete the trip. Escaping from the canyon in those days was a serious matter, but we knew that Monticello, Utah, was 35 miles away and figured we could carry enough water to make the trip, assuming the terrain was relatively gentle. We found a spot where we could climb out of the canyon, and looked out over the most *un*gentle landscape I've seen in my life. I don't think there was anywhere that you could walk 50 yards in a straight line. It was as if you had taken Bryce Canyon and laid it out on a plateau, throwing in thousand-foot-deep canyons here and there for good measure. We went back down to the junction of the Green and Colorado Rivers and waited patiently, hungrily, and eventually successfully, for someone to come by and rescue us.

The area that impressed us so much on the plateau above the river was the Needles area of present-day Canyonlands National Park. It is one of the most spectacularly eroded areas in the country. In 1936, the Canyonlands area was part of a 6,968-square-mile area of deeply entrenched canyons and eroded sandstone plateaus in southeastern Utah and northern Arizona which was proposed as an Escalante National Monument.[1] About the same time, Robert Marshall, one of the founders of what has become the National Wilderness Preservation System, proposed an Escalante Wilderness Area twice as large at 13,900 square miles, seventeen times larger than present-day Canyonlands National Park.[2] Both areas were centered on the Green and Colorado Rivers from near Moab, Utah, to Lee's Ferry at the head of the Grand Canyon. Unfortunately, both proposals were decades ahead of their time. Jeep roads for uranium exploration in the 1950's fragmented the area, and the Glen Canyon Dam, built in the early 1960's, took the heart out of it.

Still, much of the area today, outside of Lake Powell, is just as it was then. Recreation has come to the area, bringing financial rewards and leading to increased interest in preserving the area. Glen Canyon National Recreation Area was established around Lake Powell, Capitol Reef and Arches National Monuments were expanded in size and made

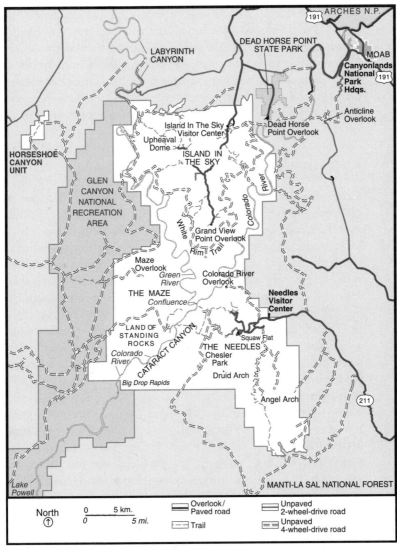

## Canyonlands National Park

national parks, and Canyonlands National Park was established.[3] In 1996 a Grand Staircase–Escalante National Monument was established, connecting Glen Canyon National Recreation Area with Bryce Canyon National Park. Much of Robert Marshall's proposed wilderness is still available on federal land in the area, although it is fragmented into many individual sections. Federal restrictions and the relatively small numbers of visitors have kept development to a minimum.

## FOUNDING THE NATIONAL PARK

Canyonlands was the first national park to be established in southeastern Utah and the first in the continental United States since World War II (Arches and Capitol Reef were established as national monuments in 1929 and 1937 and were elevated to national park status in 1971). I was at the hearings for the park in the early 1960's in Washington, and it was an amazing show.[4] It was obvious that the Canyonlands area was spectacular, on the same level as Zion or Bryce in southwestern Utah, but had somehow been forgotten in the exploration and development of the United States. When the Echo Park Dam was being debated in the 1950's, the Sierra Club suggested a larger Glen Canyon Dam in its place, feeling nothing would be lost. The filming of the first *Cinerama* (a travelogue on an enormous screen) during that period, where a B-52 bomber with cameras in its nose flew down Glen Canyon, alerted the nation to what it was about to lose. Also, the upstream area that was to become Canyonlands became known only after a series of pictures in *National Geographic*, taken at the same time that a congressional delegation was studying the area.[5] I doubt if one person in a thousand in this country knew either area existed until they were publicized.

The area under consideration for the new park supported virtually no economic use and very little recreational use. There was one ranch with attendant grazing (recently purchased by the Nature Conservancy), and a commercial jeep operation taking people into the area. There was everything to gain by establishing the new park and nothing to lose. Yet the Utah congressional delegation fought it, not so much opposing the park idea per se, but trying to reduce it in size and make sure no potential economic use would be inaccessible. Only because the Secretary of the Interior, Stewart Udall, pushed it strongly, did the Canyonlands National Park proposal manage to pass in the form we see today.

*The Colorado River in Glen Canyon before the construction of the Glen Canyon Dam downstream. Navajo Mountain is in the distance.*

## GEOGRAPHY OF CANYONLANDS

Canyonlands National Park is made up of four different areas that, because of difficulty of access, could almost be in different parts of the state. To drive to the Maze from the Needles area, for example, which adjoin each other across the Colorado River, requires a 184-mile trip, followed by several miles in a four-wheel-drive vehicle.

The most accessible section of Canyonlands is an area known as the "Island in the Sky." It provides a spectacular view of the Green and Colorado Rivers thousands of feet below, distant mountain ranges, the sandstone pinnacles of Monument Basin, and the wonderfully spectacular canyon country of southeastern Utah. John Wesley Powell, the first explorer of the Green and Colorado Rivers, wrote of the area:

> Away to the west are lines of cliffs and ledges of rock—not such ledges as the reader may have seen where the quarryman splits his blocks, but ledges from which the gods might quarry mountains that, rolled out on the plain below, would stand a lofty range; and not such cliffs as the reader may have seen where the swallow builds its nest, but cliffs where the soaring eagle is lost to view ere he reaches the summit.[6]

*Chessler Park in the Needles area of Canyonlands National Park narrowly avoided a paved highway which was proposed when the park was founded in 1964.*

Trails lead to overlooks, and to Upheaval Dome, which may be the only meteor crater preserved in a national park (its origin is still disputed). The 100-mile White Rim Trail, which follows a broad bench a thousand feet above the Green and Colorado Rivers, is one of the most popular jeep–mountain bike roads in the country, with primitive campsites along the way.

"The Needles" of Canyonlands National Park is one of my favorite areas in all the national parks. It is a wonderland of arches, spires, cliffs, and canyons, in myriad shapes and colors. Unlike "single-view parks," which a visitor might tire of quickly, this area could accommodate endless visits, with new discoveries every trip. Much can be seen from the road, but even more than at most national parks, the treasures of the Needles area—Chessler Park, Druid Arch, Angel Arch, Elephant Canyon—are reserved for the off-road enthusiast, the mountain biker, and the hiker. The area is also rich in Anasazi Indian ruins and pictographs.

Every national park needs a "Maze." This area has been called by the NPS "one of the most remote and inaccessible regions in the United States."[7] The Maze is a continuation of the amazing landforms of the Needles area, separated by the Colorado River, yet with silence and solitude hard to find today even in the national parks.

There are actually two kinds of rivers in the park: two placid, the Green from the north and the Colorado from the northeast, and one wild, the Colorado River below the junction of the two rivers. Cataract Canyon has some of the most difficult rapids in the entire Colorado River Basin. Unfortunately, the outstanding views along the Green and Colorado above the junction are available only with motors (unless you're willing to paddle upstream to get out), or are followed by a trip through Cataract Canyon. Of course, for professional river running services this is perfect: a float through a wonderland of towering sandstone cliffs, a thrilling ride through Cataract Canyon, and ending with a few miles on the blue waters of Lake Powell.

## VISITATION

The tourist bonanza that some had hoped for did not come to Canyonlands for several years after the establishment of the new national park. Only 57,000 people per year entered the park as late as 1980. However, this number had doubled by 1985 and doubled again only three years later.[8] The 1996 figure, 447,527, was almost eight times that of sixteen years previously.[9] Canyonlands' reputation as a very special place is beginning to be widely known, but to visit it requires more than just a "drive through" sight-seeing tour. The two major sight-seeing areas in the park—the Needles area and Island in the Sky—require 32- and 76-mile drives, respectively, to reach from park headquarters in Moab.

The problems of Canyonlands are different from those of most national parks, especially those of the lower forty-eight. The relative isolation of the major attractions of the park and the fact that beyond the visitor centers and small campgrounds there is no development in the park, have spared the park the usual problems of overcrowding. A lot of this was planned. Being a relatively new park, Canyonlands was established after visitor facilities were already in place in the adjacent towns of Moab and Monticello, and there was no real pressure to build any inside the park. A paved highway was planned to be built into Chessler Park in the Needles area, but once the park's first superintendent, Bates Wilson, got a look at the destruction a major road would cause in such a fragile area, he decided against it, and was popular enough in the area to make the decision stick.

*The dirt road following a geologic feature called a graben in the Needles area of Canyonlands National Park does far less damage than a paved highway and is used by four-wheel-drive vehicles, mountain bikes, and hikers.*

## RECREATIONAL USE

Canyonlands National Park is one of the premier backcountry parks in the country. Although Canyonlands is thirty-fourth among the 54 national parks in total visitation, it is sixth in backcountry recreation, ahead of even Yellowstone.[10] One of the primary reasons for the large amount of backcountry use is that jeeps were used almost exclusively to visit the area before it was a national park, a tradition carried over into the new park. There are 196 miles of unpaved roads in the park, a majority of which are four-wheel-drive roads, and about 40 percent of the total backcountry use is by jeep or other four-wheel-drive vehicle.[11] They impact the natural environment more than other backcountry uses, visually and through noise pollution, but the controls are the same: permits must be obtained, off-road use is prohibited, and camping is limited to designated sites. Expansion of backcountry road mileage is far less likely than its reduction, as evidenced by a recent environmental

154

The White Rim Trail in the Island in the Sky area of Canyonlands National Park, following the edge of the canyon in this photograph, is one of the best-known mountain bike trails in the country.

assessment, which includes suggestions for closing roads into fragile canyons in the Needles area.[12]

The exploding popularity of mountain biking in the 1980's took everyone by surprise. The national parks had less trouble with mountain bikes than many federal agencies, because they limited them to roads. In most parks this would mean that there would be little change in the popularity of mountain bikes compared to touring bikes, but in Canyonlands there are all those unpaved roads, a strong allure to the mountain bike enthusiast. Biking here, and outside the park around Moab, has reached such a high level that some are calling it the mountain bike capital of the world.

Another factor in the increasing use of Canyonlands' backcountry is the popularity of river running. Canyonlands not only has Cataract Canyon, with its impressive rapids, but a lot of flat water and relatively easy put in and take out points. To handle the increasing river use the NPS has established a registration system for river runners and a quota for both private and commercial trips, and has set regulations to prevent deterioration of the river resource.[13]

Canyonlands National Park contains high-quality hiking country, and half of the park's visitors in 1991 took at least a short day hike on part of the 125 miles of hiking trails in the park. The complexity of the

155

landscape is unequaled, and going from point A to point B on any trail in the park is going to open up a constantly changing series of new vistas. Problems occur, however, when hikers go off-trail. On the one hand, with miles of bare rock in the park, cross-country use can have virtually no impact on the environment. On the other hand, the prevalence in the region of cryptobiotic soils, which can be severely damaged by minimal trampling, makes off-trail use more serious than usual.[14] Cryptobiotic soils are bound together by microscopic plants of fine threadlike rootlets and fibers. Tires, human feet, and the hooves of domestic livestock can destroy in an instant crusts that will take years to mend. We can hope that the information programs in place informing visitors of the fragility of the soils, along with rules to protect them, can preserve the environment of Canyonlands National Park.

Finally, there is a long list of commercial companies, most of them with headquarters in Moab, which have the expertise and equipment to take even beginners on boat trips through Cataract, bike trips across the slickrock, and jeep trips to the most challenging four-wheel-drive destinations. Concessioners in Canyonlands National Park include seventeen specializing in white water rafting and float trips, and five which offer four-wheel-drive and backpack trips.[15] There is also a growing list of trail guides and maps on the park available at bookstores in Moab and visitor centers in the park.

## EXTERNAL THREATS

It is a paradox that many of the people in Utah who fought so vociferously against Canyonlands National Park and, indeed, all efforts on federal land that would preserve the quality of the landscape by limiting economic activity, still cannot see what is happening. Moab, which was so shattered by the loss of jobs following the slowdown in uranium development that it seemed ready to embrace a nuclear dump in the area, has been experiencing an incredible tourist boom as people recognize the beauty and the recreational potential of the area. Recreational use around Moab increased 300 percent during a five-year period in the 1990's; mountain bike use on the nearby Slickrock Trail, for example, went from 140 bike rides in 1983 to over 100,000 in 1994.[16] Yet antienvironmental groups seem to control the legislative power in the state, preventing the preservation of southeastern Utah's landscapes, which are what draw the tourist in the first place.

To make the situation adjacent to Canyonlands even more desperate, tourism is expanding so rapidly that the land management agencies, financially strapped in the best of times, cannot begin to keep it under control. The beauty and (ironically) the uncrowded nature of this country, coupled with all the new recreational toys—mountain bikes, four-wheel-drive vehicles—have attracted visitors and new residents alike.[17] Environmentalists in the area are afraid that unless controls are established quickly, the cure (tourism) is going to be worse than the disease (ranching and mining). In 1992, several thousand four-wheel-drive enthusiasts met near Moab, and during a night of heavy drinking, used trucks to pull up trees for a bonfire. Attempts at control led to a riot, arrests, and a lot of soul searching among local residents.[18]

## SUMMARY

Salvation for the entire canyon country of southeastern Utah is going to require more than the NPS. If the NPS makes no progress toward solving the overuse problem with its public support and mandate, however, the rest of the area certainly stands no chance. One ray of hope is a program started by former Superintendent Noel R. Poe of Arches National Park, called the Visitor Experience and Resource Protection Plan (VERP).[19] Arches National Park is adjacent to Canyonlands, with their headquarters only a few miles apart. The two parks obviously face the same external threats, and because of the nature of the terrain, many of the same internal problems as well. The VERP program attempts to establish a level of visitation which visitors feel gives them a high-quality experience, and which the NPS feels can be sustainable. Visitation can often be controlled by limiting parking areas. The program has gotten a good start and may be the ray of hope that this outstanding area needs and deserves.

# 10 Care and Feeding of Visitors

$T$AKING care of the creature comforts of visitors has always been part of the national park experience. The original act establishing Yellowstone National Park called for leases to allow accommodations to be provided, a policy clarified by the act establishing the National Park Service.[1] An NPS management guide refers to all visitor services this way: "The National Park Service will provide, through the use of concessions, those commercial facilities and services within the parks necessary for the visitors' use and enjoyment of the park."[2] In the first half-century or so of the national parks this would have meant hotels, restaurants, and all sorts of recreational facilities. Now, although the policy might be the same, accommodations have been frozen at current capacity for several decades, and new parks are brought into the system with no accommodations and minimal facilities. New hotel units are being built, but they are only replacements for old, undesirable, or poorly located facilities.

## ACCOMMODATIONS

Hotels, lodges, and cabins are found in only 46 units in the entire National Park System, yet they are found in 29 of the 54 "National Parks."[3] The reasons for this supposed imbalance are age and size. These 29 national parks tend to be the oldest and the largest units in the National Park System. Yellowstone, Yosemite, and Grand Canyon National Parks, for example, together contain over half the overnight lodging in the National Park System.[4]

The situation relating to accommodations has changed through the years. The ease with which we tour the national parks today is in marked contrast to the situation half a century ago. Until the early 1950's, when the massive federal interstate highway program made traveling cross-country much easier, staying overnight in some of the national parks was almost a necessity. The real heyday of park accommodations, however, was before the 1920's, when the Ford Motel T made automobiles affordable to everyone and led to a democratization of the national parks. Before then, the small numbers of traveled elite enjoying the parks led to a situation that will probably never be equaled. How beautiful and leisurely a trip to the parks must have been in those days, before the hordes of visitors arrived with their noise and congestion, and while the landscape still had an unsullied, pristine look. Travel went slowly by coach, and a trip through the parks was measured in days or weeks rather than hours. Those who could afford the travel came by guided tour and enjoyed a camaraderie not generally obtainable today. After a day's travel they could retire to structurally massive and thoroughly beautiful hotels with an excellent degree of service. Not all accommodations were like that, of course. But with labor costs that allowed high-quality work at low costs, and railroads that built hotels in the national parks partly as advertising, a number of hotels were built that are as interesting, architecturally impressive, and well designed as any in the country.[5]

Old Faithful Inn is a good example.[6] It was built in 1903 and remains one of the world's largest "log cabins." It was built entirely of native materials, including countless pieces of twisted logs polished and fitted together for banisters and stairways. There is an 85-foot-high fireplace, built of rocks quarried nearby, which amazingly withstood the Madison River earthquake in 1959. Old Faithful Inn, a national historic landmark, would be saved for its architectural and historic interest even if its normal use somehow had to be suspended.

The era of building big hotels outlasted the early automobile period to some degree because of the first director of the NPS, Stephen Mather. Although his goal was to get as many people to visit the parks as possible, he also recognized the importance of attracting visitors of wealth, power, and prestige. The Ahwahnee Hotel in Yosemite, for example, was opened with his support in 1927. Finally, the last of the big hotels to be opened in the national parks was the Jackson Lake Lodge, built in the Grand Teton National Park in 1953, on land bought by the builder's father, John D. Rockefeller Jr., and given to the park.

*Luxurious hotels are no longer considered necessary or even desirable in the national parks, but one as beautiful and unique as the Ahwahnee Hotel in Yosemite Valley is unlikely to ever be removed.*

The most dominant feature of the early hotels was not the architecture but the location. Early builders could pick any spot they wanted, so obviously picked only the finest: next to Old Faithful, the rim of the Grand Canyon, Yosemite Valley, Paradise Valley on Mount Rainier, and the shores of Yellowstone Lake. When the mobs of visitors started arriving after World War II it was obvious that the NPS had made mistakes in where they allowed the hotels to be built, because they usurped prime visitor locations. Moving them, however, proved a difficult task, even though most of the hotels were old and expensive to maintain. Old Faithful Inn, for example, had a high fire danger, and Paradise Inn at Mount Rainier, located in the world's snowiest location, was virtually buried in snow each year. However, they had supporters, and attempts at relocation usually failed. Besides, Old Faithful Inn faced its worst nightmare, the enormous Yellowstone fires of 1988, and emerged intact.

The number of people visiting the national parks expanded dramatically in the 1930's and even more so following World War II. The big, expensive hotels no longer fitted the needs of the touring public; what was needed was a "full range of overnight accommodations," from basic to opulent, with the majority of accommodations somewhere in between. The low end of the range was represented in Yellowstone National Park by "camper cabins" at several places in the park, the preferred accommodations for this writer and his family when we lived near Yellowstone in the 1960's. The price was cheap (at $3.50 for four), the cabin kept out the bears (assuming they didn't really want in), and it was fun to stay in a single, uncluttered cabin whose furnishings consisted of a table, wood burning stove, sink with cold-water faucet, beds with covered mattresses, a single 60-watt unshaded light bulb, and no insulation on the walls. The camper cabins have been removed, although even more basic accommodations still exist in the tent cabins of Yosemite National Park.

An innovation in the care and feeding of park visitors occurred in Grand Teton National Park in the 1960's when Colter Bay was constructed. The theory was to remove accommodations and services from scenic parts of the park and concentrate them in a pretty but not outstanding part of Jackson Lake. Jackson Hole was filling up with hotels, bars, and dude ranches when Rockefeller bought up the land to present it to the NPS, and the NPS was in the process of removing many of the buildings found there, especially from the shores of scenic Jenny Lake. Colter Bay contained one of the largest campgrounds in the National Park System, with 520 sites, 175 cabins, 75 tent cabins (a blend of camping and cabins), and 112 trailer sites, for an approximate overnight population of 3,500. There were also a store, a bar, a laundry with showers, a cafe, a cafeteria, a large visitor center with an Indian museum, two gas stations, and a marina. All this occupied a few hundred acres, with the wilderness immediately adjacent to the camp. Relocation of park facilities from sensitive sites ran into two major problems. One, closing accommodations, anywhere, was going to be a problem. No matter how many Colter Bays you built, people would fight to retain some of the facilities being replaced. Secondly, moving buildings away from scenic areas would not satisfy an increasingly vocal minority that wanted them out of the park altogether.

Yosemite National Park has been the scene of perhaps the longest running battle in the National Park System to remove accommodations. Yosemite not only has more overnight lodging visitors than any other park but has nearly twice the number of the park with the next-highest total— Yellowstone (1,030,368 vs. 550,768).[7] Yosemite's accommodations make up many of the close to 1,000 buildings that clutter the floor of the Yosemite Valley. Something—hotels, services, housing, maintenance—is

*Colter Bay in Grand Teton National Park was developed under Mission 66 during the 1960's to replace development in more sensitive areas.*

going to have to go if the quality of the valley is to be maintained in the face of increasing visitor totals. Hotels seem an obvious choice.

The massive hearings on the 1980 Yosemite General Management Plan, held in the mid-1970's, left no doubt that people felt some of the accommodations should go; some were in the floodplain or on rockslide aprons from which they ought to be removed anyway. Yet, sixteen years after the acceptance of the Yosemite General Management Plan, the "last" word in management of the park, not a single hotel building has been removed. Why not? Partly it was politics: Ronald Reagan became president at the same time the GMP was adopted, and his Secretary of the Interior, James Watt, took the tack exactly opposite that of the environmentalists. Not only did the concessioners want to retain their full complement of pillow count, but they also wanted to upgrade their facilities — to replace the tent cabins, for example, with rooms with baths. According to their records these were the first rooms to be rented and therefore the most popular with the public. Presidents come and go, as do concessioners, and it looks as if something will happen in the next few years. Current plans call for some upscaling, and an overall reduction of 20.4 percent in the number of accommodations in the valley.[8] The floods of 1997 have hastened this process, which will be discussed in the case study on Yosemite.

In summary, the park service has not increased the pillow count significantly in the national parks for half a century. Except for Jackson Lake Lodge, there have been no big hotels built in the parks in seventy-five years. Only one-seventh of the units in the National Park System have overnight accommodations, but 29 of the "National Parks" do, including the most famous parks like Yellowstone. In parks with accommodations and overcrowding, hotels and cabins are obvious targets for removal. So far, however, few accommodations have been removed.

## FOOD AND SERVICES

Years ago, when I was completing a questionnaire on which services I thought should be available in Yosemite Valley, my daughter looked over what I had checked. "Dad," she said, "Do you really think the only things that ought to be sold in Yosemite are liquor and ice cream?" I was kidding, of course, but one person's necessities might be the pure indulgences of another. There is no "must have" list for any park. It is obvious you could enjoy Yosemite and not starve if everything were moved out of the valley. The last to go, however, would have to be food (without the liquor and ice cream perhaps). The provision of food in the national parks has followed in a large degree the pattern of the accommodations: from "elegant dining" to fast food. While the beautiful dining rooms are still there, in the Ahwahnee of Yosemite or Lake Hotel in Yellowstone, the growth in recent years has certainly been in cafeterias, or cafes serving hamburgers and pizzas. Grocery stores are also there, including the enormous Babbit store on the South Rim of the Grand Canyon, which includes souvenirs, fast food, and recreational equipment. The movement of such stores, or at least small copies of such, into campgrounds has been contemplated, as these are the only places that "need" such services.

The question of need will determine what is offered in any park. Here is that list of services in Yosemite Valley, taken from the questionnaire I was referring to above, in 1975: accommodations, fast food service, cafeteria food service, restaurant food service, grocery sales, recreational equipment rental, recreational equipment sales, emergency medical service, full hospital service, dental service, gift sales, gas and oil service, auto repair and towing, auto rental, post office, banking service, laundry, alcoholic beverage sales, photography instruction, climbing and mountaineering instruction, cross-country skiing instruction, commercial tours of park, clothing sales, barber and beauty services, dry cleaning services, kennel service, bike rental, and pack animal rental. How many *should* be offered in the park, or in any park? Video rentals have been added to the list above, reflecting the fact that there is a population of 1,900 workers in the valley in summer months (this would also account for banking, and barber and beauty shops) in addition to all the visitors.[9]

Every item on the list above offers some convenience or increases the enjoyment of those in Yosemite for a few hours or for a season. The ultimate question is the seriousness of the NPS in returning Yosemite Valley, or any of the national parks, to their natural state. It is obvious that Yosemite Valley does not have to have bars, any more than it has to have ice cream outlets. I enjoy walking down the trail from Vernal Falls to Happy Isle and having an ice cream cone, but I would readily forgo it if the urban scene I was about to encounter at Curry Village were lessened.

## CAMPING

In two successive summers I sat at group campfires in campgrounds in the national parks and heard environmental discussions deteriorate into diatribes against motor homes. Luxury motor homes with their inhabitants inside watching TV hardly correspond to my view of camping, either, but the depth of feeling of my fellow tent campers amazed me. Of course, the term "camping" has far different meanings for different people, and has certainly changed over time. Forty years ago, a campsite would house a tent, a fire, a rustic table, perhaps a gas stove or lantern, and people who were obviously on close terms with the out-of-doors and its occasional discomforts. Now there are campers, large pickups with metal homes fitted onto their beds, tent trailers, whose "tents" are often made of fiberglass, house trailers of every dimension, and finally, the self-propelled motor homes, some as large as buses and some simple, home-designed vans. Spilling out of these myriad vehicles are tents, electric lights, boats, motorcycles, folding chairs, CD speakers, stoves, refrigerators, cots, sometimes even cars that have been towed behind the "camper." The NPS has not, however, succumbed to the demands implied by the escalation in size of recreational vehicles. It has provided minimal hookups in a few parks, in what amount to large barren parking lots, but beyond that the vehicles must fit into existing facilities. Actually, recreational vehicles probably cause more problems outside the campgrounds than in them, requiring several parking places or infuriating traffic caught behind them on narrow park roads.

While the majority of campers were moving to more luxurious accommodations in recreational vehicles, lightweight and colorful materials have led to a resurgence in plain old tent camping. The result has been a boom in camping, which hit the national parks especially hard in the 1960's. During that period campsites were free and the NPS was building new campsites, complete with flush toilets and heated "comfort stations," as fast as it could, especially during Mission 66. The NPS did not take long to see that this was an endless task, as campground use escalated much higher than even visitation during that period. Existing campgrounds were showing signs of age and would eventually have to be closed. Money was always short. Something had to be done. At the same time, campgrounds still filled and campers were still unhappy. I remember an experience in the summer of 1968 when I went with a ranger to a campground in Grand Teton National Park to move a "Campground Full" sign to a better location. It was 8:30 P.M. on the Fourth of July, still light in that part of the country. In the process of putting the sign up, the ranger was accosted by a person, pulling a house trailer and a boat, who was hopping mad because there was no campsite waiting for him. It did little good to explain to him that if campsites were provided for everyone who wanted one late at night on the most popular night of the year, it would mean excess capacity 99 percent of the time, that campsites cost money, and that all the "vacant" land sweeping up to the Tetons had values which would be lost if converted to campgrounds.

Just as it has with all accommodations, the NPS has frozen the construction of new campgrounds. It is removing campgrounds from scenic locations and areas where conflict with wildlife is a problem, relocating them, if necessary, to less sensitive locations. It is cleaning and repairing the most overcrowded and deteriorating campgrounds. Most importantly, it is charging fees, comparable to minimum-service campgrounds outside the parks. Finally, it is requiring reservations at the most popular parks. I feel the situation has improved.

If you have made your reservation, you pull into your vacant site at whatever time you arrive. The noisiest things in the campground are generators, and they must be turned off by 10 P.M. in most parks or earlier in others. Smoldering campsites seem to be on their way out, as few parks allow the gathering of wood anywhere near the campground and bought wood burns a lot cleaner than green or wet wood. The nightly excursion of bears has been slowed with bear-proof garbage containers and rigidly enforced rules about securing food. In short, camping in the national parks should be as good a hundred years from now as it is today, a sustainable situation that is exactly as it should be. For persons who rail against the rules that allow the campgrounds to be sustainable, numerous campgrounds are available around most of the parks, public and private, a situation that was not present before the current boom in camping.

## CONCESSIONERS

When Yellowstone National Park was established, it was fondly believed by the government that there would be no costs involved. Until the NPS was established in 1916, very little money was appropriated, mostly to the U.S. Army, which ran most of the parks after 1883. Certainly there was no money to furnish comfort to the visitor, such as with hotels or food, even if the U.S. government had shown any desire to go into the hotel or restaurant business. Private enterprise was ready and willing from the first, however, almost beating the tourists to some park areas. The Yellowstone Act of 1872 allowed leases, although only for ten years, and the facilities that followed were very minimal. Here, for example, is a partial list of buildings in Yellowstone in the 1880's:

> An earth-roofed, loop-holed cabin, 16 × 20 feet in diameter; a log house upon the point just above the Forks of the Yellowstone, built by C. J. Baronette in the spring of 1871; an earth-roofed log house, and also a cabin bath-house, built by M. McGuirk in 1871–72, near Mammoth Hot Springs.[10]

The leases allowed by the Yellowstone Act would include not only hotels and accommodations but also services. As early as 1878, saddle and pack animals were offered at Mammoth Hot Springs, by 1880 stage lines carried visitors into the park, and by 1891 a steamer operated on Yellowstone Lake. A permit to build an elevator to the foot of Yosemite Falls was turned down, but the environment still suffered as game was hunted, fish were caught for visitor meals in the hotels, and trees were cut down for their construction.[11] To attract more tourists the concessioners did everything from fencing wildlife and feeding grizzlies in Yellowstone to providing the nightly firefall in Yosemite.

The major problem concessioners faced was that most national parks were in areas where providing services entailed high costs and a short season. Presumably, by reducing the competition the concessioner could give much better service, as well as cooperate with the NPS in protecting the environment. This change was effected with the founding of the NPS and the coming of Stephen Mather, its first director. Mather had no problem with visitor development in the national parks. One of his most widely quoted statements was: "Scenery is hollow enjoyment to a tourist who sets out in the morning after an indigestible breakfast and a fitful sleep on an impossible bed."[12] The statement about an "indigestible breakfast" was no exaggeration in the early days of the national parks. Yellowstone Superintendent Horace Albright, making an unannounced inspection of a camp kitchen in Yellowstone, concluded that it would have turned the stomach of a black ant. That day the camp reported twenty cases of ptomaine poisoning.[13] In Yosemite, more than two dozen concessioners provided services, leading to intense and cutthroat competition. Mather forced the merger of these and other concessioners, leading to the policy of granting monopoly control in each park.

The policy worked well for a while until dismal profits by the concessioners during the Depression and World War II, and a further decline in service because of the hordes who descended on the parks in the postwar period, led to the Concession Policy Act of 1965. In this, the concessioners had not only monopoly rights but preferential rights in retaining contracts after their expiration, longer-term contracts, and possessory interest, which gave them de facto ownership of all their holdings. Concessioners whose leases were terminated for whatever reason must be bought out.[14]

Many agreed with Representative John Dingell's remark that his investigations had shown that "concessioners, not the National Park Service, are running the parks."[15] The statement reflects the battle, especially heated from the 1970's on, between environmentalists trying to reduce pressure on the parks from visitors and development, and the concessioners, naturally, trying to increase park visitation and their profits. Every time a plan was unveiled to reduce human impact on the national parks, the concessioners were there to oppose it. The problem was particularly acute in Yosemite.

Yosemite Valley in the 1960's and early 1970's represented all that was wrong with the national parks to many environmentalists. There were no controls on the number of people pouring into the valley, and the deterioration of the natural scene was obvious. The NPS started several programs to improve the situation, but much of the problem lay with the concessioners. It was hoped that an official master plan would give direction to an overall decrease in the pressures of accommodations and services in the park. Instead, when the master plan did come out in 1974, it specified no changes in either visitor totals or accommodations.[16] It appeared obvious that the Music Corporation of America (MCA), the owner of the Yosemite Park and Curry Company, had had undue influence in producing the plan.[17] Consequently, NPS Director Ronald Walker killed the plan, partly because of the widely publicized actions of MCA in painting rocks in Yosemite to enhance TV commercials and the start of a network television show, *Sierra*, which seemed to capitalize on the park.[18] Later Delaware North (Yosemite Concession Services) took over the concessions in the park, and the situation improved, as will be discussed later in the case study on Yosemite.

Despite Yosemite Park and Curry Company's undue influence on the park, there were few complaints about its ability to take care of visitors. In Yellowstone, however, an NPS report, "leaked" to the press in 1977, accused the Yellowstone Park Company of some of the worst service in park history. Employees were underpaid, overworked, and often hostile to employer and guests; facilities were falling apart, and the company had no intention of improving the situation, only profits. Congress approved the buyout of the company in 1979, a partial step in the improvement of a difficult situation.[19]

While the concession situations in Yosemite and Yellowstone National Parks appeared to be victories for environmentalists and park supporters, it is hard to speculate on the future. A concessions reform bill that would increase concession fees and return them to the parks, establish competitive bidding for contracts, and reform possessory interest came close to passage during the 103d Congress. A bill that would continue, or worsen, the present situation was offered in the 104th Congress. Neither bill became law.

## Individual Concessioners

There are hundreds of concessioners in 139 parks, grossing $650 million a year in 1994.[20] With 374 units in the National Park System, this means a little more than a third of the parks have concessions. Most of the historic parks and the smaller parks have no need of concessions. Forty-six of the 54 "National Parks," on the other hand, have concessions. Canyonlands (river and jeep guides), Glacier Bay (tours), Grand Canyon (boat trips and services), and Grand Tetons (boat trips and lodging) have 141 concessions among them.[21] The number of concessions can give a false impression of the amount of commercial activity in a park, however. Glacier Bay National Park has 32 concessioners, which are mainly charter boats and cruise ships. Yosemite National Park, on the other hand, lists only 4 concessioners, but this includes lodging for thousands of visitors, dining rooms, restaurants, cafeterias, snack bars, stores, gift shops, ski shops, swimming pools, river rafting, trail rides, horseback riding, pack horses, sight-seeing tours, coin laundry, showers, bicycle rentals, and transportation services. While there is still considerable competition among concessioners in certain fields, like river running and cruises, the most important concession services, like food and lodging, were long ago taken over by conglomerates. Some, like Yosemite Concession Services, specialize in one park. National Park Concessions, Inc., however, operates on Blue Ridge Parkway, and in Olympic, Mammoth Cave, and Isle Royale National Parks. TW Services, Inc., operates in Bryce, Death Valley, Everglades, Yellowstone, and Zion National Parks.

## SUMMARY

Sustainability is obviously easier at parks like Bryce Canyon or Crater Lake, where visitors drive to the rim, take a good look, and leave, than it is in Yosemite Valley, where many people would live permanently if they had the opportunity. Sight-seeing, while basic, is only part of what many of us want a good national park experience to be. We want to camp in a grove of giant Douglas firs in Mount Rainier National Park, or enjoy striking views of the mountain from our room at Paradise Inn. We want to eat a sandwich while feeling the spray from a waterfall along the Merced River in Yosemite, or enjoy a pizza at Colter Village as we watch deer graze in Stoneman Meadow. We want to hike among the awesome and color-splashed cliffs of Zion, or see the same sights in the comfort of our automobile. We want to be thrilled by the plunge into Sockdologer Rapid in the Grand Canyon as the soaring walls of the canyon glide by, or look down into the unfathomable gorge while flying over it.

I believe the argument on the level of services in a national park goes well beyond whether or not we can drive in the park, fly over it, or spend the night there, to the *level* of that experience. Whatever we do in the national parks, the bottom line will always be how well we take care of them. A simple room in a compact hotel development that blends perfectly into the environment would have far less impact on the park than the same room in a big gaudy hotel perched on a lakeshore, brow of a hill, or edge of a canyon, for example. A fancy sit-down restaurant conspicuously sited would have a much greater impact and serve far fewer people than a well-located fast food place. Making these kinds of decisions on the care and feeding of visitors to the national parks will ultimately decide the future quality of our park experiences.

# Case Study:
# Yosemite National Park

THE incredible beauty of Yosemite Valley in the Sierra Nevadas of California has helped make it perhaps the most intensely used "living space" in the National Park System. The valley's combination of some of the world's tallest and most spectacular sheer cliffs with some of the world's tallest waterfalls provides a national treasure which has lured visitors to the valley for over a century. It seems as if sustainability can work in Yosemite Valley it can work anywhere in the National Park System.

The Yosemite National Park established in 1890 didn't even include Yosemite Valley. The Sierras surrounding Yosemite, the beautiful valley and canyon of the Tuolumne River, and impressive groves of giant sequoias were considered reason enough, by themselves, to establish a national park. Yosemite Valley is the prime raison d'être of the park today and is also probably the best place in the National Park System to study sustainability as it applies to scenic natural areas. Fortunately, the valley has been under some form of protection since shortly after it was first entered by non-natives in 1851.

In 1864 the valley had been visited by enough people to support it as a protected area. The Yosemite Park Act of 1864, signed by President Lincoln, gave Yosemite Valley to the State of California to manage as a public park, "inalienable forever."[1] In 1890, the most scenic portion of the Sierra Nevadas, surrounding but not including Yosemite Valley, was made a national park through the urging of John Muir and others. The valley itself, although accounting for only 0.7 percent of the total acreage of the park, was the primary goal of most of the visitors to the Sierra Nevadas and was included in the national park in 1905. Although the act establishing the park protected it from development, the greatest loss suffered by any national park occurred in 1913 with the disappearance of a valley comparable to Yosemite—Hetch Hetchy—under a water supply reservoir for San Francisco. Perhaps due to greater public attention after the establishment of the National Park Service in 1916, Yosemite National Park has remained inviolate ever since.

The reason Yosemite Valley was remitted to Yosemite National Park was that the State of California never really protected the valley as many felt it should. To build and operate the hotels in the valley, timber was cut, livestock fenced, and the valley floor itself was farmed.[2] The real "lost opportunity" for the state was not accepting a proposal for a more protected Yosemite Valley by Frederick Law Olmsted in 1865, which would have produced a much more natural valley than we have now.[3]

Other than stopping the farming and lumbering, the National Park Service did not, at first, adopt many plans which we would applaud today. It penned animals for viewing, built as many roads as it had money for, looked the other way when bears were fed, stocked streams and lakes for fishing, and felt that the more people that visited the park, the better. The number of visitors to Yosemite was modest at first, less than 10,000 a year up to 1905. Then it doubled in ten years, doubled again in five years, and kept climbing until it reached a million in 1954.[4] The increases have averaged 82,000 visitors a year since, more than the total number of visitors in the first thirty-five years of the park's existence.

The result of all these numbers was a steadily deteriorating natural environment. There were over a thousand structures built: hotels; lodges; cabins; homes for the rangers, concession staff, and the thousands of seasonal workers; grocery stores; restaurants; gift shops; a bank; and a beauty parlor. There were warehouses, vehicle maintenance buildings, ranger stations, administration buildings, a school, and even a magistrate court. There was everything associated with automobiles: roads, parking lots, gas stations, and a garage. And finally, there were the human impacts created as people walked through the meadows, prevented fires, and pitched their sea of tents. Very little of Yosemite Valley has escaped. Even the cliffs, among the most popular in the world for rock climbers, are festooned with bolts and slings, discolored with chalk, and contain cracks scarred by pitons and cleared of vegetation by legions of climbers.

Some of this impact was the result of simple ignorance, or the lack of support from the public for what the environmental experts were telling the park service it ought to do.[5] Much, however, was the result of a steadily rising visitation, which continues to be accepted by the NPS today for public support and potential funding increases. Unfortunately, politics is very much a part of park operations, and it takes a brave superintendent indeed to turn visitors back at the gate, remove a park attraction that the public loves, or do anything which would decrease tourist income in surrounding communities.

The statement "parks are for people" was finally dropped as a guiding symbol for the National Park System because of what happened in Yosemite Valley in the late 1960's and early 1970's. "Yosemite City" was an apt nickname for the valley in those days. The upper 4 miles of the

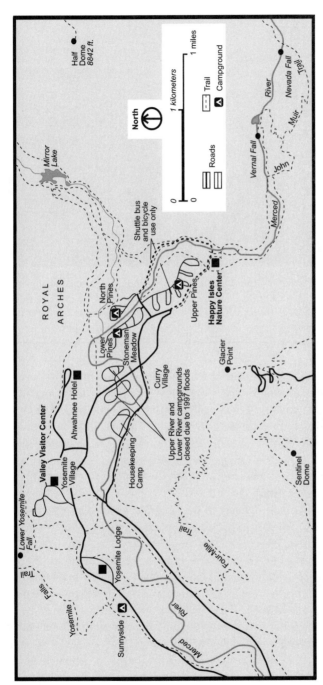

**Yosemite Valley, Yosemite National Park**

*The upper 4 miles of Yosemite Valley, an area about twice the size of Central Park, contains most of the development and visitation of Yosemite National Park. Fortunately, in this view from Columbia Point, forests screen most of the roads and buildings.*

valley, about twice the size of Central Park in New York City, contained all the campgrounds, hotels, cabins, and services of the valley and an overnight population density equal to that of most cities. With this density the usual urban problems of crime, pollution, and noise would be expected, and the NPS was forced to rethink its whole attitude toward visitors. This was the "hippie era" in American culture, and there were almost as many counterculture people here as in Haight-Ashbury, 200 miles to the west.

I visited Yosemite Valley in 1967 in what remains as my most unforgettable national park experience. Finding a camping place was a matter of shoehorning your place among other campers, or finding someone in the process of moving; there were no camp*sites*, reservations, campground hosts, or campground rangers. That year, one-seventh of all the camping in the National Park System in the United States took place in Yosemite Valley.[6] We found a few square yards for our tent and sat back to watch the show. In a site next to ours there were fifty hippies, complete with rugs hung to delineate the site, music from a stereo system, incense burning, and enough secondhand marijuana smoke to get high just standing around. It was hard enough to breathe anyway with all the smoldering campfires and auto exhausts. There was a motorcycle race

*Yosemite Valley in the summer of 1967, when a campground contained as many people, tents, and cars as could be packed into it. "Parks are for people" reached its unhealthy peak in Yosemite National Park in the late 1960's.*

at 3 A.M. and a "wake up call" from teenagers in a convertible with megaphones at daybreak. Campers today, in sites where fires are only permitted between 5 and 10 P.M. and generators are not allowed after dark, should be happy for all they're missing.

The changes the NPS was starting to make were hastened by a full-scale riot in the valley in 1970, when a motorcycle group appeared on July 4th looking for a campsite, and decided Stoneman Meadow, off-limits for forty years, would do nicely.[7] The NPS had to call in outside help to clear the meadow after an attempt by the untrained, unarmed park rangers failed. The NPS eventually trained and armed its rangers, but knew this would not be enough to take care of the growing over-crowding problem in Yosemite and elsewhere in the National Park System. Fortunately, the "age of ecology" was born about that time, and preserving the park would climb to a number-one priority with the NPS.

The major problem with restricting numbers in Yosemite Valley

*Stoneman Meadow was the location of the infamous July 4th riot of 1970. Restoration has improved the quality of the meadow since this photo was taken in the 1980's. Curry Village is in the lower half of the picture.*

is that, in addition to its beauty, it is so *livable*. The valley floor is flat, covered by pine, oak, or meadow, has a cold mountain river flowing through it, and has a climate that is essentially California perfect. Furthermore, San Francisco is 200 miles away, Los Angeles 300, and the Central Valley, one of the fastest-growing sections of the country, is adjacent. It is one of the most desirable summer camping locations in the country.

The NPS has attempted to diminish overcrowding pressure by reducing overnight use of the park, lessening the impact of cars in the valley, influencing visitor behavior, and turning away visitors at peak travel periods. Camping was the main target in reducing overnight use, as the pillow count at hotels and cabins has remained relatively stable for decades. In 1968 the NPS prohibited all camping outside of campgrounds, including sleeping in cars in parking lots, and completed the process of *unitization*, which divides the campgrounds into specific sites. The capacity of some of the campsites in the valley dropped by two-thirds. Wilderness permits were also required for roadless areas adjacent to the valley, stopping the scene, according to one ranger, of "wall-to-wall bodies" in popular places like Little Yosemite Valley.

People can crowd an area, but their cars can crowd it even more. The philosophy at one time seemed to be that if there wasn't enough room

*The Yosemite National Park shuttle service has allowed roads and parking lots to be closed in the upper end of Yosemite Valley. The 1980 General Management Plan for Yosemite National Park envisions extending the system to the entire valley.*

for everyone who wanted to stay in the valley, they could at least drive there and visit for the day. The day when the upper valley would be completely paved over with parking lots became a distinct possibility. Recognizing this, the NPS combined with the park concessioner, the Yosemite Park and Curry Company, to start a shuttle bus system. The buses were immensely popular, so much so in the beginning when the buses were topless, that joy riders would spend all day on them, sometimes with loud music and water balloons. The buses were considered the opening wedge of an auto-free valley.

In an overcrowded valley it makes little sense to have attractions like golf courses, tennis courts, and swimming pools, all of which are easily obtainable outside the park, or a totally unnatural show like the famous Yosemite firefall. A golf course near the Ahwahnee Inn was closed, with few objections. In 1968, however, the removal of the firefall drew fierce opposition. In 1872 a concessioner got the idea of building a bonfire on Glacier Point, just above the valley and easily reached by road, and pushing the coals off the cliff. The firefall was certainly spectacular, but the thousands of people who showed up at 9 P.M. for the brief show were causing a crowding problem in the Curry Village and Ahwahnee areas, going and coming.[8]

The NPS made a start toward a more natural valley in the 1970's, supported by an environmentally active public. The goal of moving toward a completely auto-free valley and reducing shops and hotels soon ran up against a powerful foe, however: the concessioner. A master plan for Yosemite, published in 1974, was rejected because of undue influence in writing the plan by the Yosemite Park and Curry Company (YPCC).[9] The new master plan, the General Management Plan of 1980 (GMP), seemed to have widespread public approval but ran up against the philosophy of a new Secretary of the Interior, James Watt. In a speech to park concessionaires on March 9, 1981, in Washington, D.C., he said that in cases of conflicts over park use: "I will err on the side of public use versus preservation."[10] The public, however, has reaffirmed its desire to see the GMP completed by reacting against a 1989 review of the plan which stated that the people who prepared the plan had "grayed" and no longer wanted to ride on buses or do without hotels.[11] Also, the Yosemite National Park superintendent in the early 1990's, Mike Finley, made a statement exactly the opposite of Watt's concerning concessioners: "Making an honest determination about a visitor's experience is a very difficult balancing act. I will always err on the side of the natural resource."[12]

The crucial part of the GMP dealt with making the valley auto-free. The first draft of the 1980 plan called for parking lots at the entrance to the valley across from El Capitan at a place called Taft Toe, where noncrucial space is available, and shifting all day-use traffic to a shuttle system extending to the entire valley. Visitors with campground or hotel reservations would drive directly to their sites but shift to buses for sight-seeing. The final draft, however, located parking in areas near the park entrances, making the changeover to public transportation much more difficult and, at the time, effectively killing the proposal.[13] A new study (1994), however, restores the parking lot at Taft Toe, and examines the feasibility of a rail system, probably the ultimate solution to Yosemite Valley traffic problems.[14]

Another proposal for reducing park overcrowding calls for moving housing for park employees and rangers to places outside the valley. Currently 1,900 employees live in the valley, many of them in bleak, substandard quarters. The proposal would have up to 345 employees moving out of the valley, depending on the severity of the problems associated with the resultant commuting. The problems include safety, increased parking requirements, costs, the uncertainty that such a program could pass air-pollution requirements in an environmental impact statement, and the environmental impact on the area where the new quarters would be located.[15] Some ranger housing has been moved to El Portal at the West Entrance to the park, where various amenities not available to rangers in the valley, like building equity in their own homes and better schooling for their children, would be available. However, living in Yosemite Valley is a strong employment inducement for rangers, and most of the ranger houses have been put on the National Registry of Historical Places, making their removal unlikely.

The housing problem can be simplified by moving as much administrative and maintenance work as possible outside the valley. The Yosemite Park and Curry Company, for example, moved all its reservation activity to Fresno. Much of the NPS's administrative work, especially that pertaining to personnel, was moved to El Portal, just outside the park. Maintenance work not directly tied to Yosemite Valley is being moved out as funds become available. The reasoning behind all this, of course, is to reclaim the priceless beauty of Yosemite Valley, and to increase the amount of usable recreational space in the most scenic part of the valley. Visitors often wander into the central maintenance area or into employee housing and wonder if they're still in Yosemite National Park. Even the better concessioner housing looks little different from suburban housing anywhere, and it can usurp some of the most scenic areas in the valley, such as those at the edge of Ahwahnee Meadows with striking views of Half Dome.

Visitor accommodations and services are to be reduced under the GMP mandate, and here, too, there has been resistance to change.[16] The reduction in rooms is to be 20.4 percent, which will be met primarily by moving units out of the floodplains and rockfall zones.[17] The services to be removed, such as video rentals, beauty shops, car maintenance, and banking, don't seem to belong in a natural national park anyway. The plan also calls for an increase in some visitor services, such as campground showers and fast food capacity. All await funding and the operations of the new concessioner.

One of the more hopeful events in recent years has been the selection of a new concessioner for Yosemite National Park. The former concessioner, the Yosemite Park and Curry Company (YPCC), was exemplary on some environmental matters, such as helping to start the Yosemite Valley shuttle service and being one of the first organizations in the country to buy back beverage containers and to quit using Styrofoam. It also, however, fought any changes which might have resulted in fewer people and shorter stays. Furthermore, it was returning only

*This road, at the edge of the Ahwahnee Meadows in Yosemite National Park, may be removed under one of the recent park restoration proposals, making the experience for the biker and hiker even more natural.*

0.75 percent of its $92.6 million gross in exchange for enjoying monopoly use of the valley. It is estimated that the new concessioner, Delaware North (Yosemite Concession Services), will pay close to 20 percent in fees, which will allow the purchasing of all the assets of the former concessioner, cleaning up toxic waste sites, and funding some of the relocations mentioned above.[18]

Restoration has moved to the forefront of park improvement plans as donations and volunteer work enable smaller, long-term projects to take place. The two largest groups working in the park are the Yosemite Fund, which has spent over $7 million in the park since 1986, and the Yosemite Association, which has donated $3.3 million since 1984.[19] Cleaning up backcountry campsites, repairing trails, saving the disappearing California black oak, returning the black bear to a more natural state by installing bear-proof metal boxes in all the campsites, and restoring and protecting the meadows of the valley are all examples of such projects. Restoring the Merced River is one of the larger projects. The project has involved removing riprap along the stream banks, replanting willow and other streamside trees, allowing fallen trees, at one time removed, to remain in the stream channel, and rebuilding bridges to improve stream hydraulics.[20] Education has been an integral part of the program, as the streamside is a favorite place to play and camp and rafting is a very popular Merced River activity.

180

## THE YOSEMITE FLOODS OF 1997

Just after reserving a campsite in the Lower River Campground in Yosemite National Park by phone for my national park field trip in 1997, I saw the first photographs of the January 1–3 flood in Yosemite Valley. *All* of the Lower River Campground was under 3 feet of water. When we showed up in late April (to a different campsite), the Lower and Upper River Campgrounds no longer existed—what the flood didn't take out, and this included soil and roads, the NPS had removed. Dramatic changes, by humans *and* nature, were taking place.

The 1980 GMP, high in purpose and conception, had slowly begun to cause significant change by the mid-1990's. The flood might be the catalyst to accelerate that process. Flood damage to highways, sewer systems, campgrounds, and housing totaled $176,000,000. Past experience would have relegated that total to an ever-increasing backlog of deferred maintenance and decaying infrastructure. This time, however, the full amount was funded by an Emergency Supplemental Appropriations Bill

*Substandard tent accommodations for employees had been slated for replacement when nature, in the form of the January 1997 flood, hastened the process.*

*The small cabins in the clearing at Yosemite Lodge, used for employee housing, were damaged by flooding of the Merced River in January 1997 and are slated to be replaced in a safer location. Most of the land shown in the photo was underwater during the flood.*

signed into law June 12, 1997, and recovery efforts will be geared to the 1980 GMP.[21] Two campgrounds which were most damaged by the flood, for example, will not reopen. The removal or relocation of the campgrounds should make restoration of the Merced River easier, and will reduce overnight crowding. Employee housing in the Yosemite Lodge area, severely damaged by the flood, will be removed and compacted in a less sensitive area. Detailed plans for recovery projects will be based on the Yosemite Valley Implementation Plan, which was still being reviewed in early 1998.[22]

## SUMMARY

I believe Yosemite National Park represents a potentially sustainable tourist destination. Yosemite Valley is not a place for the environmental purist, especially in the summer, given that this is one of the earth's greatest natural attractions, which will continue to be visited by hordes of people. Nevertheless, the NPS has done a remarkable job in keeping the quality of the valley's natural environment high. Wilderness is available in the park's backcountry, and urban amenities are available just outside the park; neither *has* to be in the middle of Yosemite Valley.

People probably won't be able to travel directly into the valley in their autos in the future, and day-use reservations will be required, but the scene when they arrive should be as good, or if all the potential restoration projects are completed, even better, than today. Money will continue to be tight and administrations can change, but if the past is any indication, even the worst situations will only slow, not stop, the movement toward an even more natural and beautiful national park.

# 11 Administration, Politics, and Finance

THE agony of Hetch Hetchy, where a Yosemite-like valley floor disappeared under an unnecessary reservoir in 1915, represented, to some, the birth pangs of the NPS. For several years it had been recognized that the national parks were not doing well on their own. Some parks had army officers in charge and some had civilians. The policy for each park was often set by local politicians. There were few tourists and the accommodations were rudimentary. "Park barrel," as we now know it, where spending often depends on what park is in whose political district, existed to an absurd degree. Parks which today are not even well known as local scenic areas, like Sullys Hill in North Dakota or Platt in Oklahoma, came in as full-fledged national parks.[1] Financing was very sparse and protection of the natural landscape (except for the army-run parks) weak. There had been earlier attempts at setting up a new "park bureau," but neither public nor congressional interest was enough to see it completed.

Ironically, one of the individuals who was instrumental as Secretary of the Interior in getting Hetch Hetchy approved, Franklin K. Lane, also helped create the National Park Service, perhaps as penance for what he had done to the parks by supporting the dam. When he took over as Secretary of the Interior in 1913 after his appointment by President Wilson, he brought in a professor from Berkeley named Adolph C. Miller to be Assistant Secretary of the Interior in charge of the 31 existing parks, which included Yellowstone, Yosemite, Sequoia, Mount Rainier, Crater Lake, and Rocky Mountain National Parks.[2] Miller, in turn, brought his reader at Berkeley, twenty-three-year-old Horace Albright, to be his assistant, a man who later became the second NPS director.[3] A friend of Lane, Stephen Mather, was brought in to be the first director of the NPS, and Albright was made his assistant. As discussed in the history chapter, it is hard to imagine the NPS as we see it today without the efforts of Mather and Albright.

## THE NATIONAL PARK SERVICE

The National Park Service is a bureau in the Department of the Interior headed by Robert G. Stanton and with a budget of $1.6 billion. The NPS is in the midst of a massive restructuring and downsizing based on recommendations of the Vail Agenda—an NPS seventy-fifth anniversary symposium which brought together seven hundred experts in Vail, Colorado, in October 1991 to plan the future of the national parks.[4] The restructuring was intended to meet the president's goal of reducing the size of the federal government while increasing efficiency.[5] In 1994, before the reorganization, the NPS had 19,286 "full time equivalent" (FTE) employees. This was made up of a Washington headquarters with 1,091 FTE employees, ten regional offices with a total of 1,903 FTE (Boston, Philadelphia, District of Columbia, Atlanta, Omaha, Santa Fe, Denver, San Francisco, Seattle, and Anchorage), the Denver Office of Design and Construction with 680 FTE, the Harpers Ferry (West Virginia) office with 247 FTE, other NPS centers and miscellaneous facilities with a total of 795 FTE, and the parks themselves with an FTE count of 14,570.[6] This gives three levels of management: the headquarters, the field offices, which work directly with the parks, and the 374 parks.[7] The Denver Office handles architectural design and construction, as well as restoration of historical sites, for all units of the National Park System. The center employs "architects, landscape architects and engineers, historians, economists, social scientists, naturalists, graphic artists, topographers, photographers and energy specialists" with the ability to design anything from "garbage cans to hospitals and to restore structures that range from Fort Laramie on the Oregon Trail to Independence Hall in downtown Philadelphia."[8] The Harpers Ferry center handles interpretive materials, slide shows, and graphics for all the parks. There are also centers for basic NPS training (Albright Center at the Grand Canyon), for interpretation (Harpers Ferry), and for other specialized needs such as weapons training and fire fighting.

The reorganization was necessary (in the words of the NPS):

Because the National Park System has changed substantially since the current regional office based organization was implemented in the 1930's, because the nature of our mission has been dramatically expanded over time by Congress, because the threats to the National Park System are increasing at an alarming rate and because financial resources cannot be expected to increase dramatically in the foreseeable future.[9]

The major complaints about the old system were that it had become top-heavy and that there were too many layers of bureaucracy between the bosses and the rangers in the field. The new system would reduce the Washington headquarters from 1,091 to 653 FTE, the regional offices from 1,903 to 1,176, and other offices from 1,177 to 883.[10] The end result would be more rangers in the field, and less paperwork.[11] Opponents of the restructuring worry that politicians will now be able to bring increased pressure on local superintendents.[12]

## RANGERS

In the early years of the NPS the position of ranger took on an almost spiritual quality, as individuals were put in direct control of some of the most beautiful places on earth and charged with protecting them. The makeup of the job, to be at one and the same time a frontiersman like Daniel Boone, a naturalist like Thoreau, and a salesman for natural America like Mather, led to a pride in position seldom found in an increasingly desk-bound work culture. The rangers didn't take long before building a legend as the "last of the mountain men." The first job description published in 1926 said a ranger's duties included "knowledge of methods of fighting forest and prairie fires; packing horses and mules; habits of animals; ability to ride and handle horses; construction of fire lines and trails; reading of topographic maps and compass; tact in handling people; cooking; use of firearms; driving motor cars and motorcycles; and in those parks where needed, skill on snow shoes and skis; incidental clerical and information work."[13] As our world becomes more systematic and our jobs more narrow, the wide background of rangers, and especially the close contact with nature, make them stand out even more.

The number of people who would fit that description might be limited, but the number of people applying for ranger positions ran to many times the demand and led to the NPS being able to pick and choose among excellent candidates. Unfortunately, the general nature of rangers' jobs has worked against them when it comes to civil service personnel standards, which tend to favor highly trained specialists.[14] In 1991, half of the full-time rangers were classified at the GS-7 level, with an annual salary of $21,906 (some rangers took second jobs or used food stamps).[15] Rangers live in wonderful places and have jobs which many envy, but they also might live in a remote place with poor housing, difficulties in shopping and sending children to school, and the near impossibility (particularly for the young ranger) of the American dream of home ownership.[16] Difficulties of advancement, the effects on morale generated by the strong antigovernment feelings in recent years, and other negative factors have led to a turnover rate which jumped from 3 percent in the 1970's to 8 percent in the early 1990's.[17] The reorganization plan might help the ranger situation some, but only a substantial increase in the NPS budget is going to cause marked improvements.

## PERSONNEL DUTIES

Rangers may dream of working in the backcountry of Sequoia, preserving the trees and wildlife for posterity, but end up dealing with law enforcement in crowded urban parks. The law enforcement will probably be part of their duty no matter where the parks are located. The national parks are crowded, and crowds invariably mean crime. In national parks there are also many activities, such as riding a bicycle on the trails, picking flowers, or feeding the animals, which may not be crimes outside the parks. Rangers find their world defined by people—not nature. To be exact, rangers deal with people *in* nature, which should be a joy, but in understaffed, overcrowded parks, often is not.

There are many jobs in the National Park System besides those filled by rangers. About a quarter of the full-time permanent staff of the NPS are rangers, with the remainder of positions in 288 separate occupational classifications.[18] Many are in various administrative and clerical positions—secretaries, financial and personnel clerks, clerk-typists, administrative officers—and even more in the various maintenance positions—motor vehicle operators, mechanics, electricians, painters, plumbers, custodians, and security personnel. Rangers and maintenance workers are often at odds because they are competing for the same limited resources—the rangers for resource protection, while the maintenance people are worried about money for roads, buildings, and sewage plants.[19] Another group that always feels, with some justification, that it is being neglected is the park scientists. In any long-range plan based on sustainability, the environment must be thoroughly understood, which involves a sizable investment in research. Only 2 per cent of the NPS budget goes to research, however, according to a 1992 study by the National Academy of Science.[20]

## PARK PLANNING

Planning is an essential element in balancing preservation with visitor use in the national parks for a sustainable future. Fortunately, the NPS has been into planning for a very long time, founding one of the first divisions of landscape architecture in the U.S. government.[21] Everything from roads to buildings to campgrounds to trails were sited for the least possible interference with the environment. By 1926 the formal development of "master plans" had begun, with the goal of having every park operating under some kind of plan. In 1969 the National Environmental Policy Act was passed, requiring public participation in planning efforts and leading to a far different way of creating what are now called General Management Plans.

### Yosemite National Park Planning

The planning history of Yosemite National Park shows the problems and benefits of park planning. The park has some of the greatest problems with visitor use and resource protection of any national park, and planning is an absolute necessity. Working with a citizens' advisory team and park concessioners, the NPS prepared the first draft master plan for Yosemite in 1971, with the goal of removing all auto traffic from Yosemite Valley and relocating NPS and concessioner facilities from the valley.[22] A mammoth bridge across the Merced River gorge to keep cars out of the valley was strongly opposed, however, even in the unlikely event that money for building the bridge could be found. Costs were also a factor in the failure of the proposal to move facilities from Yosemite Valley to El Portal, 14 miles down a winding and often crowded road.[23] An "official" master plan was then written by an NPS team in 1974 but was never adopted because of accusations of undue influence on the master plan by the Music Corporation of America, the concessioner of Yosemite. The plan called for an increase in and upgrading of facilities in Yosemite Valley, while the public seemed to want just the opposite.[24] This fiasco led the NPS to seek unprecedented public involvement in preparing the 1980 Yosemite General Management Plan.

To get the true feelings of the public for the Yosemite master plan, the NPS made several changes in its usual way of gathering information from the public. For one, instead of having the hearings in a gateway community or large city near the park, where people with a financial stake in the parks might have undue influence, the NPS held thirty-four public workshops in California and another fourteen throughout the United States in 1975.[25] Also, instead of having just a series of statements by businesses, organizations, and individuals, as is usually the case, each meeting was broken into discussion groups where everyone was heard on a variety of issues affecting the park. Following these hearings, and partly based on them, the NPS sent out sixty thousand workbooks to everyone who asked for them.[26] Twenty thousand seven hundred individuals and groups spent an average of four hours each to complete the four oversized sheets ($2 \times 3$ feet, printed on both sides) which made up the workbook.[27] As a geographer I was delighted with the workbook, which asked you to choose and make comments on several different management options for the park as a whole, Yosemite Valley, the park wilderness, and several other locations in the park. Under transportation, for example, there were sixty-eight options, which included such choices as eliminating all autos from Yosemite Valley, inaugurating helicopter flights into the valley, and deciding whether or not shuttle bus users should pay a fee. In general, the workbooks were arranged so that a person could easily choose between options that would favor the most natural park and those that would favor maximum human activity. All options conformed to current rules and regulations affecting the park.

The tallying of the results of the workbooks, every one of which was supposedly read, took two years and was followed by traditional hearings where different proposals developed by the NPS were also examined.[28] Finally, in 1980, the General Management Plan (GMP) was released, ironically just in time for the Reagan era of reduced spending on environmental matters. The plan called for a more modest realization of the goals set by the 1971 plan: an auto-free valley and fewer NPS and concessioner employees living in the valley.

The GMP was called into question by a 1989 NPS study which said that people had perhaps changed their minds about riding in buses and staying in modest accommodations. The uproar that followed this pronouncement, and the subsequent assertion of the NPS that it had no intention of reneging on the 1980 plan, helped underline the importance of the plan. Since then several detailed studies of segments of the plan have been made, ending with the Yosemite Valley Implementation Plan, discussed in the Yosemite Case Study. There has been frequent criticism of the length and cost of the Yosemite study, but I feel that in this one case, we know about as certainly as we're ever going to know what people really want in a sustainable Yosemite National Park. Considering all the money we will eventually spend in the park, it is information we *have* to have.

## POLITICIZING THE NPS

One way to judge the increasing politicizing of the NPS is to note that while there were only seven directors of the NPS in the fifty-six years up to 1972, there have been eight directors in the twenty-four years since.[29] A second indicator is the loss of professionalism. From Mather until the end of George B. Hartzog's term in 1972, only one director, Newton T. Drury from 1940 to 1951, was not from the NPS, and he was an executive of the Save-the-Redwoods League and the California State Park Commission.[30] After Hartzog, half of the directors were not from the NPS, although Reagan's appointee, William Penn Mott, had been a successful director of the California state parks.[31] Ron Walker, who turned out to be a good director, admitted he knew nothing about the national parks when he took the job, and Bush's appointee, James Ridenour, had never been to the Grand Canyon, Yellowstone, or Yosemite. Ridenour, in all fairness, had considerable park management experience on the state level, and worked hard at improving the national parks while he was in office.[32] Clinton's first appointee, Roger Kennedy, had no experience with the national parks, but as the director of the Smithsonian Institution, had considerable managerial expertise and the personality for this high-profile job.[33] The new director, Robert G. Stanton, has thirty-five years total service in the NPS, and is its first black director.

Saying that the National Park Service was above politics before 1972 is perhaps too strong a statement. The NPS is part of the Department of the Interior, and as the Secretaries of the Interior are political appointees, there could often be problems. Mather threatened to resign at one point when Secretary Lane supported a dam in Yellowstone National Park. That problem was solved when Lane himself resigned. Albright quit at least partially because he didn't want to work with the often cantankerous Secretary Harold Ickes, who was particularly hard on Albright's successor, Arno Cammerer.[34] Cammerer's successor, Drury, was forced to resign because he strongly opposed Echo Park Dam in Dinosaur National Monument, which his boss, Secretary Oscar Chapman, supported.[35] Still, if people within the NPS were doing their job, from the director on down, they could feel they would not be let go for purely political reasons. Since 1972 they have not been so sure.

## MICROMANAGEMENT OF THE NPS

Whether the president was Hoover or Roosevelt, Kennedy or Nixon, Johnson or Ford, the NPS was considered a national treasure and more or less left alone. After all, the NPS is usually at the top in polls that rank government bureaus, with some 80 percent of the responses favorable.[36] The antigovernment rhetoric that intensified with the Reagan presidency and has continued with the 104th Congress, however, is affecting even the national parks. Although the NPS seemed to have a favored position under Reagan, with its budget staying relatively intact, the antienvironmental fervor of the administration was bound to have an effect. Stories of James Watt will undoubtedly continue as long as there are parks or an environmental movement. If you worked for the NPS it was probably wise not to speak out too strongly for the environment during Watt's tenure. Motors on boats going through the Grand Canyon, an airport runway extension in the Grand Teton National Park, a potential coal mine adjacent to Bryce Canyon National Park, a nuclear dump near Canyonlands National Park, and attempts to privatize sections of the national parks, were all issues that rangers, superintendents, and even directors spoke out against at their own peril.[37] Howard Chapman, the director of the Western Regional Office of the NPS, refused to knuckle under to antienvironmental actions of the administration and was forced to resign.[38]

The 104th Congress proved to be a nightmare for supporters of the parks and the environment. This was illustrated by the Utah Public Lands Management Act of 1995, which would have opened 1.4 million acres of currently protected wilderness in Utah to oil and gas exploration, mining, off-road vehicles, and possibly dams. The bill was withdrawn in the House when it looked as if it would be defeated, then suddenly reappeared in the Senate as part of an Omnibus Park and Recreation Bill. This bill, without the Utah rider, had wide support, including a measure to protect the Presidio in San Francisco, and to purchase a private forest for a park in New York state.[39] Senator Bill Bradley of New Jersey started a filibuster against the bill, which was withdrawn when a vote to stop the filibuster failed. The Omnibus Park and Recreation Bill later passed, without the rider.

Clinton's establishment of the Grand Staircase–Escalante National Monument in Utah a few months later continued the drama of Utah's public lands.

For the national parks the park closure bill was the scariest action of the 104th Congress. There had been criticism about the addition of certain national parks to the system, especially the more expensive urban parks. The former director of the NPS, James Ridenour, even wrote a book about it.[40] Turning a group with anti-park, antigovernment sentiments loose on the National Park System, however, with a mandate to find "inferior parks" and those which could be better managed by the states, could well have been "the greatest threat to the National Park System since it was established in 1916," according to the president of the National Park and Conservation Association.[41] While the avowed purpose of the bill was to improve the National Park System, it seemed to be only a pretext to find parks to close, especially urban, Alaskan, and historical parks. The bill was voted down by the full House, after which Rep. James Hansen placed the bill as a rider on an appropriations bill, the exact tactic that he had accused pro-park people of using to gain extra parks (actually, only Steamtown National Historic Site came into the system that way, out of 374 parks).[42] The House Budget Committee later removed the park closure bill from the budget reconciliation package, after President Clinton had vetoed the original bill.[43]

## FINANCING THE PARKS

The NPS has been trying do more with less money for a number of years now. According to a study by the Natural Resources Defense Council, the NPS budget has declined $635 million, in constant dollars, from 1978 to 1996.[44] The reaction to this by those who have the power to change the situation has often been to call for even more government austerity. If this continues, hope for an improvement in the quality of protection and enjoyment of the national parks becomes faint indeed. Many, however, agree with the Western writer Wallace Stegner that establishing the National Park System was "the best idea we ever had," and would like to see more money spent on the parks. According to a Citibank poll, two-thirds of the public want more money to go to the national parks.[45] This seldom translates, however, into a push for higher taxes to pay for the parks.

Several factors make the financial situation of the national parks worse than might even be expected. The most critical factor is the increasing popularity of the parks, which means that every year the rangers have to deal with more visitors, and with all the increased demands on facilities, interpretation, services, and law enforcement. This can also mean greater deprivation for certain aspects of park spending than for others, as the more visible aspects of park operations, such as the campgrounds or roads, will tend to be the "squeaky wheels that get greased," rather than, say, wildlife protection. This in turn leads to ranger dissatisfaction as it becomes obvious that preservation is not the primary goal of the NPS.[46]

The second factor worsening the national parks' financial situation is park expansion. In the 1980's the National Park System enjoyed its greatest expansion in history. Much of this took place in Alaska, where visitation tended to be low, but some 25 new units were also added to the National Park System elsewhere.[47] Most park supporters applauded these additions, but they also expected funding to go along with the new parks. Instead, it has meant more responsibilities for the NPS for the same amount of money. There were also a few "park barrel" projects in the national park budget, such as Steamtown National Historic Site in Pennsylvania. This park, the "bête noire" among park barrel parks, at 62 acres in size with a visitation of 145,000, had a larger budget at $2,325,000 than half of the national parks.[48] Whether or not this park will someday prove to be a good addition to the National Park System, as supporters claim, it serves today as a lightning rod for those who claim reducing the size of the system would cure the parks' financial problems.

The financial crisis of the national parks also includes critical delayed maintenance. The backlog for maintenance and construction is $5.6 billion, for protection of resources $2 billion, and $1.5 billion for land acquisition.[49] The Yellowstone road system would cost $300,000,000 to fix, for example, while the park was able to allocate only a thirtieth of that amount to road repair in 1994.[50] Deteriorating sewage systems, collapsing buildings, and substandard housing for rangers are part of a long and growing list of problems that require more money to solve.[51] This is in addition to the funds needed to complete purchases of inholdings in the parks, to meet the external threats of air and water pollution, and to meet the increased demands of rising visitation.

The proposed national park budget for 1998 is $1.6 billion, a slight increase over the last two years.[52] Although cuts are not anticipated, as in past years, Congress usually includes projects not requested by the NPS (park barrel as usual), and uses the budget to handicap projects some members do not like, such as, in the past, cutting funds for the gray wolf program in Yellowstone National Park and the new Mojave National Preserve in California. The proposed budget provides for a funding increase of at least 1 percent for each unit in the system, but does almost nothing to decrease the tremendous funding backlog mentioned above. Funds to improve the Everglades ecosystem and remove dams in Olympic National Park, however, are in the budget. Even assuming these funds are left intact by Congress, many more imaginative financial solutions must be sought, while park supporters pray for better days.

The backlog of authorized but unpurchased lands in the national parks, including some 423,000 acres of inholdings, should have long since been paid for by a congressionally authorized method, the Land and Water Conservation Act.[53] The act, which provides funds for acquisition of public recreational land on all governmental levels, has, since its inception in 1965, provided most of the funds for whatever land the NPS has acquired.[54] The fund provided up to $736 million a year (only part of which went to the national parks) until the Reagan-Watt era, when further requests for spending were suspended, despite the growing backlog and increasing costs of authorized recreational land. The fund continues to be healthy, with $900 million available each year, including money from federal offshore oil leases and entrance fees to federal lands. Appropriations have averaged less than $300 million each year, with the NPS receiving about $50 million. The 104th Congress resolved to eliminate the fund altogether, then reconsidered and included $49.1 million in the 1996 budget it submitted.[55]

Raising entrance fees is another logical way of providing money for the national parks, and several proposals for doing so are in various stages of enactment. The problem is twofold. Fees go directly into the U.S. Treasury, with no direct benefits to the national parks from the fee increase, and many would argue that these are "national treasures" for which there should be no fees. The result is fees that have not changed much since the parks first opened, such as the 1996 $10 fee for a car full of people to visit Yellowstone. Entrance fees were an insignificant portion of most visitors' vacation expenditures. Congress authorized a new plan in 1996 as a test project, which may help the parks. It authorizes increases at up to a hundred parks, including Yosemite, Yellowstone, and Glacier, where the fee will increase to $20 per car per week. Eighty percent of the extra revenue will remain in the parks for specific improvements, such as new shuttle buses in Yosemite, with the remaining 20 percent going to sites with the most need.[56] Early reports indicate almost no opposition to the fees.[57]

Increasing concession fees could raise significant moneys which would go directly to the parks. In 1993 concessioners returned only 2.8 percent in franchise fees to the parks, $18,600,000 out of revenues of $657,200,000.[58]

*One method of stretching budgets in the national parks is by extensive use of volunteers, like this hatless ranger in the Fiery Furnace area of Arches National Park.*

A bill to raise the percentage that concessioners pay almost made it through the 103d Congress. The 104th Congress presented a bill preserving the current situation and insuring that none of the money collected would remain in the park where it is collected, and it, too, was defeated.[59]

Volunteers in the national parks have made an overwhelming contribution to the quality of the national parks. On the last two trips I've made to Arches National Park, I've taken the delightful nature walk through the Fiery Furnace with volunteer rangers. They did excellent jobs, and although they receive no salary, they do receive funds for room and board, spend a summer doing what they want to do, and expand their résumés. Unfortunately, all this still costs the parks in scarce housing and supervision time, limiting the number of volunteers they can manage. In a large city park adjacent to San Diego State University, where I teach, the four-person ranger staff is bolstered by two hundred part-time volunteers. The chief ranger of Mission Trails Regional Park, Randy Hawley, says there is no way the park could be operated without these volunteers. Increasingly, national parks are approaching the same situation.

Draconian measures for curing the parks' financial problems are frequently espoused by antigovernment groups. The park closure bill was discussed above. The proposals with perhaps the greatest support are to close the urban parks, two of which—Golden Gate National Recreation

Area in San Francisco and Gateway National Recreation Area in New York City—are among the most expensive units in the National Park System to run. In terms of money for acquisition, Santa Monica National Recreation Area would also be at or near the top. The main argument against them is that we can only afford the "crown jewels among parks"—the Yosemites, Yellowstones, and Grand Canyons. Privatization of the national parks is also a possibility, usually mentioned by the same people. There are resources in the national parks—timber, minerals, grazing land, water—which could be sold to pay for the parks. More seriously, who would doubt that Disney could quickly turn a profit at the most popular national parks? Of course, in paying $50 a person to see the Grand Canyon, for example, you'd expect a fireworks display and a laser light show down in the canyon! If Las Vegas can support several of the largest hotels in the world in a flat desert environment, think how many rooms could be filled on the floor of Yosemite Valley. At a lower level of exaggeration there are many who felt that McDonald's would have done a superlative job as concessioner for Yosemite National Park, and that national chains, with only a slight relaxing of advertising regulations in the parks, should be given a shot at various services within the parks.

## SUMMARY

Increasing park budgets is the obvious and best solution for the financial problems faced by the national parks, but given the current budget situation, might have to be put on hold. As one writer put it: the "rise in inequality between the rich and poor, the increasing poverty overtaking whole segments of the population, the enfeebling effects of drug addiction, the decline of the public school system," and finally, wholesale environmental degradation, are bound to have an impact on all future budget requests.[60] With the national parks consuming only 0.1 percent of the national budget,[61] an amount equal to half what we spend on federal prisons, and about the same as cotton subsidies, I still believe we can afford it.[62] In the meantime, adversity can build strength and new directions such as an expanded volunteer program, and increased park and concession fees may keep the parks together until budgets do increase. The public is hearing the message of park impoverishment in an unprecedented wave of articles; some improvement seems inevitable.[63]

# Case Study:
# Grand Teton National Park

No one ever has to ask why the Teton Range of northwestern Wyoming is in a national park. Driving into Jackson Hole from any direction, you are faced with one of the country's most dramatic landscapes. The Teton Range rises precipitously 3,000–6,500 feet out of the valley, classic fault block mountains with glacial erosion presenting views of alpine grandeur. The Cathedral Group of the Teton Range— the Grand Teton, Mount Owen, and Teewinott Mountain—will stand comparison with mountains anywhere.

It is its situation that makes the Teton Range so dramatic. Jackson Hole, relatively flat, provides the perfect platform from which to view the mountains. The North Cascades from Puget Sound and the Sierras from the Central Valley are examples of spectacular peaks that are hidden by distance or other mountains. Not only is the Teton Range dramatically visible, but the scene is enhanced by a series of lakes and the Snake River. The question is not why the area is in a park but why it took until 1950 to complete Grand Teton National Park as we see it today. Few parks have been more affected by politics.

## FOUNDING THE PARK

A bill to include much of today's Grand Teton National Park in an expanded Yellowstone National Park passed the House unanimously in 1919 and seemed headed for a quick victory in the Senate. A group of Idaho sheepherders thought the bill might somehow affect them, however (it wouldn't have), and convinced an Idaho senator to oppose it. Under a filibuster then in effect, his one vote was all that was needed. A thirty-one-year battle for the protection of the Teton Range and Jackson Hole in a national park had begun.[1]

The antagonists in the fight over Grand Teton National Park seem little changed from those in the battle for parks and wilderness lands today. Most of us have identified at one time or another with the dichotomy in this country between private and public land use, between cooperation and freedom to do exactly what we want, between the environmentalist and the cowboy. It's almost the irresistible force and the immovable object. We can identify with the person who wants a nice home on the shores of Jackson Lake, while at the same time recognizing that national parks would be impossible if all the better places were in private hands. It helps us understand how an area as outstanding as Jackson Hole was almost left out of Grand Teton National Park.

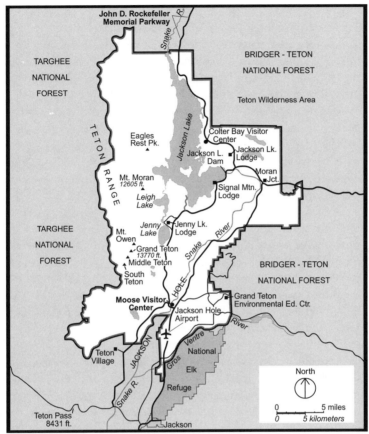

# Grand Teton National Park

The Teton Range without Jackson Hole was never that controversial. There was opposition from the U.S. Forest Service, but in 1929 a 150-square-mile park was established around the most impressive part of the range. Interestingly, a no-roads, no-hotel provision was written into the law, making it the first national park established with wilderness provisions, to satisfy dude ranch interests in the area who feared Yellowstone-type hotels and services.[2] A much larger park was already being planned, however, starting with a 1926 visit to the Teton Range by Yellowstone Superintendent Horace Albright and John D. Rockefeller Jr. at a spot commemorated today as Lunch Tree Hill near present-day Jackson Lake Lodge. Rockefeller expressed an interest in buying Jackson Hole and presenting it to the nation.[3]

The purchase of much of Jackson Hole was accomplished more or less as planned, but when Rockefeller tried to give the NPS the 32,000 acres he had purchased, all hell broke loose. The U.S. Forest Service led the fight against the expanded parks, but there were many people who, for political, financial, or personal reasons, were happy to join in. As today, protecting the "little people" against the rich (Rockefeller) and the powerful (U.S. government) was a sure route to political fame. At a hearing in 1943 at Jackson, Wyoming, 644 were against the extension out of the 650 people at the hearing (the other 6 were neutral).[4]

The park would probably never have prevailed against such opposition if the pugnacious Harold Ickes had not been Secretary of the Interior and Franklin Roosevelt the president. The environmental movement, which was to become a force after World War II, was also quietly building at the time. Rockefeller threatened to sell back the land if it was not accepted in the park, leading Roosevelt to establish a national monument including Jackson Hole in 1943. Congress, well into an anti-Roosevelt mood at that time, voted to abolish the national monument, but Roosevelt pocket-vetoed the abolition bill and the anti-park movement slowly died.

Grand Teton National Park will celebrate its fiftieth anniversary as a full park in the year 2000, and park detractors will probably be as hard to find as supporters were back in the 1940's. It is easy to see why. Jackson has been one of the fastest-growing communities in the West since then, and without a park it isn't difficult to imagine what Jackson Hole would be like. There are recreational slums throughout the West, but somehow I think Jackson Hole, with development scattered along its rivers, lakes, and terraces, would be one of the worst. As it is, the national park is the homeowner's dream, providing a beautiful view and a neighborhood which should never deteriorate (except with more and more neighbors).

## DEVELOPMENT

In the beginning, park supporters had to fight environmental organizations over making Jackson Hole part of the national park. In many people's minds, the existence of Jackson Lake Dam, built in 1906 and 1911, was a fatal flaw. Remembering Hetch Hetchy, many park supporters were afraid that the coexistence of water resources development and a national park would open the way for other dams in other parks.

Idaho irrigation farmers had their eyes on the Yellowstone–Grand Teton area long before the Teton Range became a park. The farmers were unable to divert the Yellowstone River into the Snake River via a tunnel from Yellowstone Lake, or build a dam on the Bechler River in the southwestern part of Yellowstone, as they had proposed, but they were able to develop the Snake River for irrigation in the cheapest and best way possible for them. The project on Jackson Lake was called an outlet improvement. By lowering the lip of the outlet of Jackson Lake into the Snake River, and by building a dam to raise the outlet, the entire surface of the lake could be used for storage. When the gates of the dam were first closed, 7,234 acres of lodgepole pines were flooded and killed (later cleaned up by the Civilian Conservation Corps). Currently, during low-water periods, often coinciding with the tourist season, the lake is drawn down, leaving an unattractive shoreline. The possibility always exists of buying out the irrigation rights of the Idaho farmers, subsidized by the Bureau of Reclamation in the first place, but this likelihood is only a little greater than removing the Hetch Hetchy dam from Yosemite.

The original highway through Jackson Hole skirted Jackson and Jenny Lakes, areas that the NPS rightly decided were unique areas which should be spared as much traffic as possible. Consequently, a bypass highway was built in the eastern part of the park on land ecologically less important, but with spectacular views. People in a hurry could skip the often crowded conditions along the lakes and still "see" the park.

Along Jenny Lake an earlier bypass had been built, as straight and cheap as possible, avoiding the narrow road which followed the lake. As the years went by RVs had increasing trouble negotiating the narrow road, leading to the possibility of extensive widening of what, in my opinion, is one of the most beautiful roads in the park system. The solution was to make the road around Jenny Lake one-way, widening it slightly, and to make the bypass a more aesthetically pleasing curving road.

With the town of Jackson so close by, it seems logical that lodges, hotels, and cabins would be banned from the park, just as in the original park bill. However, one of the first orders of business for the newly expanded park was the building of Jackson Lake Lodge by one of John D. Rockefeller's sons, Laurance, on the site where the senior Rockefeller first conceived of the park expansion. Not everyone was happy with the architecture of the hotel, or even convinced of its need, but the views from the main lobby have to be among the most impressive from any hotel in the world.[5]

The NPS pursued the idea in the 1950's of moving facilities away from the major points of interest, where they would naturally gravitate when the park was new, to "less scenic" areas. Colter Bay, quite beautiful, but untouched compared to popular Jenny Lake, where they were closing down cabins and stores, became the location for a huge complex encompassing stores, cabins, a visitor center, a marina, a trailer park, and a campground. The area fits the landscape well enough, but just as with Grant Village in Yellowstone to the north, the building of Colter Bay seemed more to be based on adding facilities to the park than trading for a more pristine scenic area.

Whatever the NPS might do to attract tourists to the park or discourage them, the addition of the Teton Village Ski Resort, the explosive growth of Jackson, and the increasing popularity of air travel have presented the park with massive problems. The location of the Jackson Hole Airport is the best, and some say only, location for an airport in the Jackson–Grand Teton area. It has become one of the busiest airports in the state of Wyoming, showing a 270 percent increase in passengers in the decade since jet service began.[6] The park is committed to maintaining a natural environment, however, which many feel is inconsistent with the landing of jets. There have been hearings, environmental impact statements, and more or less constant pressure from environmental groups, but proposals still surface to increase the length of the runway in the interests of safety.[7] It might be left to another generation, if ever, to restore the natural quiet to Jackson Hole by moving the airport some distance away, but restricting the number and size of jets landing could be done today.

## RECREATIONAL USE OF THE PARK

Grand Teton is a wonderful park for recreational travel, by car, bike, foot, or boat. I have never seen a national park where the overlooks seem so perfectly located, whether you stop just south of Jackson Hole Lodge, looking over Willow Flats to the lake and the Teton Range in the near distance, or at the dramatic Snake River Overlook on the John D. Rockefeller Parkway, or at the close views of the Cathedral Group from the one-way road next to Jenny Lake. Because the terrain is mostly flat and the newer roads have good shoulders, biking is very popular in the park. Hiking is also superlative, either along the lakes in front of the mountains or up into the peaks themselves.

Back in the late 1950's a few of us used to float the Snake River, feeling it was our little secret. There weren't any bad rapids between the dam and Menors Ferry at park headquarters, the river ran fast enough to be exciting, the scenery was incredible, and seeing a moose, or an eagle, or a bison was almost certain. Well, it hasn't been a secret for a long time; 104,152 persons floated the river in 1995,[8] following guidelines on where to put in, take out, and land during the trip.[9] The numbers, so far, have not had to be limited. Fortunately, like a sandy beach, a river can handle a very high number of users without impact if they don't stop en route and boats are spaced where people can still have a wilderness experience.

The Teton Range has long been a prime destination for mountaineers. The peaks are accessible, the rock excellent, the views unexcelled, and a guide service has been available since 1931, one of the oldest in America. Exun Mountain Guides, named after the founder who first climbed the ridge that is the standard route to the summit, guided 1,437 clients on the Grand Teton in 1994.[10] The NPS is in the rescue business but no longer requires skill and equipment checks or even registration for climbs, although overnight backcountry use still requires a permit. Voluntary registration exists, but registrants often do not sign in, "causing administrative complications and occasional costly searches."[11]

## INHOLDINGS

The major reason for Rockefeller's buying land in Jackson Hole and adding it to an expanded park was to prevent the inevitable sleazy "recreational villages" which had already begun to develop in the area. When the national park was founded in 1950, dude ranches were scattered around the valley and clusters of buildings were found in the small village of Moran below Jackson Lake Dam, at Signal Mountain south of the dam, around one side of Jenny Lake, near the crossing of the Snake River, and at various other places in Jackson Hole. The park immediately started clearing the land it owned, removing the town of Moran, and several dude ranches and stores around Jenny Lake. Of the original 44,856 acres of private land in Jackson Hole, Rockefeller acquired 32,419 acres, leaving thousands of acres of private land in the park.[12] Some of these lands have proved to be more of a headache than others—I well remember one highly visible chuck wagon–bar– store complex with the word "EAT" written in enormous letters on its roof.

On the other hand, there are some inholdings that seem innocuous or even beneficial to the park. When my daughter was in high school she attended the Teton Science School in a former dude ranch in the valley; the cabins were used as simple housing for students from all over the country, while the main building contained a library and large guest room where lectures took place. There are other university and school properties in the park, plus private land which has not been touched and thus is indistinguishable from parkland. Rockefeller kept one piece of property in the southern end of the park nestled against the mountains (2,333 acres), which seems only fair.

As of 1990, 7,572 acres of private inholdings in Grand Teton National Park had been purchased for $29,124,282.[13] Proceedings to acquire most of the remainder will continue, despite a chronic shortage of such funds. If the land cannot be purchased outright, restrictive easements can often be obtained. The NPS lists several reasons for the incompatibility of such land with the park: cattle and sheep grazing, hunting and shooting, pets, garbage disposal, gravel extraction, snowmobiling, irrigation, vegetation management, and visual intrusion.[14] The greatest problem, however, relates to the park's being "legally required to provide rights-of-way for roads and utilities to private lands in the park."[15] A high-standard road was constructed across the park to a new subdivision in 1980. Furthermore, the NPS plows many of these roads in the winter, and provides some or all of the fire protection, police protection, garbage disposal, and road maintenance for the inholdings.

## JENNY LAKE

Jenny Lake, as one of the most beautiful and popular places in the park, has received a great deal of attention from efforts to restore it to its original natural condition. When I used to climb there in the early to mid-1950's, few climbers bothered with a formal campsite in the campground. They would just pitch their tents on a ridge between campsites where a climber-writer used to have a large teepee and tables and would host climbers all summer long. The shoreline between the road and lake was narrow and mostly barren from overuse. There were a studio, a ranger station, cabins, a cafe, and a guidehouse in the area. The cabins and cafe were the first to be removed, followed by the studio and guide-

*Two highways in this aerial photograph of Jenny Lake have been removed in an attempt to restore one of the most popular places in Grand Teton National Park. The campground, however, remains, and a parking lot was built near the upper end of Jenny Lake.*

house. The ranger station was moved away from the lake in the early 1990's, and more importantly, part of the road next to the lake was moved inland. To serve the heavy visitation to the area, a dispersed parking area was built a short distance from the lake, and hardened trails built to it.[16] A small store and restrooms are also in the area. The campground was upgraded and slightly enlarged to include a walk-in campground. As an act of landscape architecture, it is probably the best that can be done to preserve the shoreline of this beautiful lake against the hordes that undoubtedly will continue to come.

## SUMMARY

Jackson Hole, with the splendid Teton Range to the west, gorgeous lakes at the mountains' base, and the Snake River winding through it, has long been known as one of the most beautiful valleys in the country. It seemed inevitable that Jackson Hole, consisting mostly of private land, would deteriorate in time, with uncontrolled businesses competing for the tourist dollar. Writing a scenario for the area seventy-five years ago, where a wealthy and public-spirited individual would buy the area and give it to the NPS, would have strained credulity. Even fifty years ago, when I first saw the valley, a person would have been hard pressed to imagine the area with actually *less* development today, as most of the structures from that period were removed. Finally, to imagine the park being accepted by nearly everyone in the area, after the bitter battles of midcentury, would be hardest to believe of all.

Difficult choices, unfortunately, are still to come. Like any population explosion, the constantly climbing visitation which has prevailed since the park was established will someday have to stop. Perhaps, however, that day is still a long way in the future. Grand Teton National Park came into the system after one of the most acrimonious fights in the National Park System and with more operating restraints than almost any other park. That the park is in good shape despite all this, in the face of crowds and limiting budgets, says worlds about the truth of the original park concept.

# 12 Conclusions

WHEN the first national park was established in 1872 the nation contained enormous areas of wilderness, especially in the West. With few roads or little development in the western United States, there weren't too many places you *couldn't* establish a wilderness area, using today's criteria. The Colorado River through the Grand Canyon had just been traversed by Major John W. Powell, and first ascents were available on most of the nation's large mountains, including Mount Whitney and the Grand Teton. As late as the mid-1930's there were nine roadless areas larger than Yellowstone National Park in the conterminous United States; today only one remains—the High Sierra Wilderness.[1] Alaska was virtually untouched.

For all this, in 1872 wildlife depredation in this country was already well advanced, resources were disappearing at an accelerated rate, and almost no one was speaking for the environment. John Muir would be heard from in a few years, but Aldo Leopold didn't start writing until the 1920's and the Sierra Club, founded in 1892, would not really become powerful until the Echo Park controversy in the 1950's. The first Earth Day in 1970 is considered by many as an unofficial "beginning" to the current environmental movement. In short, in 1872 there were no National Park System, no wildlife refuges, no national forests, no National Wilderness Preservation System, no state parks, no Environmental Policy Act, no Endangered Species Act, no Wild and Scenic Rivers System, and few people who really cared.

We are far advanced in environmental laws, support, and consciousness over what we were 125 years ago. The natural landscape is much reduced, but it is not gone, thanks partially to what happened on the Yellowstone Plateau at that time. Nor have the exploiters gone. Timber companies are cutting some of the last of the ancient redwoods, and we could have lost up to half of the country's precious wetlands under bills introduced in the 104th Congress. The environmental debate is as sharp and acrimonious as it has ever been, but this is far better than silently watching the world deteriorate as people did for years.

Our national parks are as solid as our government itself. This doesn't mean that individual parks will not receive a lot of attention, but almost all of the parks are certainly safe. I believe Stephen Mather was right in believing that the more people see the parks, the safer they are going to be. People standing for the first time at the rim of the Grand Canyon, or in front of the Liberty Bell in Independence National Historic Park in Philadelphia, have got to feel the $6 per person that the National Park System is costing them per year is well worth it.

## INTERNATIONAL LANDSCAPE PRESERVATION

The example set by the United States in establishing national parks has been adopted by all but a handful of nations in the world. Out of 237 countries included in a United Nations survey of protected areas in the world, only 19 of them had no national parks.[2] Most of the world's protected areas have been established in the last twenty-five years, with the five-year period starting in 1970 being the most productive.[3] A few countries followed America's lead in the nineteenth century, notably Canada, Australia, and New Zealand, which had large areas of open land, small populations, and spectacular scenery. But whether early or late, some 2,000 national parks and reserves had been established in 120 nations by the early 1980's.[4] The International Union of Conservation of Nature (IUCN) counts 9,832 areas with some kind of protection in the world, with almost a billion hectares of land involved.[5] The categories which the IUCN uses are similar to the different categories used in the national parks. Any real attempts by nations or individuals at saving the natural or cultural landscape and making it available for enjoyment are recognized.

Several of the U.S. national parks have been listed as World Heritage Sites (WHS), including the first—Yellowstone National Park. World Heritage Sites are established by the Convention Concerning the Protection of the World Cultural and Natural Heritage, an organization founded by the General Conference of the United Nations Educational, Scientific, and

*Sagarmatha National Park, one of some 2,000 national parks and reserves in the world, protects the Nepalese side of Mount Everest.*

Cultural Organization in Paris in 1972.[6] World Heritage Sites number over 400 in 90 countries and include everything from the Great Barrier Reef to the Tower of London.[7] Other World Heritage Sites in the United States are the Everglades, Grand Canyon, Great Smoky Mountains, Hawaii Volcanoes, Mammoth Cave, Olympic, Redwood, Wrangell–St. Elias, and Yosemite National Parks. The category is strictly honorary and informational, and not a plot for world domination, as feared by some "conspiracy theorists and wise use groups."[8]

## RESTORATION

In the summer of 1996 I stood on Stoneman Bridge in Yosemite National Park and looked upstream over the Merced River, swollen by snowmelt. On the left was a Yosemite streambank I had long been familiar with—bare dirt, the legacy of over a hundred years of walking, playing, and trampling. On the right bank was an area which had been closed for a decade with a simple split-rail fence—as rich and lush as you would expect a sunny, well-watered strip of soil to be. I would assume that no one has been deprived of a place to walk and play, as there was a big natural sandy beach just below it. People who were sitting in front of their trailers adjacent to the protected area were enjoying a scene more natural and more beautiful than even their parents would have enjoyed two or three decades before. A year later and the campground here is gone, washed out by the 1997 flood, and recovery of a natural streambank in the midst of a valley with millions of visitors now seems assured.

Such a scene should be possible anywhere in the National Park System, even where use is heaviest. After all, it is nature doing most of the restoring. We accepted the wear and tear on the national parks as we made way for visitors in an endless stream—visitors who someday would love and understand the parks and want them to be as nature intended. The multiple-trail blight of Paradise Valley on Mount Rainier, the thousand buildings of Yosemite Valley, "the longest moving parking lot in America" at the South Rim of the Grand Canyon, the mass of people and buildings around Old Faithful, even the drowned beauty of Hetch Hetchy, should be restorable if the will, and the money, are there.

## THE FUTURE OF THE NATIONAL PARKS

Despite many of the negative undertones in this book I think the parks are going to improve in the years ahead. If the national parks were being run sloppily, or if the public were unhappy with them, there would be plenty of reason to worry. But the primary reason for most park problems is simple neglect, which can be ended anytime we choose. The following eight measures, in my opinion, would bring the national parks up to a level of quality where they belong.

1. *Improve funding.* The national parks seem almost to have "hit bottom" as far as funding is concerned. Articles are beginning to appear with regularity in mainstream publications about the deplorable way we have been treating our national treasures, both natural and historic. This could, if it continues, signal a turnaround in park fortunes. The foundation is there in new programs to obtain funds and operate more efficiently; now the budget has to increase.

2. *Improve environmental education.* National parks are places where people come willingly and eagerly into a learning situation. People are on vacation, they are surrounded by beautiful and interesting things, and they are curious. They want to talk to a ranger, to ask questions, and to listen. Yet seeing rangers outside of the usually crowded visitor centers is rare, and when you spot them, they are usually surrounded by people. Most everyone agrees that environmental information is important, yet one of the perfect places for it to be taught is handicapped by lack of personnel and, inevitably, lack of money. As with all the measures to follow, NPS budgets must increase.

3. *Slow visitation growth.* This book is mostly about exploring the ways that the maximum number of people can enjoy the national parks in the most natural conditions possible. Overcrowding occurs in the parks, however, and it will continue to occur despite all that can and should be done to improve the parks. Eventually, people will have to be turned back at the gates when a predetermined number, which has been proven to harm a particular park, has been reached. This has already happened in Yosemite and will have to be done in several other parks in the future. If the reasons for such closures are given through improved educational programs, and advance reservation systems expanded, negative response should be minimal.

4. *Nonautomotive transportation in the national parks should be improved.* An important method of allowing more people to see the national parks with no loss in environmental quality is to replace private with public transportation. Such changes have already had dramatic positive impacts on Yosemite Valley, with even greater improvements planned for the future. Most of the high-density national parks, such as Grand Canyon, which has an underfunded system in place, could profit from public transportation. More and better bike paths and trails are also important future additions to the parks.

5. *The national parks should become less political.* This is probably just wishful thinking, but the actions of the 104th Congress give some hope that the parks might become less political in the future than they've been in the past. All of the anti-park legislation offered in that Congress was either defeated or withdrawn, reaffirming the fact that national parks have widespread bipartisan support. Furthermore, the closing of the national parks during the governmental shutdown of 1995, which might have helped Clinton's reelection, was one of the most damaging events of the shutdown. Everything that needs to be done to insure quality national parks in the future will be much more certain if the parks are taken out of the political arena.

6. *Be prepared for changing forms of outdoor recreation.* I don't believe anyone could have anticipated the tremendous increase in popularity of rock climbing, river rafting, mountain biking, and snowmobiling in this country. No one knows what new sports, or what improvements in the technique or equipment of old sports and activities, will do to the recreational use of the national parks. By trying to anticipate such changes, however, we can avoid immense headaches in the future. The firm regulations on mountain biking on trails in the national parks, for example, have kept it from being a problem in the parks, just as the lack of up-to-

date plans for rock climbing has led to ongoing conflicts over that sport in the national parks.

7. *Park restoration should continue until pre-European landscapes prevail.* Looking at a landscape which has been almost trashed after a century of visitation and feeling that this was the price that had to be paid for a National Park System are no longer necessary. If Yosemite Valley can be restored to an approximation of what the original visitors saw there, it can happen anywhere. Unfortunately, it will cost money, although imaginative funding and volunteer work projects can help.

8. *Expand the National Park System.* As Americans continue to become more aware of the beauty of natural landscapes—lakeshores, wetlands, prairies, ancient forests, and wild rivers—they're going to become more appreciative of the National Park System. The special expertise of the NPS allows areas of special beauty to be seen, appreciated, interpreted, and indeed saved, for generations to come. The tiny percentage of the

*North Cascades National Park, which contains spectacular mountains like Forbidden Peak, was not founded until 1968, nearly a full century after Yellowstone. Other areas, just as scenic and even more ecologically diverse, await our attention in the years ahead as we become willing to pay for the expansion of our beloved National Park System.*

American landscape that is in the National Park System might be large enough to accommodate the "crown jewels" of the country, most of the most important historical areas, and a sampling of ecological and recreational areas, but there is much more in this country deserving of national park treatment. I don't expect us to pull up the streets of our cities, or lay fallow valuable farmland to create more national parks, but certainly *some* of the vast acreage of this country can be converted to areas which are so important to the quality of our lives.

## SUMMARY

People are aware of the global environmental crisis and want to do something about it. They also want to hang onto as much of the natural world as they can. There are others, perhaps, for whom the world is a brief stopping place on the way to a truly magnificent eternity. Without belittling what may be out there, many of us are impressed with what is here on earth. Protecting the natural and the beautiful places of the world, although of less immediate importance than preventing poisoning of the earth or global warming, is essential to making this a life worth living.

The question long ago stopped being about the existence of national parks, which is about as solid as our freedom or democratic way of life, but about the quality of those parks. The numbers visiting our national parks will continue to escalate, and keeping the quality of the park experience high will become more difficult. I hope our expectations for the parks will also increase in time, meaning we will move into a new era of caring for our parks, and a truly sustainable National Park System.

# Notes

ABBREVIATIONS

NM     National Monument
NP     National Park
NPS    National Park Service
NRA    National Recreation Area
USGPO  United States Government Printing Office


1. INTRODUCTION

1. U.S. Bureau of the Census, *Statistical Abstract of the United States 1992* (Washington, D.C.: USGPO, 1992), p. 8.

2. Stewart Udall, *The Quiet Crisis and the Next Generation*, pp. 54–68.

3. S. 392, H.R. 464, 42d Cong., 2d sess., Stat. 17, 32.

4. The literature of ecotourism is growing rapidly. A simple introduction is Tensie Whelan, ed., *Nature Tourism* (Covelo, Calif.: Island Press, 1991).


2. NATURE OF THE SYSTEM

1. NPS, *The National Parks: Index 1995.*

2. Comparing *units* of the National Park System, Lake Mead NRA has twice as many visitors at 9,350,847 visitors as the Grand Canyon NP's 4,537,703 visitors, and Golden Gate NRA had 14,043,984 visitors in 1996. NPS, *National Park Service Statistical Abstract, 1996*, pp. 4–17.

3. Stat. 34, 225.

4. NPS, *The National Parks: Index 1995*, p. 13.

5. Barry M. Buxton and Steven M. Beatty, eds., *Blue Ridge Parkway: Agent of Transition* (Boone, N.C.: Appalachian Consortium Press, 1986).

6. NPS, *NPS Statistical Abstract, 1996*, pp. 1, 5.

7. Eliot Porter, *The Place No One Knew: Glen Canyon* (San Francisco: Sierra Club Books, 1963).

8. Michael E. Long, "The Grand Managed Canyon," *National Geographic*, July 1997, pp. 134–135.

9. Tim Palmer, *Endangered Rivers and the Conservation Movement* (Berkeley: University of California Press, 1986).

10. Ronald A. Foresta, *America's National Parks and Their Keepers*, p. 178.

11. Ibid., p. 172.

12. Ariel Rubissow, *Golden Gate National Recreation Area Park Guide* (San Francisco: Golden Gate National Park Association, 1990).

13. NPS, "Reveille, The Newsletter of the National Park Service Presidio Planning Process," May 1990.

14. Terry Trucco, "San Francisco's Urban Retreat," *New York Times*, October 15, 1995.

15. Timothy Eagan, "Peacetime Vision for the Presidio in Jeopardy," *New York Times*, February 21, 1995.

16. Dwight Rettie, *Our National Park System*, pp. 268–269.

17. Randal O'Toole, "The National Pork Service," *Forbes*, November 20, 1995, p. 160.

18. National Park and Conservation Association, "House Approves Presidio Trust," *National Parks Magazine*, November/December 1995, pp. 14–15.

## 3. HISTORY

1. Udall, *The Quiet Crisis*, pp. 54–68.

2. Ibid., p. 57.

3. George Catlin, *Illustrations of the Manners, Customs, and Conditions of the North American Indians* (London: H. G. Bohn, 1851), 1:262.

4. NPS, *The National Parks: Shaping the System*, pp. 14–15.

5. Alfred Runte, *Yosemite, the Embattled Wilderness*, pp. 10–21.

6. Ibid., pp. 21–27.

7. John Ise, *Our National Park Policy*, p. 74.

8. Aubrey L. Haines, *The Yellowstone Story*, 2 vols. (Boulder, Colo.: Yellowstone Library and Museum Association, 1977).

9. NPS, *Winter Use Plan Environmental Assessment* (Washington, D.C.: USGPO, 1990), p. 8.

10. Alfred Runte, *National Parks: The American Experience*, pp. 48–64.

11. Nathaniel Pitt Langford, *The Discovery of Yellowstone Park* (Lincoln: University of Nebraska Press, 1972; reprint of 1905 ed. printed by the Haynes Foundation in St. Paul).

12. Paul Schullery, *Searching for Yellowstone* (Boston: Houghton Mifflin Co., 1997), pp. 56–64.

13. Langford, pp. 117–118.

14. Ferdinand V. Hayden, *Twelfth Annual Report*, U.S. Geological and Geographical Survey of the Territories, 2 vols. (Washington, D.C.: USGPO, 1883).

15. Schullery, pp. 56–64.

16. Runte, *Yosemite*, p. 40.

17. Louis C. Cramton, *Early History of Yellowstone National Park and Its Relation to National Park Policies* (Washington, D.C.: USGPO, 1932), p. 39; Runte, *Yosemite*, p. 38.

18. Richard A. Bartlett, *Yellowstone: A Wilderness Besieged*, pp. 19–20.

19. H. Duane Hampton, *How the U.S. Cavalry Saved Our National Parks* (Bloomington: Indiana University Press, 1971), p. 88.

20. Bob R. O'Brien, "The Yellowstone National Park Road System: Past, Present and Future" (Ph.D. dissertation, University of Washington, 1965).

21. Stephen Fox, *John Muir and His Legacy* (Boston: Little, Brown and Co., 1981).

22. NPS, *The National Parks: Shaping the System*, pp. 1–17.

23. Ise, *Our National Park Policy*, p. 49.

24. Ibid., pp. 307–317.

25. Ibid., pp. 193–194.

26. Ibid., p. 191.

27. William C. Everhart, *The National Park Service*, p. 21.

28. Ise, *Our National Park Policy*, pp. 296–297.

29. Executive Order 6166, signed June 10, 1933.

30. Horace M. Albright, *The Birth of the NPS*, pp. 285–297.

31. Everhart, *The National Park Service*, p. 24.

32. Jack Haynes, *Haynes Guide* (Bozeman, Mont.: Haynes Studios, 1966), p. 34.

33. Ise, *Our National Park Policy*, p. 450.

34. Bernard DeVoto, "Let's Close the National Parks," *Harper's Magazine*, October 1953, pp. 49–52.

35. The best description of Mission 66 comes from its originator, the sixth national park director: Conrad Wirth, *Parks, Politics, and the People* (Norman: University of Oklahoma Press, 1980).

36. Douglas Strong, *The Conservationists* (Menlo Park, Calif.: Addison-Wesley Publishing Co., 1971), pp. 166–178.

## CASE STUDY: YELLOWSTONE NATIONAL PARK

1. Sandra Blakeslee, "Facing the Peril of Earth's Cauldrons," *New York Times,* August 26, 1997.

2. In a 1989 visitor survey 93 percent of those interviewed listed viewing wildlife as one of their activities in the park, while 85 percent listed viewing thermal features. Margaret Littlejohn et al., *Yellowstone National Park Visitor Study,* University of Idaho, March 1990, p. 11.

3. NPS, *NPS Statistical Abstract, 1996,* pp. 2–19.

4. O'Brien, "The Yellowstone National Park Road System." The "maximum preservation road system" is presented on pp. 154–156.

5. "Maximum utilization road system," ibid., pp. 152–154.

6. Ibid. Map on page 100.

7. Christopher Tunnard and Boris Pushkareu, *Man-made America: Chaos or Control?* (New Haven, Conn.: Yale University Press, 1963), p. 175.

8. In 1915, 86.6 percent of the park visitors used public transportation to enter and tour the park. U.S. Department of the Interior, *Report of the Acting Superintendent of Yellowstone National Park to the Secretary of the Interior for the Year 1915* (Washington, D.C.: USGPO, 1915), p. 6.

9. NPS, *Alternative Transportation Modes, Feasibility Study, Yellowstone National Park* (Denver: NPS Denver Service Center, July 1994), 3:ES-8.

10. Haynes, *Haynes Guide,* pp. 56–63.

11. NPS, *Alternate Transportation Modes,* 3:ES-22.

12. NPS, *Parkwide Road Improvement Plan Environmental Assessment, Yellowstone National Park* (Denver: NPS Denver Service Center, Draft, February 1992), p. 7.

13. NPS, "Yellowstone Today" (information leaflet handed all visitors to the park), Spring 1996, p. 1.

14. NPS, *Canyon Village, Environmental Assessment* (Denver: NPS, February 1988), p. 9.

15. Littlejohn et al., *Yellowstone National Park Visitor Study,* p. 12.

16. NPS, *Old Faithful Development Concept Plan* (Denver: NPS, January 1985).

17. Kathleen M. Davis and Robert W. Mutch, "The Fires of the Greater Yellowstone Area: The Saga of a Long Hot Summer," *Western Wildlands,* Summer 1989, p. 2.

18. NPS and U.S. Forest Service, *The Greater Yellowstone Postfire Assessment of Research Needs,* August 1990, pp. 1–2.

19. Conrad Smith (interview), "Yellowstone and the News," *Yellowstone Science,* Winter 1994, pp. 9–14.

20. Paul Shullery and Don Despain, "Prescribed Burning in Yellowstone National Park: A Doubtful Proposition," *Western Wildlands,* Summer 1989, pp. 30–34.

21. NPS, *Yellowstone National Park Wildland Fire Management Plan,* March 1992.

22. Lee H. Whittlesey, *Death in Yellowstone* (Boulder, Colo.: Robert Rineharts Publishers, 1995), pp. 28, 30.

23. "Protecting Geothermal Areas Rests with Old Faithful Protection Act," *Greater Yellowstone Report,* Winter 1994, p. 4.

24. Bob Ekey, "Wonder upon Wonder," *Greater Yellowstone Report,* Winter 1994, pp. 1, 4–5.

25. Ibid., p. 5.

## 4. PRESERVING THE PARKS FROM COMMERCIAL USE

1. 39 Stat. 535. National Park System Organic Act was signed by President Woodrow Wilson on August 25, 1916.

2. The value of tourism, in relation to other basic industries like logging, mining, agriculture, and manufacturing, is taken from *The World Almanac of the U.S.A.* by Allan Carpenter and Carl Provorse (Mahwah, N.J.: Funk and Wagnalls, 1993).

3. National Park and Conservation Association, *National Parks,* May/June 1995, p. 11.

4. Carol Estes, "Sea of Grass," *National Parks,* March/April 1995, pp. 38–44.

5. NPS, *The Redwoods* (Washington, D.C.: Strant Lithograph, 1964), p. 30.

6. Melville Bell Grosvenor, "World's Tallest Tree Discovered," *National Geographic,* July 1964, pp. 1–9.

7. John G. Mitchell, "Unfinished Redwood," *Audubon,* September 1988, pp. 63–64.

8. G. Tyler Miller, *Living in the Environment,* 8th ed. (Belmont, Calif.: Wadsworth Publishing Co., 1994), pp. 395–397.

9. NPS, "Redwood Renaissance" (undated leaflet).

10. Miller, *Living in the Environment,* p. 281.

11. Wildland Research Center, University of California, Berkeley, *Wilderness and Recreation: A Report on Resources, Values, and Problems* (Washington, D.C.: USGPO, 1962), pp. 109–110.

12. Philip S. Barnett, "The Mining in the Parks Act: Theory and Practice," Chap. 15 in *Our Common Lands,* ed. David Simon (Washington, D.C.: Island Press, 1988), pp. 415–424.

13. Miller, *Living in the Environment,* pp. 504–505.

14. Ise, *Our National Park Policy.* Hetch Hetchy is discussed on pp. 85–96 and the Yellowstone dam proposals on p. 433.

15. Russell Martin, *A Story That Stands like a Dam,* pp. 43–74.

16. Ibid., p. 66.

17. An organization rising from the sagebrush rebellion of the 1980's, of anti-government, land-rights people, found mostly in the West, who would like to do away with the national parks or at least to allow lumbering, grazing, and mineral development in the parks. William R. Lowry, *The Capacity for Wonder*, p. 33.

## 5. EXTERNAL THREATS

1. Henry David Thoreau, "Walking," quoted from the title of Eliot Porter's *In Wildness Is the Preservation of the World* (New York: Sierra Club/Ballantine Books, 1962).

2. John L. Harper, *Mineral King* (Arcata, Calif.: Pacifica Publishing Co., 1982).

3. John Muir, *My First Summer in the Sierra* (Boston: Houghton Mifflin, 1911), p. 211.

4. Don Despain et al., *Wildlife in Transition*, p. 35.

5. Ibid., pp. 14–36.

6. Runte, *Yosemite*, pp. 67–82.

7. Bob R. O'Brien, "Recreational Resources," in Art Getis, ed., *The United States and Canada* (Boston: Wm. C. Brown Publishers, 1995), p. 317.

8. Even today, when a cold front blows away the pollutants, visibility can exceed 200 miles. NPS, *Draft General Management Plan for the Grand Canyon* (Denver: NPS Denver Service Center, March 1995), p. 138.

9. Elizabeth A. Fayad, "The Clean Air Act: New Horizons for the National Parks," in Simon, ed., *Our Common Lands*, pp. 293–330.

10. Ibid., p. 309.

11. Ibid.

12. Grand Canyon Trust, "Government Delays Threaten Crystal Clear Vistas," *Colorado Plateau Advocate*, Winter 1993, p. 7.

13. Ned Burks, "Shenandoah Park on the Brink," *American Forests*, November/December 1994, p. 20.

14. Lowry, *The Capacity for Wonder*, pp. 183–187.

15. Todd Wilkinson, "Fool's Gold," *National Parks*, July/August 1994, pp. 30–35.

16. Bob Ekey, "Clinton Tours New World Mine," *Greater Yellowstone Report*, Summer 1995, p. 1.

17. Editorial, "Canceling the New World Mine," *New York Times*, December 10, 1995.

18. Yellowstone Center for Resources, "President Announces Settlement on New World Mine," *Yellowstone Science*, Fall 1996, p. 20.

19. Phil Pryde, "Dilemma of the Everglades," in Getis, ed., *The United States and Canada*, p. 37.

20. Kim A. O'Connell, "Gore Unveils Everglades Plan," *National Parks,* May/June 1996, pp. 13–15. Also William Stevens, "Everglades Paradise Not Quite Lost," *New York Times,* March 22, 1994.

21. Miller, *Living in the Environment,* pp. 606–607.

22. Christopher Reynolds, "Helicopters Churn Up Noise, Safety Questions," *Los Angeles Times,* June 20, 1993.

23. Brent Israelsen, "Canyonlands, Arches Are Invaded from Above," *High Country News,* March 21, 1994.

24. Dennis Glick, Mary Carr, and Bert Harting, eds., *An Environmental Profile of the Greater Yellowstone Ecosystem* (Bozeman, Mont.: Greater Yellowstone Coalition, 1991), p. 9.

25. Rick Reese, *Greater Yellowstone,* Montana Geographic Series (Helena, Mont.: American and World Geographic Publishing, 1991), pp. 8, 11.

26. Greater Yellowstone Coordinating Committee, *Vision for the Future* (Washington, D.C.: USGPO, 1991).

27. Ibid., part 4, p. 1.

28. Lowry, *The Capacity for Wonder,* pp. 56–57.

29. Ibid.

30. Lang Smith, "The Land Rush Is On," *Greater Yellowstone Report,* Winter 1993, p. 1; Ray Rasker, "The Emerging Economy," *Greater Yellowstone Report,* Winter 1992, pp. 4–6.

## CASE STUDY: GRAND CANYON NATIONAL PARK

1. Peter Matthews, *Guinness Book of World Records* (New York: R. R. Donnelly & Sons, 1994), p. 19.

2. Douglas Hillman Strong, "The Man Who 'Owned' Grand Canyon," *American West,* September 1969, p. 36.

3. J. Donald Hughes, *In the House of Stone and Light,* pp. 67–68, 111–112.

4. Robert Brewster Stanton, *Down the Colorado* (Norman: University of Oklahoma Press, 1965), pp. xv–xvi.

5. Hughes, *In the House of Stone and Light,* p. 66.

6. NPS, *NPS Statistical Abstract, 1996.*

7. *Grand Canyon National Park Establishment Act,* 40 Stat. 1175, sec. 7.

8. Martin, *A Story That Stands like a Dam,* pp. 250–252.

9. Ibid.

10. Michael E. Long, "The Grand Managed Canyon," *National Geographic,* July 1977, p. 126.

11. Martin, pp. 247–279.

12. Steven W. Carothers and Bryan T. Brown, *The Colorado River through the Grand Canyon,* p. 52.

13. Michael Collier et al., *Dams and Rivers*, U.S. Geological Survey Circular 1/26, 1996, p. 65.

14. Julie Gale, "Downstream of a Dam," *Colorado Plateau Advocate*, Spring/Summer 1994, p. 5.

15. Tom Moody, "Good News for the Canyon," *Colorado Plateau Advocate*, Fall 1995, p. 6.

16. "Artificial Flood Created to Rejuvenate the Grand Canyon," *New York Times*, March 27, 1996.

17. Personal communication from Gary O'Brien, Grand Canyon boatman, who has made several trips through the canyon since the 1996 flood.

18. Carothers and Brown, *The Colorado River*, pp. 64–66, 146–148.

19. Andrew Murr and Sharon Bagley, "Dams Are Not Forever," *Newsweek*, November 17, 1997, p. 70.

20. Ibid.

21. Greg Hanscom, "Reclaiming a Lost Canyon," *High Country News*, November 10, 1997.

22. Fayad, "The Clean Air Act," pp. 293–323.

23. Martin, *A Story That Stands like a Dam*, p. 308.

24. Roger Clark, "Protecting Crystal Clear Vistas at the Canyon," *Colorado Plateau Advocate*, Spring/Summer 1994, p. 4.

25. The flights cost about $50 per half-hour. James Sterngold, "Limits on Aircraft Set for Grand Canyon" (subtitle), *New York Times*, January 1, 1997.

26. Julie Galton Gale, "NPS Natural Quiet Report Released," *Colorado Plateau Advocate*, Fall/Winter 1994, p. 5.

27. Public Law 100-91.

28. NPS, "Aircraft Overflights," Briefing Statement to the 102d Congress, January 1992.

29. Julie Galton Gale, "Quiet Skies—When?" *Colorado Plateau Advocate*, Fall 1995, p. 7.

30. Robert L. Arnberger (superintendent of Grand Canyon NP), "The Grand Canyon: Celebrate Its Past, Invest in Its Future," *Toward a Geography of Hope* (Grand Canyon Symposium, Flagstaff, Ariz., October 6–8, 1994), p. 8.

31. Sterngold, "Limits on Aircraft Set."

32. Reynolds, "Helicopters Churn Up Noise, Safety Questions."

33. NPS, *Draft General Management Plan: Environmental Impact Statement* (Denver: National Park Service, 1995), pp. 161, 164.

34. Jon Margolis, "With Solitude for All," *Audubon*, July/August 1997, pp. 49–50.

35. "Federal Plan Would Ban Cars in National Parks to Ease Crowding," *San Diego Union Tribune*, November 26, 1997.

36. NPS, *Draft General Management Plan: Environmental Impact Statement*.

37. Ibid., pp. 293–306. This also includes spending throughout the park.

38. "Vision for Grand Canyon National Park" (proposal by Grand Canyon Railway, undated).

39. Rick Moore, "Watch Those Elbows," *Colorado Plateau Advocate*, Fall 1995, p. 5.

40. NPS, *Colorado River Management Plan* (Grand Canyon National Park, September 1989), pp. C1–C6, D18–D23.

41. *U.S. Code Annotated*, title 16, sec. 29b, pp. 118–119.

42. Lowry, *The Capacity for Wonder*, pp. 169–170.

43. Ibid.

44. NPS, *Backcountry Management Plan* (Grand Canyon NP, September 1988).

45. Julie Galton Gale, "Grand Canyon Wilderness Proposal Bogged Down?" *Colorado Plateau Advocate*, Spring/Summer 1994, p. 3.

46. Frederic H. Wagner et al., *Wildlife Policies in the U.S. National Parks*, p. 61.

## 6. WILDERNESS

1. *Wilderness Act*, Public Law 88-577, Section 2(c).

2. Horace M. Albright, "Annual Report for Yellowstone National Park" (typed) (Yellowstone National Park, Wyoming, 1923), p. 8.

3. The vote on the Wilderness Act was 373 to 1. Fox, *John Muir and His Legacy*, p. 289.

4. Dyan Zaslowsky and T. H. Watkins, *These American Lands*, pp. 195–228.

5. NPS, "Wilderness Management Plan, Yosemite National Park," 1989, p. 1.

6. Ibid., pp. 91–93.

7. *Wilderness Act*, Public Law 88-577, Section 4(c).

## CASE STUDY: DENALI NATIONAL PARK

1. NPS, "Denali Alpenglow" (Denali National Park and Preserve, Summer 1995), p. 8.

2. NPS, *Denali, Statement for Management* (Denver, September 8, 1995), p. 61.

3. Ibid., p. 22.

4. Charles I. Zinser, *Outdoor Recreation* (New York: John Wiley & Sons, 1995), pp. 112–127.

5. Ibid., p. 123.

6. NPS, *Denali, Statement for Management*, p. 7.

7. Ibid., p. 12.

8. Glenn Randall and Harry Johnson III, *Mt. McKinley Climber's Handbook* (Talkeetna, Alaska: Genet Expeditions, 1984), p. 105. Also Mountaineering

Rangers of Denali NP, *Mountaineering, Denali National Park and Preserve* (n.p.: Alaska Natural History Association, 1944).

9. Lisa Morgan, "Where Did All the Money Go?" *Climbing*, November/December 1995, pp. 29–30. Also see pp. 243–244.

10. Mountaineering Rangers, *Mountaineering*, p. 4.

11. Danny Westneat, "Animals Even More Grand than McKinley," *San Diego Union Tribune*, May 11, 1997.

12. Douglas Chadwick, "Denali, Alaska's Wild Heart," *National Geographic*, August 1992, p. 70.

13. Paul M. Tilden and Nancy L. Machler, "The Development of Mt. McKinley National Park," *National Parks*, May 1963, pp. 10–15.

14. An adult round-trip fare to Wonder Lake, a full day trip, is $26, with under twelve free. Concession tours are more expensive. NPS, *Denali Digest*, May 1, 1995, p. 11.

15. NPS, *Denali Final Entrance Area and Road Corridor Development Concept Plan* (Denver: NPS Denver Service Center, December 1996), p. 29.

16. Denali Task Force, "Findings and Recommendations for the National Park System Advisory Board," October 21, 1994, pp. 13–20.

17. NPS, *Denali, Statement for Management*, p. 26.

## 7. WILDLIFE

1. Paul Schullery, *Searching for Yellowstone*, pp. 42–43.

2. Ise, *Our National Park Policy*, p. 19.

3. Ibid., p. 25.

4. Ibid., p. 45.

5. Haines, *The Yellowstone Story*, 2:80–82.

6. Adolph Murie, *Ecology of the Coyote in the Yellowstone* (Washington, D.C.: USGPO, 1940), p. 15.

7. Ibid., pp. 146–148.

8. Ise, *Our National Park Policy*, p. 594.

9. Wright, *Wildlife Research*, p. 173.

10. T. H. Watkins, "Desert Extraordinaire," *Audubon*, March–April 1995, pp. 42–57. There was virtually no hunting in the area before the park; the national preserve status was to satisfy the National Rifle Association and allies.

11. Michael Milstein, "The Quiet Kill," *National Parks*, May/June 1989, pp. 19–25.

12. "Yellowstone Resource Notes," *Wilderness Profile* (The Yellowstone Association), Summer 1995, pp. 12–13.

13. Douglas H. Chadwick, "U.S. Imperative: Networking Habitats," *Defenders of Wildlife,* September/October 1992, pp. 26–33.

14. Wright, *Wildlife Research,* p. 122.

15. Paul Schullery, *The Bears of Yellowstone,* pp. 199–200.

16. Wright, *Wildlife Research,* p. 122.

17. Mary Meagher and Jerry R. Phillips, "Restoration of Natural Populations of Grizzly and Black Bears in Yellowstone National Park," *International Conference on Bear Research and Management* 5: 152–158. For an opposing view see Wagner et al., *Wildlife Policies in the U.S. National Parks,* pp. 66–67.

18. Suzanne Charlé, "To Bears in Yosemite, Cars Are like Cookie Jars," *New York Times,* November 30, 1997.

19. Carla Neasel, "People Who Chase Bears Feel Better," *Yosemite* (Journal of the Yosemite Association), Winter 1988, pp. 1–3.

20. Charlé, "To Bears in Yosemite, Cars Are like Cookie Jars."

21. Richard Knight et al., "Final Report, Ad Hoc Committee to Investigate the Need and Feasibility of the Supplemental Feeding of Yellowstone Grizzly Bears," December 5, 1983.

22. Kerry A. Gunther, "Bear Management in Yellowstone National Park, 1960–1993," *International Conference on Bear Research and Management* 9(1): 549–560.

23. R. R. Knight et al., "Mortality Patterns and Population Sinks for Yellowstone Grizzly Bears, 1973–1985," *Wildlife Society Bulletin* 16 (1988): 121–125.

24. Kerry Gunther and Hopi Hoekstra, "Bear-inflicted Human Injuries in Yellowstone, 1970–1994," *Yellowstone Science,* Winter 1996, pp. 2–9.

25. Norman Bishop, research interpreter, Yellowstone National Park, personal communication, May 1996.

26. Jack Olsen, *Night of the Grizzlies* (New York: Putnam & Sons, 1969).

27. Ted Williams, "Deregulating the Wild," *Audubon,* July/August 1997, pp. 56–63, 92ff.

28. Tim Stevens, "Grizzly Mortality Rate in Greater Yellowstone Highest since 1972," *Greater Yellowstone Report,* Winter 1996, p. 19.

29. Tom Lemke and Francis J. Singer, "Northern Yellowstone Elk: The Big Herd," *Bugle,* Fall 1989, p. 115.

30. Despain et al., *Wildlife in Transition,* p. 25. Also: Bartlett, *Yellowstone,* p. 385.

31. A. Starker Leopold et al., "Wildlife Management in the National Parks," *Transactions of the North American Wildlife and Natural Resources Conference* 28 (1963): 27–45.

32. NPS, *Yellowstone's Northern Range* (Mammoth Hot Springs, Wyo.: NPS, 1997), pp. xi–xiii. Also: Sam McNaughton (interview), "Grazing in Yellowstone," *Yellowstone Science,* Winter 1996, pp. 12–17.

33. Land Smith, "Land Exchange on Fast Track," *Greater Yellowstone Report,* Spring 1993, pp. 16–17.

34. Stephen Budiansky, "Yellowstone's Unraveling," *U.S. News and World Report,* September 16, 1996, pp. 80–83. Also several sections in Wagner et al., *Wildlife Policies,* and nearly all of *Playing God in Yellowstone* by Alton Chase (Boston: Atlantic Monthly Press Books, 1986).

35. Wright, *Wildlife Research,* p. 88.

36. Montana Fish & Wildlife, Yellowstone National Park, U.S. Forest Service, *Yellowstone Bison: Background and Issues,* May 1990, p. 10.

37. Mary Meagher, "Yellowstone's Free-Ranging Bison," *The Naturalist* 36, no. 3 (1985): 20–26.

38. Where bison hunting regularly takes place the bison develop survival techniques and provide better "sport." Despain et al., *Wildlife in Transition,* pp. 36–45.

39. Jim Robbins, "Montana's Policy of Killing Bison Brings an Outcry," *New York Times,* March 25, 1996.

40. Marvin Jensen, "Buffaloed," *National Parks,* July/August 1997, p. 43.

41. Doug Peacock, "The Yellowstone Massacre," *Audubon,* May/June 1997, p. 41.

42. Winston E. Banko, *The Trumpeter Swan* (Washington, D.C.: USGPO, 1960), p. 146.

43. "Yellowstone Resource Notes," *Wilderness Profile,* Winter 1996, p. 8.

44. "Trumpeter Swans' Existence Remains Tenuous," *Yellowstone Science,* Summer 1997, p. 19.

45. "Executive Summary," *The Yellowstone Lake Crisis: Confronting a Lake Trout Invasion* (Mammoth Hot Springs, Wyo.: Yellowstone Center for Resources, October 1995), pp. 2–3.

46. Bob Ekey, "Lake Trout Infestation Has Frightening Consequences," *Greater Yellowstone Report,* Winter 1996, p. 13.

47. Kerry Murphy (interview), "The Yellowstone Lion," *Yellowstone Science,* Spring 1994, pp. 8–13.

48. "Big Cats and Big Questions," *Approach* (The Journal of the Yosemite Fund), Spring/Summer 1996, pp. 1, 11.

49. Jameson, *The Story of Big Bend National Park,* pp. 92–93.

50. Jackie Hutchins, "Cougar Mauls Youngster," *Estes Park Mail-Gazette,* July 23, 1997.

51. William K. Stevens, "Howl of the Wolf Is Being Heard Once Again in Old Haunts," *New York Times,* January 31, 1995.

52. Pat Cole, "They're Back! Wolves Finally Return to Yellowstone Park," *Wilderness Profile,* Winter 1995, pp. 1–4.

53. "Livestock-Killing Wolves Removed," *Yellowstone Science,* Fall 1997, pp. 20–21.

54. Jim Robbins, "Ranchers Welcome Ruling on Yellowstone Wolves," *New York Times*, December 14, 1997.

55. Ibid.

56. John Muir, *The Yellowstone National Park* (Golden, Colo.: Outbooks, 1986), p. 35.

## 8. VISITATION

1. NPS, *NPS Statistical Abstract, 1996*, p. 1.

2. NPS, "Public Use of the National Parks: A Statistical Report, 1904–1940" (Washington, D.C.: Conservation and Protection Branch, NPS, reprint, 1963).

3. William R. Eadington and Valene L. Smith, *Tourism Alternatives* (Philadelphia: University of Pennsylvania Press, 1992), pp. 1–3.

4. Milton D. Rafferty, *A Geography of World Tourism* (Englewood Cliffs, N.J.: Prentice Hall, 1993), p. 2.

5. Michelle Dawson, "Pact Launches Partnership with Western States Tourism Industry," *People, Land and Water*, November 1997, p. 9.

6. "Ecotourism: A Good Trip?" *Economist*, August 30/September 5, 1997, p. 48.

7. Robert C. Scace, "An Ecotourism Perspective," in J. G. Nelson et al., eds., *Tourism and Sustainable Development: Monitoring, Planning, Managing*, (Waterloo, Ont., Canada: University of Waterloo, 1993), p. 64.

8. Fox, *John Muir and His Legacy*, pp. 106–107.

9. NPS, *Statistical Abstract, 1996*.

10. Ibid.

11. Wallace W. Atwood, *The Physiographic Provinces of North America* (New York: Ginn & Co., 1940), p. 392.

12. Jim Dugan, ranger, Natural Bridges NM, telephone interview, November 28, 1995.

13. Grant W. Sharpe, Charles H. Odegaard, and Wenonah F. Sharpe, *Park Management*, 2d ed. (Champaign, Ill.: Sagamore Publishing, 1994), pp. 419–422.

14. NPS, "Yosemite Guide," March 29–June 18, 1995, p. 2.

15. Douglas M. Knudson, *Outdoor Recreation* (New York: Macmillan Publishing Co., 1984), p. 500.

16. Schullery, *The Bears of Yellowstone*, pp. 140–141.

17. NPS, *Alternative Transportation Modes, Feasibility Study*, 3:ES-8.

18. L. J. Ritter and R. J. Paquette, *Highway Engineering* (New York: Ronald Press Co., 1951), p. 111.

19. "More Visit National Parks despite Jump in Entry Fees," *San Diego Union Tribune*, August 14, 1997.

20. Yosemite Association, "1993 Highlights," *Yosemite*, Spring 1994, p. 16.

21. David Seideman, "Going Wild," *Time*, July 25, 1994, p. 28.

## 9. RECREATIONAL LAND USE

1. NPS, *Management Policies* (Washington, D.C.: USGPO, 1978), sec. VII, p. 7.

2. Ibid., p. 8.

3. NPS, *The National Parks: Index 1995*, p. 115.

4. Kim A. O'Connell, "Air Tour Industry Awaits Decisions," *National Parks*, May/June 1996, p. 18.

5. NPS, *Yosemite: Official National Park Handbook* (Washington, D.C.: USGPO, 1989), p. 138.

6. Outdoor Recreation Resources Review Commission, *Outdoor Recreation in America* (Washington, D.C.: USGPO, January 1962), p. 4.

7. U.S. Department of the Interior, NPS, *Hearings on Proposed Boating Regulations for Yellowstone Lake* (Washington, D.C.: USGPO, 1960).

8. Lily Whiteman, "Making Waves," *National Parks*, July/August 1997, pp. 22–25.

9. Whittlesey, *Death in Yellowstone*, p. 28.

10. NPS, *General Management Plan, Yosemite*, pp. 38, 40, 44.

11. NPS, *The National Parks: Index 1995*, pp. 37, 38.

12. Greater Yellowstone Coalition, "Noise from Snowmobiles Can Shatter the Peaceful Silence of a Yellowstone Winter," *Greater Yellowstone Report*, Winter 1966, pp. 5–6.

13. NPS, *Winter Use Plan Environmental Assessment: Yellowstone and Grand Teton National Parks, John D. Rockefeller, Jr. Memorial Parkway* (Denver: NPS Denver Service Center, 1990), pp. 28–29.

14. Greater Yellowstone Coalition, "Noise from Snowmobiles," pp. 5–6.

15. David Cowan, "Yellowstone Park: Speedway or Sanctuary?" *Greater Yellowstone Report*, Fall 1997, p. 5.

16. Paul Schullery, "A Reasonable Illusion," *Rod and Reel*, December 1979.

17. NPS, "Joshua Tree National Monument Climbing Management Plan 1993" (n.p., February 1993), p. 11.

18. Jon Krakauer, "Mean Season on Denali," *Outside*, August 1992, p. 57.

19. Lisa Morgan, "Where Did All the Money Go?" *Climbing*, November/December 1995, pp. 29–30.

20. NPS, "Joshua Tree National Monument Climbing Management Plan 1993," p. 11.

21. Rich Roberts, "A Rocky Situation," *Los Angeles Times*, May 26, 1993.

22. Charles Levendosky, "Group Sues to Stamp Out Tolerance and Diversity," *High Country News*, April 15, 1996, p. 17.

23. Norm Bishop, "Book Reviews," *Yellowstone Science*, Summer 1997, pp. 13–15.

24. Everhart, *The National Park Service*, p. 51.

25. Yosemite Association, *Yosemite Field Seminars, 1994* (El Portal, Calif., 1994).


## CASE STUDY: CANYONLANDS NATIONAL PARK

1. Lloyd Pierson, "The First Canyonlands New Park Studies: 1958 and 1960," *Canyon Legacy*, Fall 1989, pp. 9–14.

2. Foreman and Wolke, *The Big Outside*, p. 467.

3. NPS, *The National Parks: Index 1995*, pp. 82–83.

4. 87th U.S. Congress, "Hearings before the Subcommittee on Public Lands of the Committee on Interior and Insular Affairs, U.S. Senate" (Washington, D.C.: USGPO, March–April 1962), 2 parts.

5. W. Robert Moore, "Cities of Stone in Utah's Canyonlands," *National Geographic*, May 1962, pp. 653–676.

6. John W. Powell, *The Exploration of the Colorado River and Its Canyons* (New York: Dover Publications, 1961; first published in 1895), p. 212.

7. NPS, "Canyonlands" official map and guide (Washington, D.C.: USGPO, 1992).

8. NPS, "Statement for Management, Canyonlands National Park," August 1990, p. 12.

9. NPS, *NPS Statistical Abstract, 1996*, p. 5.

10. Ibid., pp. 18–23. Backcountry use was 70,963 overnight stays for Canyonlands, compared to 45,769 for Yellowstone.

11. NPS, "Statement for Management, Canyonlands National Park, May 1993," p. 20. Also, NPS, "Backcountry Permit Reports," 1992.

12. NPS, "Environmental Assessment for Backcountry Management Plan, Canyonlands National Park and Orange Cliffs Unit of Glen Canyon National Recreational Area," December 1993, pp. 34–37.

13. NPS, "River Management Plan, Canyonlands National Park, 1981" (n.p.).

14. F. A. Barnes, *Canyon Country Hiking* (Salt Lake City: Wasatch Publishers, 1977), p. 21.

15. National Parks Hospitality Association, *National Parks Visitor Facilities and Services*, pp. 94–96.

16. Sarah B. Van de Wetering, "Doing It the Moab Way," *Chronicle of Community*, Autumn 1996, p. 7.

17. Timothy Egan, "New Feud on the Range: Cowman vs. Tourist," *New York Times*, September 18, 1994.

18. Ibid.

19. Todd Wilkinson, "Crowd Control," *National Parks*, July/August 1995, pp. 36–40.

## 10. CARE AND FEEDING OF VISITORS

1. Act of August 25, 1916, 39 Stat. 535.

2. NPS, "Management Policies," 1978, p. VIII-1.

3. National Parks Hospitality Association, *National Parks Visitor Facilities and Services.*

4. NPS, *NPS Statistical Abstract, 1996*, pp. 20–23.

5. Jeffrey Limerick et al., *America's Grand Resort Hotels* (New York: Pantheon Books, 1979).

6. Bartlett, *Yellowstone*, pp. 178–184.

7. NPS, *NPS Statistical Abstract, 1996*, pp. 20–23.

8. NPS, *Draft, Yosemite Valley Implementation Plan* (Denver: NPS Denver Service Center, September 1997), p. 18.

9. NPS, *Yosemite Valley Housing Plan* (Denver: NPS Denver Service Center, May 1992), p. 4.

10. This is a sampling of the twenty buildings listed. Ise, *Our National Park Policy*, pp. 33–34.

11. Ibid., p. 43.

12. NP Hospitality Assn., *National Parks Visitor Facilities*, p. 129.

13. Everhart, *The National Park Service*, p. 111.

14. NP Hospitality Assn., *National Parks Visitor Facilities*, pp. 131–133.

15. Everhart, *The National Park Service*, p. 115.

16. NPS, "Yosemite, Master Plan, Preliminary Draft" (n.p., August 12, 1974). "Rejected" stamped in large red letters on front of document.

17. Maura Dolan, "Who Owns Yosemite?" in *Los Angeles Times Magazine*, September 30, 1990, pp. 11–27, 37ff.

18. Everhart, *The National Park Service*, pp. 114–115.

19. Ibid., pp. 116–119.

20. NP Hospitality Assn., *National Parks Visitor Facilities*. Income of concessioners from testimony by Roger Kennedy before the Senate Energy and Natural Resources Committee on September 15, 1995.

21. NP Hospitality Assn., *National Parks Visitor Facilities.*

## CASE STUDY: YOSEMITE NATIONAL PARK

1. Runte, *Yosemite*, pp. 21–27.

2. Stanford E. Demars, *The Tourist in Yosemite, 1855–1985*, pp. 49–50.

3. Victoria Post Ranney, ed., *The Papers of Frederick Law Olmsted*, vol. 5, *The California Frontier, 1863–1865* (Baltimore: Johns Hopkins University Press, 1990).

4. Demars, *The Tourist in Yosemite*, p. 123.

5. Runte, *Yosemite*, pp. 160–180.

6. NPS, "Public Use of the National Parks: A Statistical Report," December 1968, pp. 13, 23.

7. Runte, *Yosemite*, p. 202.

8. Frank Bonaventura, "Slowly Die the Embers," *Yosemite* (newsletter of the Yosemite Association), Winter 1988, pp. 4–5.

9. Dolan, "Who Owns Yosemite?" pp. 10–27.

10. Michael Frome, *Regreening the National Parks*, p. 41.

11. NPS, "Draft Yosemite GMP Examination Report: A Review of the 1980 GMP," August 1989, pp. 13, 17.

12. "Going Wild," *Time*, July 25, 1994, p. 27.

13. NPS, *General Management Plan, Yosemite*, pp. 19–20.

14. NPS, *Alternative Transportation Modes, Feasibility Study*, Executive Summary, June 1994, 4:ES17–24. Also Christopher Swan and Chet Roaman, *YV 88: An Eco-Fiction of Tomorrow* (San Francisco: Sierra Club Books, 1977).

15. NPS, *Yosemite Valley Housing Plan*. "Draft Addendum, Supplement to the Final Environmental Impact Statement for the General Management Plan" (Washington, D.C.: USGPO, 1996).

16. NPS, *Concession Services Plan: Environmental Impact Statement*, December 1991.

17. NPS, *Draft, Yosemite Valley Implementation Plan*, p. 18.

18. Gene Rose, "A New Era in Park Concessions," *Yosemite* (newsletter of the Yosemite Association), Winter 1994, pp. 6–7.

19. NPS, "Yosemite Guide," March 18–June 16, 1996, p. 1.

20. Mary All Madej et al., *Analysis of Bank Erosion on the Merced River, Yosemite Valley, Yosemite National Park* (Arcata, Calif.: Redwood National Park, November 1991).

21. NPS, "Yosemite National Park Planning Update," vol. 3, Winter 1997.

22. NPS, *Draft, Yosemite Valley Implementation Plan*.

## 11. ADMINISTRATION, POLITICS, AND FINANCE

1. Ise, *Our National Park Policy*, pp. 136–142.

2. NPS, *The National Parks: Shaping the System*, pp. 16–17.

3. Albright, *The Birth of the National Park Service*.

4. NPS, *National Parks for the 21st Century*.

5. NPS, "National Park Service Reorganization Marks Most Significant Organizational Change in Agency's 79-Year History," news release, May 15, 1995.

6. NPS, *Restructuring Plan for the NPS* (Washington, D.C.: USGPO, 1994), p. 61.

7. Ibid.

8. Everhart, *The National Park Service,* p. 36.

9. NPS, *Restructuring Plan for the NPS,* p. 1.

10. Ibid., p. 61.

11. Ibid., p. 1.

12. Tom Wolf, "National Park Service May Be Downsized and Reorganized," *High Country News,* December 12, 1994, pp. 1, 10–13.

13. Rettie, *Our National Park System,* pp. 152–153.

14. Ibid., pp. 154–155.

15. Lowry, *The Capacity for Wonder,* p. 67.

16. Bernard Shanks, "The Endangered Ranger," *National Parks,* January/February 1991, pp. 32–36.

17. Lowry, *The Capacity for Wonder,* p. 67.

18. Rettie, *Our National Park System,* pp. 150–151, 274–281.

19. Wolf, "NPS May Be Downsized."

20. Lowry, *The Capacity for Wonder,* p. 85.

21. Everhart, *The National Park Service,* p. 57.

22. NPS, "Yosemite National Park History and Summary of Planning Documents" (unpublished), December 13, 1974, p. 1.

23. Ibid., p. 2.

24. Dolan, "Who Owns Yosemite?" p. 23.

25. NPS, *Draft Environmental Statement, General Management Plan, Yosemite National Park* (Denver: NPS Denver Service Center, 1978), p. 217.

26. NPS, "Update: Yosemite Master Plan" (Washington, D.C.: USGPO, June 1976), p. 2.

27. NPS, *The Workbook* (Washington, D.C.: USGPO, October 1975). A "guidelines" booklet of 32 pp., plus the 4 large sheets indicated.

28. Carl Irving, "Plans to Save Yosemite Drag On and On," *San Francisco Sunday Examiner and Chronicle,* February 11, 1979.

29. NPS, *The National Parks: Shaping the System,* pp. 120–121.

30. Ise, *Our National Park Policy,* p. 443.

31. Frome, *Regreening the National Parks,* p. 102.

32. Ibid., pp. 80, 105.

33. Lowry, *The Capacity for Wonder,* p. 56. Robert Redford was also in the running for the job.

34. Frome, *Regreening the National Parks,* p. 58.

35. Ibid., p. 62.

36. Lowry, *The Capacity for Wonder,* p. 6.

37. Frome, *Regreening the National Parks.*

38. Lowry, *The Capacity for Wonder,* p. 56.

39. John H. Cushman Jr., "Bradley Presses Filibuster on Public-Lands Package," *New York Times,* March 26, 1995. Also, Terry Tempest Williams, "A Cry for Wilderness," *National Parks,* November/December 1995, pp. 24–29.

40. James M. Ridenour, *The National Parks Compromised* (Merrillville, Ind.: ICS Books, 1994).

41. "Congress Takes Aim at National Parks," *National Parks,* May/June 1995, p. 10.

42. Dwight F. Rettie, "A Question of Integrity," *National Parks,* March/April 1996, p. 53.

43. "Committee Drops Park Closure Bill," *National Parks,* January/February 1996, p. 12.

44. Sharon Buccino et al., *Reclaiming Our Heritage: What We Need to Do to Preserve America's National Parks* (New York: Natural Resources Defense Council, July 1997), p. 17.

45. Rettie, *Our National Park System,* p. 125.

46. Lowry, *The Capacity for Wonder,* p. 6.

47. NPS, *The National Parks: Shaping the System,* pp. 104–105.

48. Rettie, *Our National Park System,* pp. 256–263.

49. Michael Satchell, "Parks in Peril," *U.S. News and World Report,* July 21, 1997, p. 27.

50. Martin Forstenzer, "National Parks: Heritage in Decay," *Conde Naste Traveler,* May 1995, p. 43.

51. Patricia Leigh Brown, "Trying to Save America's Crumbling 'Parkitecture,'" *New York Times,* August 10, 1995.

52. National Parks and Conservation Association, "President Unveils 1998 NPS Budget," *National Parks,* May/June 1997, p. 16.

53. Public Law 88-578.

54. Douglas Knudson, *Outdoor Recreation* (New York: Macmillan Publishing Co., 1984), p. 368.

55. National Parks and Conservation Association, "Congress Slashes Interior Spending," *National Parks,* November/December 1995, pp. 18–19.

56. *Omnibus Consolidated Recessions and Appropriations Act of 1996,* Public Law 104-134.

57. "More Visit National Parks despite Jump in Entry Fees," *San Diego Union Tribune,* August 14, 1997.

58. Bruce F. Vento, "Dollars and Sense," *National Parks,* November/December 1996, p. 50.

59. "Concessions Battle Part of Budget War," *National Parks,* January/February 1996, pp. 12–13.

60. NPS, *National Parks for the 21st Century,* p. 73.

61. National Park and Conservation Association, "Our National Parks" (paid advertisement), *New York Times,* May 22, 1995.

62. Buccino et al., pp. 21–22.

63. Personal observation. Environmental magazines are giving increasing coverage to the national parks' financial (and other) problems, as in the July/August *Audubon* (cover: "National Parks, National Paradox"), but so are mainstream publications: *U.S. News and World Report,* July 21, 1997 (cover: "Parks in Peril") and the June 1997 *Consumer Reports* (cover: "The Best National Parks").

## CASE STUDY: GRAND TETON NATIONAL PARK

1. Robert W. Righter, *Crucible for Conservation* (Boulder: Colorado Associated University Press, 1982), pp. 28–29.

2. 45 Stat. 1314.

3. Righter, *Crucible for Conservation,* pp. 43–65.

4. Ibid., p. 118.

5. Ibid., pp. 146–147.

6. National Park and Conservation Association, "Expansion Opposed at Jackson Hole Airport," *National Parks,* September/October 1991, p. 18.

7. Ibid.

8. Personal communication, Chief Ranger's Office, Grand Teton National Park.

9. National Park Service, "Proposed Snake River Management Plan, Grand Teton National Park," produced by NPS, Grand Teton National Park, August 8, 1975, p. 27.

10. Linda Olson, Grand Teton NP, personal communication received January 1996.

11. Linda Olson, news release, Grand Teton NP, March 21, 1994.

12. NPS, "Land Protection Plan, Second Biennial Review, Grand Teton National Park" (unpublished), January 1991, p. 20.

13. Ibid., p. 1.

14. *Resource Protection Case Study — Jackson Hole, Grand Teton National Park* (Denver: NPS Denver Service Center, June 1982), pp. 26–29.

15. Ibid., p. 29.

16. NPS, *Development Concept Plan for the Teton Corridor, Moose to North*

*Jenny Lake, Grand Teton National Park,* (Denver: NPS Denver Service Center, 1991), pp. 27–28.

## 12. CONCLUSIONS

1. Robert Marshall and Althea Dobbins, "Largest Roadless Areas in United States," *Living Wilderness,* November 1936, reproduced in *The Big Outside* by Dave Foreman and Howie Wolke, pp. 464–469.

2. International Union of Conservation of Nature (IUCN), *1993 United Nations List of National Parks and Protected Areas* (Gland, Switzerland, and Cambridge, Eng.: IUCN, 1994).

3. Ibid., pp. 251–252.

4. Everhart, *The National Park Service,* p. 157.

5. IUCN, *1993 United Nations List of National Parks and Protected Areas,* p. 246.

6. IUCN, *Masterworks of Man and Nature* (New York: Facts on File, 1994), pp. 388–392.

7. Ibid., endpages.

8. "U.N. Conspiracy Theorists Back Bill," *National Parks,* May/June 1997, p. 27.

# Selected Bibliography

Albright, Horace M. (as told to Robert Cahn). *The Birth of the National Park Service.* Salt Lake City: Howe Bros., 1985.

Bartlett, Richard A. *Yellowstone: A Wilderness Besieged.* Tucson: University of Arizona Press, 1989.

Carothers, Steven W., and Bryan T. Brown. *The Colorado River through the Grand Canyon.* Tucson: University of Arizona Press, 1991.

Demars, Stanford E. *The Tourist in Yosemite, 1855–1985.* Salt Lake City: University of Utah Press, 1991.

Despain, Don, et al. *Wildlife in Transition.* Boulder, Colo.: Roberts Rinehart, 1986.

Dilsaver, Lary M., and William C. Tweed. *Challenge of the Big Trees.* Three Rivers, Calif.: Sequoia Natural History Association, 1990.

Everhart, William C. *The National Park Service.* Boulder, Colo.: Westview Press, 1983.

Foreman, Dave, and Howie Wolke. *The Big Outside,* rev. ed. New York: Harmony Books, 1992.

Foresta, Ronald A. *America's National Parks and Their Keepers.* Washington, D.C.: Resources for the Future, 1984.

Frome, Michael. *Regreening the National Parks.* Tucson: University of Arizona Press, 1992.

Hartzog, George B., Jr. *Battling for the National Parks.* Mt. Kisco, N.Y.: Moyer Bell Limited, 1988.

Hughes, J. Donald. *In the House of Stone and Light.* Grand Canyon, Ariz.: Grand Canyon Natural History Association, 1978.

Ise, John. *Our National Park Policy.* Baltimore: Johns Hopkins Press, 1961.

Jameson, John. *The Story of Big Bend National Park.* Austin: University of Texas Press, 1996.

Keiter, Robert B., and Mark S. Boyce, eds. *The Greater Yellowstone Ecosystem.* New Haven, Conn.: Yale University Press, 1991.

Lowry, William R. *The Capacity for Wonder*. Washington, D.C.: Brookings Institute, 1994.

Martin, Russell. *A Story That Stands like a Dam*. New York: Henry Holt & Co., 1989.

National Park Service (NPS). *Draft General Management Plan: Environmental Impact Statement, Grand Canyon National Park*. Denver: NPS Service Center, 1995.

——. *General Management Plan, Visitor Use, Park Operations, Development, Yosemite National Park*. Washington, D.C.: USGPO, September 1980.

——. *The National Parks: Index 1995*. Washington, D.C.: USGPO, 1995.

——. *The National Parks: Shaping the System*. Washington, D.C.: USGPO, 1991.

——. *National Park Service Statistical Abstract, 1996*. Denver: Public Use Statistics Program Center, 1996.

——. *National Parks for the 21st Century (The Vail Agenda)*. NPS Document No. D-726. Washington, D.C.: NPS, 1992.

National Parks Hospitality Association. *National Parks Visitor Facilities and Services*, 3d ed. Washington, D.C.: National Parks Hospitality Association, 1994.

Rettie, Dwight F. *Our National Park System*. Urbana: University of Illinois Press, 1995.

Runte, Alfred. *National Parks: The American Experience*. Lincoln: University of Nebraska Press, 1979.

——. *Yosemite, the Embattled Wilderness*. Lincoln: University of Nebraska Press, 1990.

Sax, Joseph L. *Mountains without Handrails*. Ann Arbor: University of Michigan Press, 1980.

Schullery, Paul. *The Bears of Yellowstone*, 3d ed. Worland, Wyo.: High Plains Publishing Co., 1992.

——. *Searching for Yellowstone*. New York: Houghton Mifflin Co., 1997.

Shankland, Robert. *Steve Mather of the National Parks*, 3d ed. New York: Alfred A. Knopf, 1970.

Sharpe, Grant W., Charles H. Odegaard, and Wenonah F. Sharpe. *Park Management*, 2d ed. Champaign, Ill.: Sagamore Publishing, 1994.

Strong, Douglas. *Dreamers and Defenders*. Lincoln: University of Nebraska Press, 1988.

Udall, Stewart. *The Quiet Crisis and the Next Generation*. Salt Lake City: Peregrine Smith Books, 1988. Updates *The Quiet Crisis* (1963).

Wagner, Frederic H., et al. *Wildlife Policies in the U.S. National Parks*. Washington, D.C.: Island Press, 1995.

Wright, R. Gerald. *Wildlife Research and Management in the National Parks*. Urbana: University of Illinois Press, 1992.

Zaslowsky, Dyan, and T. H. Watkins. *These American Lands*. Washington, D.C.: Island Press, 1994.

# Index